Yogi Heroes and Poets

Yogi Heroes and Poets

Histories and Legends of the Nāths

EDITED BY
David N. Lorenzen and Adrián Muñoz

SUNY PRESS

Published by State University of New York Press, Albany

Printed in the United States of America

For information, contact State University of New York Press, Albany, NY
www.sunypress.edu

Production by Kelli W. LeRoux
Marketing by Michael Campochiaro

Library of Congress Cataloging-in-Publication Data

Yogi heroes and poets: histories and legends of the Naths / edited by David N. Lorenzen and Adrián Muñoz.
p. cm.
Includes bibliographical references and index.
ISBN 978-1-4384-3891-7 (hardcover : alk. paper)
ISBN 978-1-4384-3890-0 (paperback : alk. paper) 1. nathasect. 2. Yoga. I. Lorenzen, David N. II. Muñoz, Adrián. III. Title: Histories and legends of the Naths.
BL1278.54.Y64 2011
294.5'436—dc22

2011004268

10 9 8 7 6 5 4 3 2 1

Contents

Preface

Much scholarly work has been done in recent years on Sanskrit texts about yoga philosophy and yoga practices. Fewer discussions have appeared on the religious sect that has been the main carrier of yoga traditions in India, the sect known as the Nath Panth or Kanphata Panth. The principal aim of this collection of essays is to help redress this imbalance with discussions about the history of the Nath yogis and about the vernacular folklore and poetry that they have produced. The primary source materials for the essays include folktales, songs, verses, didactic texts, and oral interviews and recitations. These sources were written or spoken in a variety of languages: modern Hindi, old Hindi, Rajasthani, Bengali, Oriya, and Sanskrit.

The editors would like to thank all the contributors for their help in organizing the collection and editing their own essays. Thanks in part to the wonders of the Internet, it has been possible to efficiently assemble a team of scholars from several different countries: the Czech Republic, Great Britain, India, Mexico, and the United States. Short biographical notes on each of the contributors are found at the end of this book.

Not all the authors of the essays have used diacritics to transcribe Indian words, but where diacritics are used they follow standard practice for the languages concerned. In most chapters, personal names and non-italicized words in Hindi or other vernacular languages appear without diacritics. However, words of these languages written in italics (including book titles) do normally have diacritics. Sanskrit words (e.g., *haṭha yoga*), usually do have diacritics, even when not in italics. Sanskrit words that are common in English sometimes appear in their common English spellings (e.g., Shiva, Shakta, Vishnu, Vaishnava, Krishna, Shankaracharya) but in essays using mainly Sanskrit sources appear in their more scholarly form with diacritics (e.g., Śiva, Śākta, Viṣṇu, Kṛṣṇa, etc.). The non-aspirated "ch" sound in vernacular words is usually written as "ch" (e.g., Chand), but in Sanskrit words it is usually written as "c" (e.g., Candra). Palatal "ś" and cerebral "ṣ" in non-italicized Hindi words are both usually written as "sh."

Much help has also been received from our colleagues in the Centro de Estudios de Asia y África of El Colegio de Mexico and from its administrative staff. We particularly would like to thank the director of the Centro, Benjamín Preciado Solís, and its administrative assistant, Adriana Villanueva. Many thanks also to Nancy Ellegate and her team at State University of New York Press.

Introduction

David N. Lorenzen and Adrián Muñoz

All disciples sleep, but the Nath Satguru stays full awake.
The Avadhuta begs for alms at the ten gates.
—Gorakh Bānī *pad* 53

The Hindu religious path or sect of the Naths is variously known as the Nath Panth or the Nath Sampraday. Its followers are called Nath yogis, Nath Panthis, Kanphata yogis, Gorakhnathis, and Siddha yogis, among other names. Sometimes the term *avadhūta* is used, although this term is applied to ascetics of other Hindu groups as well. Most Nath yogis claim adherence to the teachings of the early yogi, Gorakṣanātha (in Hindi Gorakhnath). The school of yoga most closely associated with the Naths is the well-known one of haṭha yoga. In more general terms, the combined religious and yogic teachings of the Naths are called the *Nāth-mārga* (the Path of the Naths), the *Yoga-mārga* (the Path of yoga), or the *Siddha-mata* (the doctrine of the Siddhas).

The term *siddha* means "someone perfected or who has attained [spiritual] perfection." A Siddha (from the Sanskrit root *SIDH*, "to succeed, to perfect") is an ascetic who has gained different perfections or "successes" (*siddhis*), the most famous being the eight magical siddhis achieved through intense yogic practice. The word *nāth* or *nātha* literally means "lord, master; protector, shelter," and in the present context designates, on the one hand, a follower of the sect founded by or associated with Gorakhnath and, on the other hand, someone who has controlled the senses through the psycho-physical practices of haṭha yoga. The word is also often used as a name for the god Shiva. In Nath texts, Shiva is often called "Ādi-nātha," the first or primeval Lord.

Linguistically, the word *nātha* is associated with the Sanskrit root *NĀTH*, meaning "to have dominion or power" but also "to implore or beseech." *Nātha* is also explained in traditional sources according to a homiletic etymology. Thus the *Rāja-guhya* states that the syllable *nā* connotes the *anādi* (literally "without origin")—i.e., the primordial form, whereas the syllable *tha* connotes *sthāpita,* the "established." *Nātha* then would mean the primeval form or *dharma* established in the three worlds (*bhuvana-trayam*) according to this religious speculation (Dvivedi 1980, 3).

Most Naths are clearly Shaiva in orientation, but some Naths have assumed a more Vaishnava identity. In many Nath texts, their principal God tends to be *nirguṇa,* a God without form who is essentially indescribable, a semi-monistic God. In fact, a complex web of multiple religious identities has been a constituting feature of the Nath Panth. Naths have constructed their own identity with concepts taken from Hindus (both orthodox and heterodox), Buddhists, Muslims, and Sikhs alike. Usually the Naths have assumed the role of a reformist movement, while in recent times some Naths have fostered a Hindu communalist ideology, especially in the northern state of Uttar Pradesh.

The history of the Nath Sampraday is not easy to reconstruct, in part because we cannot be sure that the exemplary Naths really lived (Matsyendra, Gorakh, Jalandhar, Chaurangi, etc.). Wassiljew tried to fix the year 800 CE as the emerging point (in Chakravarti 1963, 23). However, if the Nath legendary personalities existed at all, it is rather unlikely that they lived at so early a date. It is more plausible to assume that the first Naths lived sometime between the tenth and the eleventh century, in the northern part of the continent, somewhere between Punjab and Bengal (Bhattacharya 1996, 315; Kienhle 1997; Lorenzen 1987). Although some scholars have suggested, probably rightly, that a period of decline began in the eighteenth century (Bouy 1994, 111; Dvivedi 2004, 273–74), the Naths continue to occupy important sites in both North India and Nepal: Gorakhpur, Hardwar, and Mrigasthali in Kathmandu are just a few examples.

The historical influence of the Naths often extended beyond the religious sphere. In several periods and regions they enjoyed royal patronage and were able to influence political events. In the Punjab, traditional royal support for the Nath yogis is well documented.[1] In Rajasthan, the most famous example is that of Man Singh, the raja of Marwar (Jodhpur). During his whole career, he was influenced by the ascetic Deonath, a follower of Gorakhnath and Jalandharnath. Several historical alliances of this sort existed between Nath ascetics and Rajput rulers.[2]

Tales and stories about legendary Nath yogis such as Gorakhnath, Matsyendra, Jalandhar, Gopicand, Bharthari, Kanhapa, and Chaurangi are still popular throughout most of South Asia. Contemporary Nath yogis who model their conduct on these earlier figures can still be seen in places such as Deccan, Gujarat, Rajasthan, Hardwar, Garhwal, Bihar, Bengal, Maharashtra, as well as at pilgrimage sites in Afghanistan, Pakistan, Tibet, and Nepal. Traditionally, the ideal Nath yogi is considered to be a powerful miracle worker, an expert in controlling the senses and achieving a union with the Ultimate Reality, an individual capable of exerting power over rulers and populace alike. Present-day Nath yogis, however, are often regarded simply as storytellers, singers, and religious beggars. There is evidence to indicate that some Naths began to marry and create their own families as long ago as around 1500 or even earlier. Pitambar Datt Barthwal and Hazariprasad Dvivedi have suggested that the famous fifteenth and sixteenth-century religious poet Kabir may have come from such a family.

NATH STUDIES

One of the reasons why the Naths are so interesting is that historically they have been associated with a complex mix of competing ideals, practices, and soteriologies. Their outward features (earrings, turbans, matted hair, etc.) are mere ornaments that symbolize what it means to be a Nath yogi. Many Naths are ascetic renouncers, but others are householders; some stay in temple monasteries but other spend most of their time on the road; most are devotees of Shiva but some worship this god in anthropomorphic form and others as a formless spirit; some may even combine Muslim and Nath identities.

The Nath Panth has been historically linked to several different religious movements in South Asia. Its origins are to be found in the tantric schools of diverse traditions (Shaiva, Shakta, Buddhist). As the Nath Panth became consolidated, it influenced, and was influenced by, several devotional movements, both in the north (especially with the Nirgunis) and in the south (with the Varkaris and Nayanars). They even mixed with non-Hindu traditions such as Islam and Jainism. These complex interactions still need to be much better researched and analyzed.

Possible scholarly approaches to the doctrines and practices of the Naths are many. Nath texts include yoga treatises and manuals, mostly written in Sanskrit, on the one hand, and folktales and devotional poetry, mostly transmitted in Hindi and other vernacular languages. The study of each type of source requires different skills and disciplinary approaches. The only attempt at a comprehensive study of the Nath sect and Nath literature is the now out-of-date classic by George W. Briggs, first published in 1938. This work includes a classification of Nath subsects, a discussion of Nath doctrines and practices, and accounts of their legends and folklore. Despite the limits and weaknesses of the source materials available to Briggs, his work remains a necessary reference in modern Nath studies.

Some Nath texts, particularly vernacular folktales and devotional poetry belong largely to oral tradition and are not always available in written, much less published, form. In recent years, Ann Gold (1992) and other anthropologists have collected some of this oral literature, but much more work of this sort is still needed. The musical performance of Nath songs is another underdeveloped topic, although Edward Henry (1991) has published interesting studies in this field. An important study of early Nath songs composed in Marathi has been published by Catharina Kiehnle (1997). There is new book on Nath literature, chiefly focused on vernacular folktales, by Adrián Muñoz (2010). A pioneering older study that attempts to make a complete study of North Indian vernacular literature about Gorakh and the Naths is Hazariprasad Dvivedi's *Nāth sampradāy* (1950) in Hindi. Other studies in this area written in Hindi include those of Nagendranath Upadhyay (1991, 1997) and Dharmavir Bharati (1968). Particularly important for the study of vernacular Nath literature are the collections of early Nath texts edited by Pitambar Datt Barthwal (Gorakhnath 1960) and Hazariprasad Dvivedi (1978).

The anthropological and historical study of the Nath Panth and the practices of the Nath ascetics is another large area of research. The recent work of Véronique Bouillier is notable in this regard, particularly her new book, *Itinérance et vie monastique, Les ascètes Nāth Yogīs en Inde contemporaine* (2008). Ann Gold (1989, 1991, and 1992) and Daniel Gold (1992, 1995, 1999, and 2005) have also done important work on the culture of Nath householders in Rajasthan (see also Gold and Gold 1984). Among the older studies that should be noted is a book by Shashibhusan Dasgupta (1995) which includes much information about the Naths in medieval Bengal.

Texts on haṭha yoga and yogic anatomy, sources mostly written in Sanskrit, have been much better studied and good editions and translations of the main texts of haṭha yoga such as the *Haṭhayoga-pradīpikā* and the *Gheraṇḍa-saṃhitā* are easily available. Christian Bouy (1994) has published a good study of the so-called *Yoga-Upaniṣads*. An older work that should be mentioned here is the book on yoga by Mircea Eliade (1969). Another important older volume is the collection of various Sanskrit texts attributed to Matsyendra, the guru of Gorakhnath, including the *Kaula-jñāna-nirṇaya,* edited by Prabodh Chandra Bagchi in 1934 (Matsyendranātha 1986). The detailed introduction by Bagchi provides interesting data and suggestions regarding the origins of the Naths and the religious identity of Matsyendra. Also important in this context is the edition of the *Siddha-siddhānta-paddhati* and other Nath works, with an English introduction, by Kalyani Mallik (1954)

The relations between the Naths and alchemical tradition and between the Naths and Tantric religion have been studied in recent years almost single-handedly by David G. White, most notably in his book, *The Alchemical Body: Siddha Traditions in Medieval India* (1996) and in several other books and articles he has written (1996, 2001, 2003, 2005, 2009a, 2009b). The veritable flood of recent studies on tantric religion, particularly on Kashmir Shaivism, by Mark Dyczkowski (1989, 2004), Alexis Sanderson (1988), Teun Goudriaan and Sanjukta Gupta (1981) and others also contains much information relevant to a study of the Naths. Another topic at least indirectly relevant to the Naths is that of the influence of haṭha yoga on the Muslim Sufis who wrote medieval vernacular romances such as Manjhan's *Madhumālatī.* Aditya Behl and Simon Weightman's recent translation of this work (Manjhan 2000) has a valuable discussion about this in the introduction. Many studies of medieval Nirguni sects such as those of Kabir, Dadu and Nanak also contain information about Naths and their relations to Nirguni religion (see Lorenzen 1991, 1996; McLeod 1980a; McLeod 1980b; Solanki 1966).

THE PRESENT VOLUME

The essays in this volume fill important gaps in our knowledge about the Naths. Since the pioneering studies by G. W. Briggs and H. P. Dvivedi and the recent work by Veronique Boullier, relatively little scholarly work has been done on the Naths, their vernacular literature and their institutions as historical subjects. The essays in the first part of this collection by Purushottam Agrawal, David Lorenzen, Daniel Gold and Ishita Banerjee-Dube all discuss important aspects of these topics. Work on Nath folklore and religious ideas is somewhat better covered by recent scholars, most notably by Ann Gold, but good interpretative studies of these topics are still hard to find. The essays in the second part of this collection by David White, Ann Gold, Adrián Muñoz, Lubomír Ondračka and Csaba Kiss all examine aspects of these issues.

Here, the opening chapter by Purushottam Agrawal discusses the differing ways in which various key twentieth-century literary critics looked at the early Naths, most notably Gorakh, and the vernacular poetry attributed to them. These critics include the Mishra brothers, Ramchandra Shukla, Pitambar Datt Barthwal and Hazariprasad Dvivedi. Agrawal argues that behind the writing of a history of early Hindi literature there has usually been differing understandings of Indian and

Hindu identities as well as differing literary tastes. The division between the religious poets of *bhakti* tradition and more literary, formalist poets (the *rīti* school) has been a constant theme of Hindi literary criticism, as has been the differing assessments of the role and value of Nath poetry.

Agrawal discusses how Ramchandra Shukla, in his famous 1928 history of Hindi literature, introduced the key concepts of "the Hindu *jāti*," in the sense of cultural and linguistic community, and of "*lok-dharma*," meaning a settled moral and social order. For Shukla, the promotion of this Hindu jāti and this lok-dharma was considered to be one of the chief virtues and duties of Hindi poetry. Using these concepts as a yardstick, Shukla proposed a very positive appreciation of *saguṇī* (theistic) poets like Tulsidas and a much more negative evaluation of the poetry of Nirguni (semi-monistic) critics of the medieval social order like Kabir and Dadu. Shukla tended to place Gorakh somewhere between Kabir and Tulsidas on his scale of poetic values. Shukla appreciated Gorakh's promotion of social harmony between Hindus and Muslim, but suggested that Gorakh's interests were too esoteric and lacked "natural feeling of bhakti and love."

Agrawal next analyzes the work of Pitambar Datt Barthwal on the literature of the Nirguni poets like Kabir and Dadu. Barthwal especially praised their role in fostering Hindu-Muslim unity. About Gorakh and the Naths, Barthwal argued that they had had a strong influence on Kabir and also sponsored communal harmony. Barthwal's ideas about the influence of Gorakh on Kabir were further developed by Hazariprasad Dvivedi, although Dvivedi also recognized that Kabir could not really be regarded as an "instrument of Hindu-Muslim unity" since he in fact sharply criticized both religions. According to Agrawal, Dvivedi developed his own concept of lok-dharma, one quite different from that of Shukla. Dvivedi's lok-dharma was a more descriptive concept close to ideas like "popular religion" or "little tradition" and included both the Naths and the Nirgunis. This lok-dharma was associated primarily with Hindu religion and was largely independent of Islam.

In his chapter, David Lorenzen discusses the complex ideas about religious identity found in the poetry of Gorakh and compares them with similar but contrasting ideas found in the poetry of Kabir and the Sikh gurus. All these poets proclaim a religious identity that rises above the contrast between Hindu religion and Islam. In one verse, Gorakh claims a religious identity that somehow combines Islam, Hindu religion, and yoga, although in other texts he seems to distance himself from both Islam and Hindu religion. In the poetry of Kabir and that of the Sikh gurus, there tends to be a clearer rejection of traditional practices of both Islam and Hindu religion, although both Kabir and the Sikh gurus use a theological vocabulary and metaphysical concepts that owe more to Hindu ideas than to Muslim ones. Another important difference between Kabir and Gorakh is in the role that the body plays in their respective religious ideas. For Gorakh and the Naths the human body is something to be controlled and purified. For Kabir, the body is chiefly important as the dwelling place of the formless divine spirit that Kabir usually calls Ram. Kabir's *sādhanā* (religious practice) is directed at recognizing this Ram, not at controlling the body.

In his chapter, Daniel Gold explores the interesting way in which the Nath tradition has merged into the local culture of Gwalior, Madhya Pradesh. This regional manifestation of the Naths is unique and quite separate from those in other parts of North India and Nepal. Whereas the figure of the king is present here as elsewhere in Nath culture, the Maharashtrian Naths are a curious blend of Vaishnava religious fervor and Sufi elements. This is particularly notorious in their gatherings at one temple where long, intense musical performances are conducted; these performances are played to the tune of intense drum beatings. The general ambience of these devotional gatherings is quite reminiscent of both Sufi musical practices and Vaishnava *kirtan* singing, the eventual cadence of rhythms leading to a quasi-ecstatic climax.

Gold maps the development of Nath cults in Gwalior since roughly the early eighteenth century until the consolidation of the cult of Raja Bakshar and the lineage of Dholi Buwa. As with Man Singh, king of Jodhpur, and Prithivi-Narayan Shah, in Nepal—here too a leading political figure, Maharaja Daulat Rao (r. 1794–1827), requested the aid of a follower of the Nath Panth, Mahipati Nath. The Dholi Buwa lineage began thus with Mahipati Nath and is still highly influential in Gwalior. In this way, a long-lasting association between the Scindia dinasty and a Nath lineage was established. At the same time, an interesting shift from celibate yogis to householder Naths took place.

A similar ambivalence is found in the case of the Nath lineage of Raja Bakshar as well. Some Maharashtrian Hindus claim that Raja Bakshar is but a Muslim name given to Baba Chaitanya Nath, who is traceable to a Nath yogi lineage. His tomb is thus worshipped both as a yogi *samādhi* (tumulus), and a Sufi shrine. Daniel Gold argues that through this amalgam, the common royal and popular role of Nath yogis can become a viable urban institution. In his view, this dual institution can bring about a form of cohesion and a healthy coexistence of different communal sensibilities.

Ishita Banerjee-Dube's chapter traces the influence of Nath yoga and tantra on a religious sect of Orissa known as Mahima Dharma. This sect also has much in common with Nirguni movements such as the Kabir Panth. Mahima Dharma was founded in the 1860s by a celibate ascetic known as Mahima Swami. Like the Kabir Panthis, he rejected idol worship and many caste-based practices. Some of his ritual practices such as his celibacy and his use of the hearth-fire (*dhūnī*), strongly suggest

Nath influence. He apparently also introduced the name *Alakh* or *Alekh* as the designation of the God of Mahima Dharma. This name is clearly borrowed from the Nath name of Shiva, *Alakh Niranjan.*

Mahima Swami's chief disciple and successor was a man named Bhima Bhoi. While Mahima Swami did not leave any written texts, Bhima Bhoi was a poet and religious thinker who wrote a great variety of songs, verses, and metaphysical texts. Banerjee-Dube here identifies the many Nath and tantric ideas present in the compositions of Bhima Bhoi. She also suggests that Bhima Bhoi's personal choice to live with several women and father children may have been related to his association with tantric ideas and practices. Among the Nath and tantric terms and ideas used by Bhima Bhoi, one of the most important is that of the relation between the human body (*piṇḍa*), with the body of the universe, the *brahmāṇḍa,* a theme that can also be found in the chapter by David White on a Nath text that features this same relation.

The *Siddha-siddhānta-paddhati* discussed by White is a text attributed to Gorakhnath. It is especially concerned with Nath philosophy, physiology, and anatomy. The third chapter of this work, translated in White's essay, offers what he calls a "complete and detailed identification of the human body (piṇḍa) with the universe of the 'Puranic' cosmic egg (*brahmāṇḍa*)." White makes the important point that this cannot really be called an identification of the human body as a microcosm of the macrocosmic universe. The body of the yogi is not described as a "miniaturized replica of the universal 'macrocosm.'" Rather his body is somehow identical to the universe. The full universe is located within the yogi's own body.

White further connects the ideas about the yogi's body found in the *Siddha-siddhānta-paddhati* with the discussions of the body (or multiple overlapping bodies) found in tantric sources such as Abhinavagupta and in the vernacular poetry of Gorakh. Finally, White ties these discussions to the ideas about the equivalence of the physical universe with the body of the cosmic man or Puruṣa, first found in Vedic sources, and with later ideas about the universe being contained within the body of God such as the description of the universe in Krishna found in the *Bhagavad-gītā.* The aim of all this speculation is evidently to enable the yogi to become Śiva's equal.

The Nath yogis have become a major icon in Indian folklore, bridging linguistic barriers. Throughout the Indian subcontinent, the yogis feature in a wide corpus of folktales. Whether all of these tales sprung from the yogis themselves or whether they were the elaboration of stories by others, they represent a key element of Indian folklore. Some of these tales reveal archetypal aspects of Nath personality and identity. Ann Gold has worked with oral Rajasthani/Hindi sources. Her important insights into Rajasthani folklore concerning Nath tradition are further developed in her essay here through a commentary on two Nath legends: those of Gopichand and Bharthari. In her analysis, Gold uncovers the anxieties of specific caste and religious communities. She reveals the way in which these tales are deeply embedded in the culture of rural Rajasthan and feature as leading characters, both merchants and artisans (potters). The Nath ascetics in the stories stress the contrast between the pursuit of the Ultimate Goal, i.e. Alakh Niranjan, and the ties of domestic life. One central motif in the two stories presented by Gold is that of fostering positive popular attitudes toward alms begging and alms giving.

In his chapter, Adrián Muñoz discusses a Hindi legend about Matsyendra and Gorakh and relates it to the larger body of Nath literature and uncovers unsuspected continuities in Nath literary production. Excerpts from Nath Sanskrit texts and from Nath Hindi poetry (*Gorakh-bānī*) are compared and contrasted. At the same time, Muñoz claims that narrative discrepancies among the texts possibly reveal ideological disputes experienced by competing Nath groups in different historical periods. Muñoz argues that the tale of Matsyendra's stay in the Kingdom of Women and his eventual release by Gorakh can be read as an allegory of a conscious agenda to forge a "cleansed" form of haṭha yoga and Nathism. This agenda was prominent in Nath poetry as well. In this way, a clear opposition between Kaulism (the tantric school traditionally attributed to Matsyendra) and Nathism was constructed. The key aim was to eliminate sexual rites from yoga practices. Nonetheless, the differing viewpoints found in the available Nath and haṭha-yoga texts seem to indicate a lack of any definitive institutional stance in the extended praxis of the siddhas and yogis.

In Muñoz's view, the historical Gorakh probably tried to expunge sexual practices from his own yogic school. In the end, the Nath Panth exorcised most directly sexual elements, but this was not necessarily done in haṭha yoga, a school that was not completely controlled by the Naths and had attained a much wider popularity. Haṭha-yoga practitioners were evidently able to retain or introduce sexual exercises in their religious practice. This would explain the problematic *vajrolī-mudrā,* an exercise described in the *Haṭhayoga-pradīpikā* that presupposes the active sexual participation of a woman and the emission of bodily fluids.

In his chapter, Lubomír Ondračka again discusses the efforts of Gorakh to rescue Matsyendra from sensual temptations, but bases his analysis on a Bengali version of the legend. In particular, Ondračka focuses on a key motif that lies at the very core of his Bengali text, namely the intriguing mention of four moons. According to this source, Gorakh claims that Matsyendra can escape death and decay by means of an esoteric practice employing these four moons. The identity of these four moons is precisely what Ondračka tries to elucidate. He relates the Bengali tale of Matsyendra to other religious practices found in Bengal, especially those of the

Sahajiyas. He discusses all available hypotheses and in particular addresses the question whether these moons represent esoteric or exterior ascetic processes, or even sexual fluids. This possibility suggests again a link with Kaula practices.

The chapter by Csaba Kiss discusses one of the intersecting points between Nathism and tantra. Focussing on the *Matsyendra-saṃhitā,* Kiss establishes links between tantric practice, especially that of a Shakta-oriented branch, and Nath praxis. This argument can be seen as highly controversial since most groups of the Nath Panth have made efforts to eradicate most traces of tantric religion. However, Matsyendra, Gorakh's former guru, is widely known as a reputed tantric teacher, and is said to have founded the Kaula-yoginī school, which is believed to have engaged in ritual sexual intercourse.

Kiss seeks to establish the connections of the *Matsyendra-saṃhitā* with other Kaula texts such as the *Brahma-yāmala,* the *Jayadratha-yāmala* and the *Tantra-sadbhāva.* The recurrent Kaula vocabulary is a major indication of this relation: words like *kula, kaula, kaulika* abound in the *Matsyendra-saṃhitā.* This text, in his view, belongs to a typical thirteenth-century Śaiva tantric/yogic environment. In particular, Kiss locates the *Matsyendra-saṃhitā* within the tradition of goddess Kubjikā's cult known as Śāmbhava. The Śāmbhava cult was especially popular in South India, hence the constant references to a Cola King in the *Matsyendra-saṃhitā.* Kiss then elaborates on the proper injunctions for yoginī (female yogi) worship as laid down in the text. In fact, the practices expounded in the *Matsyendra-saṃhitā* differ greatly from those of the most famous haṭha-yoga treatises. In the *Matsyendra-saṃhitā* we find rules for sexual practices and various meditations using skulls. Thus, the yoga of this Śāmbhava cult is definitely tantric and not necessarily that of the Naths.

Much more, of course, remains to be said about Gorakh and the Naths. The essays in this book give important glimpses of the ways in which the Naths historically have been a vital link between a large number of religious, metaphysical and even medical traditions in India. This philosophically and religiously Nath tradition is linked both to tantric and Nirguni religious currents, to Abhinavagupta and to Kabir. Through haṭha yoga, the Naths are also linked to the classical yoga of Patañjali, to Sufi adaptations of haṭha yoga beliefs and practices, and even to the worldwide spread of yoga exercise and meditation as aids to healthy living. In the case of Nath legends, these stories are still a vital part of the wider world of Indian folklore and offer an essential window on many basic social, metaphysical, and psychological concerns of Hindu culture. As the Naths say, "Alakh Niranjan."

PART 1

Yogis in History

CHAPTER ONE

The Naths in Hindi Literature

Purushottam Agrawal

In 1903, Mahavirprasad Dvivedi, the doyen of Hindi literature and the legendary editor of the magazine *Saraswati,* lamented that

> Hindi is in bad shape. We have not produced any work whatsoever in many areas of study. It is, therefore futile to expect a history of Hindi literature. Our lethargy and lack of enthusiasm knows no bounds. (in Sharma 1977, 321)

His opinion was shared by many. It was the temper of the times. By this time, modern Hindi had become the chief marker of the Hindu cultural community, and the literati were duty-bound to ensure its all-round development.

The need for a history of Hindi literature was organically linked with the community's need for history as such. Given India's colonial situation, this need for history had specific epistemological and teleological dimensions. Maithilisharan Gupta, a close associate of Dvivedi and a leading poet in his own right, was to give rhetorical expression to both these dimensions through an anguished remembrance of the past and a cautious, slightly pessimistic view of the future. His hugely popular work, *Bhārat Bhāratī,* first published in 1912, resonates with the questions: "Who were we? What we have become? And what has fate in store for us?" (*Ham kaun the, kyā ho gaye, aur kyā honge abhī*) (Gupta 2006, 14).

The very next year, the Mishra brothers (Ganeshbihari, Shyambihari, and Shukdevbihari) tried to provide a history of Hindi literature in their book, *Miśra-bandhu-vinod* (the [literary] appreciations of the Mishra brothers). They subtitled the book *Hindī sāhitya kā itihās tathā kavi kīrtan* (a history of Hindi literature and a celebration of poets). In the preface, they discussed the germination of their idea for the book, an idea that goes back to 1901. They intended to write a history of literature, "through one hundred critical pieces that treat both major and minor poets" (Bandhu 1956, 10).

The notion of literature informing the enterprise of Mishra brothers was rooted more in traditional than in modern ideas. The very title of the work—*Vinod*—alludes to the traditional Sanskrit saying attributed to Bhartṛhari: "*kāvyaśāstreṇa vinodena kālo gacchati dhīmatām*" (the enlightened pass their time in the appreciation of poetics). The Mishra brothers were writing their history of Hindi literature for the newly emergent colonial literati, but they were unable to convincingly appropriate traditional ideas to the needs of these "modern" literati. Their *Vinod* drew upon and improved the information contained in the nineteenth-century works of Shivsingh Sengar and George Grierson, but it failed to provide a *historical* narrative detailing the journey of the community as reflected in its literary works. This task was performed by Ramchandra Shukla some years later. For the Mishra brothers, literature continued to be primarily a polite pastime, and its history more a chronological celebration of poets than a teleological narrative. They celebrated Deva and Bihari (the leading *rīti*, i.e., formalist, stylist poets) primarily as poets, while they revered Tulsidas and Surdas primarily as *bhaktas,* as great social and religious figures rather than as poets. The Mishra brothers did try to take due note of the vagaries of the development of Hindi language and also of the social import of those whom they saw as playing some socially significant role in this process.

The *Vinod* cites samples from the compositions of six Naths: Gorakh, Jalandhar, Chaurangi, Kaneripav, Charpat, and Chunkar. Naturally Gorakhnath is treated most prominently. The authors note the uncertainty about his floruit, saying that it could be any time between "tenth, eleventh and fourteenth centuries of the Vikram Samvat." They also note the doubts that exist about the antiquity of the language of compositions attributed to Gorakhnath. The authors conclude their discussion of both these interrelated issues:

> According to some people, his language is too polished for that period. This observation will be quite acceptable, if we were to assign Gorakhnath to the period between the tenth and twelfth centuries. But if he was a contemporary of Jyotirishwar [1325 CE], then there is no point in doubting the [authenticity of his] language. Actually Gorakhnath was contemporaneous with the demise of the Sahajia Panth, which merged with the Gorakh Panth. (Bandhu 1956, 141)

According to the Mishra brothers, it was by "purifying" the erotic cults of the Sahajias through a process of merger that Gorakhnath left a "positive impact" on society. He is said to have composed eleven works in Hindi and nine in Sanskrit. The *Vinod* also credits him with introducing an element of *saguṇa* (theistic) worship to the abstract speculations of Sankaracharya's monism, thus making Gorakh's religion more comprehensible and acceptable to the people. But this led to some logical inconsistency in Gorakh's metaphysical ideas. Here, the *Vinod* seems to be anticipating Shukla's caution against attempting to find a coherent "philosophical system" in the utterances of the *nirguna bhaktas* (devotees of a formless, monistic God) like Kabir. Some years later, Hazariprasad Dvivedi characterized Kabir's philosophical system as one that directly flowed from the Nath philosophy of *dvaitādvaitavilakṣaṇavāda* (a doctrine transcending both dualism and no-dualism), i.e., a system transcending both theism and monism.

The Mishra brothers noted the contemporary fact that the followers of the Nath Panth came overwhelmingly from the "lower and illiterate classes," and also the fact that "Gorakhnath is actually worshipped like a god by his followers and devotees." The *Vinod* concludes its discussion with the significant observation that "Gorakhnathji is the first prominent Brahmin poet to have given respect to Hindi" (Bandhu 1956, 145).

From all this, we can see how the very first history of Hindi literature written by and for Hindi speakers places Gorakhnath and his whole community in the framework of what David Lorenzen quite aptly describes as "non-caste Hinduism" (Lorenzen 2006, 78–101).[1] It is significant that in the Mishra brothers' history the Naths do not play the role of "bringing Hindus and Muslims closer together." The Mishra brothers use Islamic references and legends to make their points, but do not seem much interested in "reconciling the differences" between the Islamic and Hindu communities.

In their texts, the Naths adopted the strategy of ignoring—and thus implicitly criticizing—the caste order and its social epistemology. Their ascetic mode of life facilitated their choice of this strategy. People like Kabir, on the other hand, criticized the caste order and its ideology head-on. The Hindi critic Hazariprasad Dvivedi later described the views of Kabir and other Nirguni (those who worship a formless god) poets as the logical culmination of the Nath worldview. Dvivedi placed Gorakh and other Naths at the center of his concept of the lok-dharma (literally "popular religiosity," but Dvivedi's concept is actually closer to the concepts of the "little traditions" and "non-caste Hinduism"). In *Hindī sāhitya kī bhūmikā*, first published in 1940, he talked of both Buddhism and the Smarta-Vedic traditions transforming themselves as a result of interaction with the popular belief systems and everyday cultural practices of various regions to such an extent that Buddhism actually dissolved into popular practices (Dvivedi 1969, 10). This resulted in both these traditions transforming themselves; Dvivedi used this concept of lok-dharma as the key device for his narrative of the origin and growth of Hindi literature. I will discuss this matter later in the present essay.

The Mishra brothers were praised for advancing many steps beyond Shivsingh Sengar and Grierson, but they were also criticized sharply for their archaic and arbitrary evaluation of the poets. After all, literature could no longer remain a "polite pastime." The history of literature could not be seen just as an attempt by the "enlightened" to sharpen their faculties through a leisurely appreciation of literary works. The times had changed. Now literature had to be seen as "the autobiography of the nation" and literary history as the narration of the episodes in this same autobiography. It was still a history of past events, works and authors, but one told from a vastly different viewpoint.

From this point on, the past had to be seen both as a glory and as a torture: the present had to draw the right lessons; the future had to be imagined on the basis of such lessons. History had to be perceived as a self description of the community's individuality struggling to realize its true self. The narrative of this struggle had to cover the ups and downs of the path traversed by the community in its journey from the past on toward the future goal of realizing its inherent destiny as a self-confident, powerful, modern collectivity—a nation. The history of the literature produced, preserved, and possessed by the community was considered to be a natural corollary of this struggle, ambition, and self description. The *Vinod* was a far from satisfactory product on all these counts. Hindi had to wait for several more years before a "proper" history of literature was produced, one which would place the memories, events, and authors and their work in the master narrative of the community's unique identity striving for its present and future self-realization.

Such a work, the first properly "modern" history of Hindi literature (*Hindī sāhitya kā itihās*) was produced by the eminent critic and scholar, Ramchandra Shukla, as an introduction to an ambitious dictionary in 1928 CE. It was published as an independent volume the very next year and had a second, revised edition in 1940. Since that time, this volume has been one of the most influential narratives of the evolution of Hindi language and literature. For quite some time, it was considered to be the canonical work in the field, since it put the past, present, and probable future of Hindi literature in a perspective which both reflected and modified the perspective of its intended audience: the colonial Hindi literati. Undoubtedly, Shukla's "history" embodied unacknowledged influences. The way in which he divides the literary history of Hindi into periods is clearly influenced by Grierson (1888, "Modern Vernacular Literature of Hindustan") and Shukla's paragraph introducing the "bhakti period" reminds the reader of Keay's (1920, "A History of Hindi

Literature") discussion of this topic. But these influences in no way detract from the originality, importance and uniqueness of Shukla's volume.

Shukla made his notion of literary history clear at the outset:

> Whereas the literature of any country reflects the accumulated, collective mindset *(cittavṛtti)* of the populace, it is certain that the changes in these mindsets result in changes in literature as well. To evaluate the tradition of this changing mindset and to establish its concurrence with the tradition of literature is known as the history of literature. (Shukla 1978, 1)

Shukla employed a master narrative of the "Hindu *jāti*." He was using the term *jāti* not in the sense of caste but in the sense of a cultural, linguistic community. This sense had been accepted into the modern Hindi from at least the nineteenth century. This master narrative described and evaluated the changes in the mindset of populace and established a concurrence between these changes and changes in literary tradition. The narrative presupposed the existence of a homogenized, strong, and dynamic community, not exactly as a historical fact, but as an ethical and teleological imperative. His parameters of comparative evaluation and exclusion/inclusion stemmed from this imperative only. He sought to narrate the history of the community's literary journey from the point of view of the upper caste Hindu householder, and this point of view was articulated through his concept of the lok-dharma.

Lok-dharma, in Shukla's historiography, was a normative and not a descriptive category. Not everyday practices, but right ideals were the parameters of Shukla's lok-dharma. The right kinds of poets were naturally those who, instead of merely reflecting everyday reality, tried to orient their audience toward right kind of conduct. And the parameters of this conduct were undoubtedly drawn from the ideas and ideology of *varṇāśramadharma* (the traditional hierarchical social order). Shukla's lok-dharma was a name given to the idea of a settled moral and social order, and the Hindu jati was expected to move toward the actualization of this idea. Poets, being part of the community, were expected to extend a helping hand to this move.

Shukla did not have any sympathy for the idea that mysticism or other cultural artefacts might question this settled order and its ideals. In his seminal essay "*Bhakti kā vikās*" (the evolution of bhakti), he attributed the Nirguni poets' rejection of the varnashramadharma to their unfounded malice against lok-dharma and to the "foreign," Semitic origin of their worldview. He contrasted this "foreign" style or method of bhakti with a supposedly more authentic Indian bhakti found in the poetry of the saguṇa bhaktas, and he praised the saguṇa sensibility for appropriately balancing the beauty of the *bhakti-mārg* (the path of devotion) with that of the lok-dharma:

> Only that which adequately combines the internal pursuit (*sadhana*) [of bhakti] and the external observance of the lok-dharma with the specific and general aspects of social obligations can be described as the right bhakti view. Our bhakti aesthetics takes the beauty of lok-dharma along. That is why . . . it does not harbour any rancour against the social system. This congruence with lok-dharma is the chief thing which distinguishes the bhaktas (devotees) following the Indian method from the followers of foreign ideas. One can clearly see this difference by comparing Tulsi, Sur, Nanddas, Hitharivansh, etc. with Kabir, Dadu and Malukdas. (Shukla 1973, 45)

Nonetheless, it will be a considerable oversimplification to consider Shukla "anti-Muslim" per se. His preferences and judgments were determined by two interconnected concerns. First, he felt that the Hindu poet, as a poet, should have an organic relation with the ups and downs of the "Hindu jati." Second, the poet should uphold, and not interrogate, the settled norms of hierarchy and proper behavior accepted by the community to which he belongs as an individual. It was due to these concerns that Shukla could appreciate Malik Muhammad Jayasi with enthusiasm and could demonstrate the best of his critical acumen while writing on Jayasi. He compared and contrasted the individual humility, emotional richness, and poetic competence of Jayasi with Kabir's "irritating arrogance" and his lack of universal human feelings. The resulting judgment of their comparative worth as poets can be imagined.

With respect to the mutual relations between Hindus and Muslims, Shukla undoubtedly favored a peaceful understanding between them, and here again he found Jayasi more helpful than Kabir. The interrogative character of poetry such as Kabir's was simply not acceptable to Shukla as a critic historian who was trying to come to terms with the history and tradition of literature from the viewpoint of the modern upper-caste Hindu householder.

It ought to be noted that, unlike the Mishra brothers, Shukla very successfully appropriated traditional poetics to his modern project of literary criticism and history. In fact, he gave an ingenious, "modern" social twist to several traditional concepts and categories. Most notable was his reformulation of the theory of *rasa* (flavor or aesthetic essence). Literature being the autobiography of the community, the *rīti* poets obviously could not be at the center of his canon, even though he appreciated many of them for their formalistic achievements. His central critical idea was that a work ought to posses literary merit (in traditional sense), but more importantly it ought to be useful for the Hindu jati. So far as any overall historical and critical assessment was concerned, the yardstick was lok-dharma and ideal poet was Tulsidas. In Shukla's scheme of things, Tulsidas was celebrated not only as a bhakta, but as *the* poet of the Hindu jati. Shukla's narrative of the role played by the Naths in the history of Hindi literature was governed by these considerations and concerns.

Shukla wrote his history in the latter half of the third decade of the twentieth century, a time characterized by confusion and uneasiness in the political domain The Non-cooperation Movement had ended without many tangible results, and the Hindu-Muslim unity supposedly won during this movement was proving to be quite superficial and fleeting. The nationalist movement and its sympathizers were now forced to face the "cracks in the bridge" as Rajmohan Gandhi (2006, 284) puts it. Precedents and inspirations for the bridge-building exercises were being sought for in the past experiences of Indian history. Shukla emphasizes the Naths' contribution in this regard:

> Gorakhnath's theistic pursuit *(sādhanā)* had some attraction for the Muslims as well. He could clearly see that God-oriented Yoga can be proposed as a common sadhana for both Hindus and Muslims. This Yoga did not contain the polytheism and idol-worship that were so disagreeable to the Muslims. For this reason, he explored the possibility of removing the mutual animosity and proposing a common way, and he left the imprint of the same in his lineage. (Shukla 1978, 11)

According to Shukla, this search for a "common way" also made an impact on the language of the Naths. Discarding the traditional poetic language which drew its structure from Nagar Apabhramsha or Braj, the Naths composed their works in a curious mixture of the Khari Boli and Rajasthani; Shukla described this composite vernacular (*deś-bhāṣā*) as *sadhukkaḍī i*, i.e., the dialect of the sadhus. The composite character of the Naths' compositions was reinforced by references to Haj, Namaj, etc., along with Puja and pilgrimage (ibid., 13). The subterranean presence of the nationalist notion that Indian culture is a composite Hindu-Muslim or Indo-Persian culture cannot be missed in Shukla's treatment of the Naths, but he clearly did not see literature as a site for cultural interrogation. That is why, in spite of his recognition of the Naths' role in mending the "cracks in the bridge," Shukla could not absolve them from the charge of disorienting people from the path of the true dharma. It would be inaccurate to translate Shukla's term *dharma* as "religion," in the sense of a metaphysical belief system. Most of the time, he uses dharma in the traditional Indian sense of a socio-moral code embodying norms of behavior which were, of course, drawn from the ideal norms of varnashramadharma. Just before he introduces the bhakti period, Shukla evaluates the role of Naths in the following manner:

> We have already mentioned condemnation by the Siddhas and the Naths of empty ritualism and pilgrimage, etc., but they did not intend to rescue the people out from that abyss. They actually wanted to marginalize the very idea of social duties. Instead of orienting the people towards the true welfare of the self and society, they tried to distort the very idea of duty and responsibility. They spoke instead about the mystic and the esoteric. In order to impress the credulous of their achievements, they used to talk about the esoteric inner world. Their sadhana had no place for the natural feelings of bhakti and love, as they are available to all and sundry. What impact could such teachings have on the semi-literate and the illiterate except that of taking them away from the normal course of bhakti and the proper observance of the social norms and bringing them to the mumbo-jumbo of magic formulae? Taking all this into account, Goswami Tulsidas once observed: "Gorakh's propagation of yoga has banished bhakti from the mind of people." [*Gorakh jagāyo jog, bhagati bhagāyo log*)]. (Ibid., 44)

One can see the Naths in a sort of dual role here. They did a good thing by bringing Hindus and Muslims closer, in contributing to the making of composite Indian culture, but the negative aspect of their activities and utterances far outweighed the positive contribution. The negative influence of the Naths was commented upon by no less a person than Tulsidas. In fact, Shukla, despite noting that the Naths had a big influence on Kabir, credited Kabir for rescuing a large part of the populace from the pernicious influence of the Nath Panthis (ibid., 46). Shukla was also quite clear in his assertion that the Naths deserved a consideration in the history of literature only from the language point of view, since their compositions barely contained any real life situations and genuine feelings. Their writings cannot be treated as literature as such; one ought to place them in the same sort of category as writings pertaining to "astrology, medicine, etc." (ibid., 14). A history of Hindi literature such as Shukla's that reflects the concerns and anxieties of the upper-caste Hindu householder and idealizes varnashrama was bound to at least sideline, if not totally reject, the concerns of the inquisitive wanderers who, implicitly or explicitly, were questioning crucial aspects of the householder's worldview and practices.

While discussing the works of Gorakh and other Naths, Shukla fondly mentions his "dear student," Pitambar Datt Barthwal, who deserves the rightful credit for undertaking truly pathbreaking research on the role and importance of the Nath

Panth in the history of Hindi literature. Barthwal read an important paper in the Nagari Pracharini Sabha in December 1930; it was published in the journal of the Sabha in 1931. The essay was titled "*Hindī kavitā meṃ yog-pravāh*" (the yoga stream of Hindi poetry) and was later published in Barthwal's posthumous collection of essays (1946a). This 1930 essay drew scholarly attention not only to the general significance of the Nath compositions in the development of Hindi literature, but more importantly to the powerful connection between Naths and the Nirgunis. It is also widely recognized that Barthwal's edition of the *Gorakh-bānī* (Goraknath 1946) remains the only decent critical edition of that important text so far published.

The importance of Barthwal's work lies in the fact that he combined fine textual scholarship with a sensitive awareness of everyday practices and their implications for his areas of interest. In addition to discussing the Nath-nirguni (or *sant*) connection discovered in early literary and religious texts, Barthwal also noted the fact that in some areas of Garhwal (Barthwal's native home), "Kabir is actually called Kabir-nath":

> In Garhwal, he [Kabir] is also regarded as a siddha. He is actually called Kabir-nath in some places. His ideas, as well, spread to Garhwal. The Doms who worship Narankar (*nirakar*) are actually followers of Kabir. The Jagar [the ritual "calling" to the spirit of someone] of Kabir is performed in Narankar worship. Even though Kabir himself believed in non-violence, in this worship the Doms mercilessly kill pigs by way of sacrifice. (Barthwal 1946, 204)

Barthwal refers to the legend that gives a rationale for this practice, but his own conjecture is more interesting: "When the followers of a Muslim guru (i.e. Kabir) began to be regarded by others as Muslims, they were forced to take recourse to this symbolic act to underline their non-Muslimness." Barthwal had no doubts regarding the Muslim origin of Kabir. In his work on the nirguni poets, he had pointed out the "very modern provenance" of the legend that makes Kabir's mother a Brahmin widow.

In his Nagari Pracharini Sabha essay of 1930, Barthwal described Nirguni (or *sant*) poetry as a metamorphosis of the *yog-mārg*, arguing that "the haṭha yoga of Gorakh is only an aid for focussing on God. Kabir does not actually condemn this yoga, and Gorakh did not give undue importance to the physical aspects of yoga" (Barthwal 1978: 75). Barthwal elaborated on this theme in his 1936 seminal work, *Nirguna School of Hindi Poetry* (Barthwal 1978). In it, he pointed out how Buddhism was transformed into the Nath Panth and the "ancient Ekantik Dharma" into medieval Vaisnavism. He also argued convincingly to underline the "debt" owed by the nirguna school to the Nath Panth. Comparing the terminology and ideas (like *surati, nirati, śūnya, unman, ajapājap*) common to both Naths and Nirgunis, Barthwal declared: "Nirgunis are deeply indebted to the Nath Pantha" (Barthwal 1978, 141).

Kabir and other nirguni poets were traditionally held to belong to the lineage of Ramanand, the great independent thinker in the Vaishnava tradition. Barthwal pointed out how yoga and Vaisnavism were assimilated in Ramanand's persona and works. He did this by analyzing the *Siddhānt pañchmātrā* attributed to Raghwanand,[2] the guru of Ramanand, and by highlighting the traditions of close (even if at times competitive) interactions between the yogis and the Vaishnavas. Later on, he published an edition of the Hindi compositions attributed to Ramanand, and again highlighted the Nirgunis' debt to the yogis, not only in idiom and terminology but also in epistemology. And just as in the case of the *Gorakh-bānī*, Barthwal's *Rāmānand kī hindī rachnāem* (Barthwal 1955) remains the only decent edition of the Hindi compositions attributed to Ramanand.

As we have seen, Shukla's history assigned a dual role to the Naths. They built bridges across the communities, but at the same time they disoriented the illiterate and semi-literate from the normal course of the true dharma. Barthwal was writing his magnum opus, *Nirguna School of Hindi Poetry* (Barthwal 1978), in the later half of the fourth decade of the twentieth century. At that time the antagonism between the Hindus and Muslims had been further accentuated. The bridge was now just not showing cracks, but was crumbling. The Indian National Congresss had appointed an enquiry committee to look into the communal (i.e., religio-ethnic) violence that took place in the North Indian industrial town of Kanpur in 1931. This committee was headed by the scholar Dr. Bhagwan Das, and its report was published in 1933. This report, far from being just a political document, was intentionally written as a cultural and theoretical document by its authors. The fourth chapter of this report is titled, "The National Synthesis," and the sub-chapter, "Kabir's Synthesis," approvingly quotes at length from Dr. Tarachand's *The Influence of Islam on Indian Culture* and underlines the statement that "Kabir's was the first attempt to reconcile Hinduism and Islam."[3] The report was obviously more concerned with suggesting the ways of fighting against communal animosity, and this concern was rooted in the larger anxiety of defending the composite Indian nationalism from the onslaughts of colonial attempts—including those using the medium of historiography, to deny India nationhood in both the present and the past.

Barthwal's enthusiastic reconstruction of Gorakhnath as "an instrument of Hindu-Muslim unity" (Barthwal 1978, 287) reflects not only his, but the entire national community's urgent desire and need to resolve a contemporary, political question with the help of history and collective memory. In fact, this anxiety was one of the motivating factors for his study, as becomes clear at the outset of his *Nirguna School of Hindi Poetry*:

> Fortunately, there were men in both the races, who viewed this state of things [i.e. the religious strife] with grave concern . . . The renunciates of both the races . . . felt it the most. Some disciples of Gorakh addressed two of his treatises—the *Kafir-Bodh* and the *Awali-Saluk*—to Mohammad. . . . Half a century later, Ramanand, a Vaishnava teacher, accepted Kabir as his disciple. [Kabir] was a Muslim youth who was destined to be the founder of a great unifying movement. . . . (Barthwal 1978, 8–9)

The surprising and encouraging incident of a Vaishnava taking a Muslim as a disciple could not have occurred without Nath influence, not only on the guru concerned but also on the entire intellectual environment. Significantly, Barthwal's appreciation of Gorakhnath and his lineage was not limited to his being the "instrument of Hindu-Muslim unity." Unlike Shukla, Barthwal does not find these men guilty of leading ordinary folks toward the destruction of the social order.

Nonetheless, a major problem with making Gorakh and Kabir both apostles of Hindu-Muslim unity in a modern nationalist sense becomes ironically clear in Barthwal's decision to omit *sabdī* 226 from his text of the *Gorakh-bānī* since "some communal animosity could be read in it" (Gorakhnath 1946, 73). A scholar working in 1942 could not afford to sound communal even by association.

On the other hand, Gorakh himself, this supposed apostle of Hindu-Muslim unity, did not share such strategic considerations of a modern, composite, Indian nationalism. He was critical of whatever he thought to be empty ritualism and mindless orthodoxy without bothering about its provenance, Hindu or Muslim, and without bothering about whether some people chose to read "communal animosity" into his poetry! This is even more true of the other "apostle of Hindu-Muslim unity": Kabir.

Barthwal did not write a history of Hindi literature as a whole, but he forever changed the evaluation of the Naths in Hindi literary historiography. After his researches and reflections, the direct influence of the Naths on Nirguni poets became a matter of consensus. The role of the Naths in the social and literary history also came to be seen in a more positive light.

Hazariprasad Dvivedi developed Barthwal's ideas further and elaborated upon many of his themes. In fact, Dvivedi used the siddhas and Naths to prove the indigenous provenance of Kabir's condemnation of caste and ritualism, and thus refuted Shukla's idea of Islam having caused the rise of the bhakti movement and sensibility. Dvivedi declared in 1940 with emphasis (*jor de-kar*) that, "Seventy five percent of Hindi literature would have remained the same, even if there had been no Islam on the Indian scene" (Dvivedi 2006, 16).

Thus, the Naths along with the siddhas were assigned a most crucial role in Dvivedi's historiography, a historiography that almost totally rejected the impact of Islam on the rise of bhakti in medieval North India. Here Dvivedi marks a significant departure form both Shukla and Barthwal. He does not see either Gorakh or Kabir as an "instrument of Hindu-Muslim unity." On the contrary, he is quite perplexed while writing his most famous work, *Kabīr* (1942), as to "what is meant by describing Kabir being a preacher of Hindu-Muslim unity" (Dvivedi 2000, 147). Dvivedi rightly points out that, far from being a reconciler of Hinduism and Islam, Kabir was equally critical of both.

Incidentally, Shukla's presentation of the issue of the impact of Islam suffered from positivistic simplifications, but it was certainly closer to both the facts and their role in popular memory. On the other hand, Dvivedi's method makes Islam almost irrelevant for any study of the bhakti sensibility. His idea of lok-dharma hardly takes any notice of Islam's presence in the everyday life of North India. But this is a separate issue and need not detain us here.

Dvivedi also elaborated upon Barthwal's idea of the Nirguna bhakti being a metamorphosis of the Nath Panth and the Nath Panth itself being a metamorphosis of various Buddhist sects and practices. In addition, he also underlined the contribution of other non-Vedic traditions like Jainism to the making of lok-dharma, which, according to him, ought to be taken as a reference point for describing and assessing cultural trends in medieval North India. Contrary to Shukla's usage of the same term, Dvivedi insistently uses the lok-dharma not in a normative, but in a descriptive sense. In his usage, lok-dharma carries the connotation of local, little traditions and the everyday practices of the people instead of an idealized version of the varnashrama worldview. Dvivedi recognized the dialectics between the great and little traditions, but, more importantly, he also recognized and constantly underlined the fact that in the intellectual tradition and scholarly practices of India, those that are "scriptural or standard" *(margā* or Dvivedi's *śāstradharma*) and those that are "local or lived" (*deśī* or Dvivedi's lok-dharma) are not always and necessarily "high" and "low" in the sense of embodying different or contradictory values. Most often these two concepts are the matrices of alternatives, the value of which is to be determined by practical and pragmatic considerations. This is *the* crucial fact for any understanding of Indian tradition, and Dvivedi's constant emphasis on this fact makes his work extremely significant. Dvivedi brought about a radical shift in both literary criticism and historiography by "recommending" lok-dharma (in his preferred sense of "lived religiosity, local practices and little traditions"; Dvivedi 2006, 20) as the main yardstick for assessing and historicizing literary works, events, and authors.

Barthwal had seen Nath influence on Nirguni poets (particularly on Kabir) as coming through the mediation of Ramanand, whose works expressed several kindred ideas. Dvivedi went a step further and sought to relate Kabir and others directly with the Naths. The very chapter division of his *Kabīr* clearly brings this out. Here, we find him familiarizing the reader with a host of complex Nath ideas and terms before he actually comes to talk about Kabir. His enthusiasm in this matter went to the extent of describing Kabir's metaphysics as a direct outgrowth of Nath-Panthi metaphysics, which he called the *dvaitādvaitalakṣaṇavāda* (a doctrine transcending dualism and non-dualism) (Dvivedi 2000: 37–38). Even more interesting is one of his observations in his *Madhyakālin dharmasādhanā* (1952). This volume gives an analytical introduction to the medieval religious practices. Here Dvivedi actually reduced the Nirguni poetry to an exposition of technical aspects of yoga:

> The early stage of the nirguna bhakti must have been the culmination of the tradition of these knowledge-oriented sects. An analysis of the *bānīs* (texts) attributed to Kabir, Dadu etc, logically leads to this conclusion. As a matter of fact, the *sākhīs* (verses) of these poets were composed precisely in order to explain the eight aspects of yoga. Nonetheless, a knowledge-oriented, moral tone is preponderant over yoga in these compositions. In fact, the nirguna bhakti was the attractive liana which grew when the seed of bhakti got planted in the field of this knowledge-oriented, moralist yoga. (Dvivedi 1981, 253)

In order to prove the "non-Muslimness" and, in the same measure, the "nativity" of Kabir and his ideas, Dvivedi in fact goes to the extent of arguing that "Kabir was brought up in a community of weavers which was Nath-Panthi by tradition and had only recently converted to Islam." Naturally enough, "You just can not understand the sayings of Kabir, if you do not posses knowledge of the Nath Panthi doctrines" (Dvivedi 2000, 22–24). This idea of Kabir being "born in a family of Mohammadan weavers who were most probably recent converts" also goes back to Barthwal, who had presented it as an explanation for "high Hindu ideals of Kabir and his proclivity towards Yoga" (Barthwal 1978, 250–51). Dvivedi elevates the idea to the status of an essential precondition for understanding the poetry and philosophical ideas of Kabir. The difference between "brought up" and "born" also can not be missed.

Dvivedi introduces the necessary corrective to the tendency of reducing medieval actors to solution providers for the issues faced by the nationalist narrative of Indian cultural experience, and also the tendency to make Hindu-Muslim conflict entirely a colonial creation. But, unfortunately, Dvivedi goes to the other extreme of ignoring the role of Islam both as the ideology of the ruling class and as a proselytizing, collectivist religion. This cuts into the efficacy of his concept of lok-dharma as well. Dvivedi is actually so enthusiastic about the role of Naths in the making of Kabir and others like him that while reading him at times one is left wondering whether the scholar is talking of Kabir Das or Kabir *Nath*.

The fact, nonetheless, remains that in Dvivedi's usage of the term *lok-dharma* becomes a referent to local, popular and everyday practices and their articulations. This seems quite akin to Lorenzen's idea of "non-caste Hinduism." And the role of the Naths in Dvivedi's idea of lok-dharma is crucial since it is through them that Dvivedi defines lok-dharma as the metamorphosis of Mahayana Buddhism and goes to the extent of describing the relevance of Hindi *sant* literature in terms of its being able to tell us something about this great, popular religion (Dvivedi 2006, 22).

Kabir is generally supposed to be at the center of Dvivedi's critical and historiographical venture, but a careful reading reveals that it is actually the Nath Panth which defines the contours of Dvivedi's enterprise. In Shukla's narrative, Hindi literature was reflective of the ups and downs of the Hindu jati. Dvivedi makes Hindi literature reflective of the spread and influence of Mahayana Buddhism and its later metamorphoses into the Nath and Nirguni movements. In this process, the Naths play a crucial role.

The above analysis brings out the roles assigned to the Naths in these early historiographical ventures. We see the Naths being given credit for offering due respect to vernacular language, for morally purifying the social environment; and for building bridges. At the same time, they are sometimes described as subverting the settled world of the householder and thus leaving a pernicious influence on the people. We also see them making possible the later appearance of Kabir and other religious poets and providing the missing link between the social criticism of the siddhas and the Sants. The Naths are also seen as playing a pivotal and positive role in the metamorphosis not only of Buddhism, but also those of the Hindi language and literature. In addition, we have two contrasting connotations of the same term, the lok-dharma.

It is quite disappointing to note that since the works we have discussed above were published, hardly anything new has been added about the Naths by way of research or reflection on their role in Hindi literary historiography. Of course, there have been subsequent studies of the individual Naths and the Panth as such, and many histories of Hindi literature also have been produced after Shukla, Barthwal, and Dvivedi, but no new departures have been proposed so far as role of the Naths in the history of Hindi literature is concerned. Scholars have simply chosen to highlight the points made by either Shukla or Dvivedi. In fact, the scholarly world of Hindi criticism sometimes seems to be divided into two camps, each one owing its allegiance to one or the other of these two towering figures. But, that of course, is another story.

It ought to be noted, as a second conclusion, that the most important seat of the Naths in North India, the Gorakh Math in Gorakhpur, is now one of the most important centers of the militant Hindutva and has held this dubious distinction for at least the last seventy-five years. On the other hand, in towns and villages of the Northern, Western, and Central India there still exist ascetic wanderers who pledge their allegiance to Gorakh himself and refuse to be part of the Hindutva political project. Hopefully, these contradictions of the lok-dharma or non-caste Hinduism will one day attract the scholarly attention they deserve.

CHAPTER TWO

Religious Identity in Gorakhnath and Kabir

Hindus, Muslims, Yogis, and Sants

David N. Lorenzen

Religious identities are also religious boundaries. How we define our own religious identity depends on defining who we are not. If we are Hindus, then we are not Muslims, Christians, Buddhists, or Sikhs. Or so it would seem. In practice, religious boundaries are rarely so well defined. Particularly among subaltern classes, people often participate in the religious festivals and customs of neighbors who belong to different religions. In the Punjab, for instance, many Muslims, Hindus, and Sikhs join together in the popular annual pilgrimage to the tomb of the legendary Muslim pir, Sakhi Sarvar. Among religious intellectuals, the sharing and borrowing of religious ideas is common. The Advaita philosopher Shankaracharya, for instance, borrowed key ideas from Mādhyamika Buddhism. People can, in some cases, even openly hold multiple religious identities, although this is less likely among followers of more exclusivist religions like Islam and Christianity. This essay will examine the religious boundaries and identities described in early Hindi texts written by, or attributed to, the Nath yogi Gorakhnath and the Nirguni sant poet Kabir.

The Muslim religious jurists, preachers, and holy men who lived in medieval and early modern India generally had a well-defined sense of their own religious identity as Muslims. Scholars are much less in agreement about the extent to which educated Hindus in pre-colonial India had a clear sense of their own identity as Hindus. Most, I think, would accept that such Hindus did not consider themselves to be Muslims, Buddhists, Jains, or Christians.

Some scholars, however, have argued that few if any Hindus identified themselves as Hindus in a general sense but only in terms of the more specific but still loose categories of Vaishnavas, Shaivas, Shaktas—and/or in terms of their narrower sectarian identities as Śrī-vaiṣṇavas, Śaiva-siddhāntins, Pāśupatas, Varkaris, Kabir Panthis, Vallabhacaris, and the like. Elsewhere, I have argued against this view and have tried to show that even in pre-colonial India, the Hindus had a reasonably clear sense of their broader religious identity as Hindus.[1] The source material discussed in chapter helps to explain why I feel that this is the case, although it also shows that sometimes plural religious identities were possible.

Different levels of personal religious identity are not necessarily mutually exclusive. One can easily consider oneself to be a Hindu, a Vaishnava, and a Vallabhachari at the same time. It is less likely, but not impossible, that a person would identify himself as both a Vaishnava and a Shaiva or as both a Pāśupata and a Kabir Panthi. Some persons in pre-colonial India could and did negotiate even more complex religious identities, identities that combined elements of Islamic, Hindu, Jain, and other traditions. To some extent, this is true both of the Nath yogi Gorakhnath and the Nirguni poet Kabir.

In making this claim for a complex negotiation of religious identity in Gorakh and Kabir, I am not referring to a simple syncretism, or lumping together of ritual practices and objects of religious belief (gods, saints, etc.). The mostly illiterate rural and urban populations of agricultural laborers, artisans, and service workers, certainly did practice such syncretism. Take, for instance, the already cited example of the pilgrimage to the tomb of Sakhi Sarvar. Since Gorakhnath and Kabir were religious intellectuals, however, and since we know little about their participation in popular festivals and customs, the focus here must be on their ideas, including their ideas about religious practice. In general, it is clear that Gorakh and Kabir rejected both Islam and Hinduism, as commonly practiced, and sought to construct a religious identity that allowed them to straddle both religious traditions—to somehow be both Hindu and Muslim and neither, all at the same time. To be able to do this, Gorakh and Kabir had to recognize the identity categories of Muslim and Hindu, in a clearly religious sense, and also had to attempt to supersede these categories.

The Hindi compositions attributed to Gorakh, the *Gorakh-bānī,* have yet to be edited and studied adequately. The only decent scholarly edition of this literature is the collection edited by P. D. Barthwal in about 1942 (Gorakhanath 1960). Many more Gorakh *bānī* (sayings) exist in manuscripts, most notably those found in various Rajasthani archives. Another problem is that the dates of these compositions are difficult to estimate. The historical person Gorakh, presuming he actually existed, probably lived in about the eleventh or twelfth centuries, but it is likely that the

Hindi bani attributed to Gorakh, at least in their present form, are mostly later compositions.

Linguistically, Barthwal's *Gorakh-bānī* appear to be somewhat earlier than the oldest collections of verses and songs attributed to Kabir and to Guru Nanak, but little more can be said. Dateable internal evidence in the *Gorakh-bānī* is minimal and is mostly negative evidence about what these texts do *not* mention. For instance, the bani do not mention by name Kabir or any other later poet saints. Unfortunately, the bani do not mention any other historical persons (with the exception of Matsyendranath and Mohammad) or any known historical events. Manuscripts older than the seventeenth century containing Gorakh bani have apparently not been found although this issue needs to be better investigated. The best estimate is that the earliest surviving Gorakh bani probably date from the thirteenth or fourteenth centuries or even later. It is also likely that they have been somewhat altered in the process of transmission from manuscript to manuscript.

GORAKHNATH, HINDUS, AND MUSLIMS

The most intriguing verse from the Barthwal's *Gorakh-bānī* relating to the issue of religious identity is *sabadī* 14:

> *utapati hindū jaraṇāṃ jogī akali pari musalamāṃnīṃ*
> *te rāh cīnhoṃ ho kājī mulāṃ brahmā bisn mahādev māṃnīṃ* //
> By birth [I am] a Hindu, in mature age a Yogi and by intellect a Muslim.
> O kazis and mullahs, recognize the path accepted by Brahma, Vishnu and Shiva.

The translation of this verse, like that of almost any text in the Gorakh bani, involves some speculative interpretation, but the only word that is seriously problematic is *jaraṇāṃ.* The meaning "old age" or "maturity" is most likely, but it could alternatively mean "by burning" (*jalan*), implying "by ascetic practice." Either sense would be acceptable.

What makes this passage significant is, first, the clear recognition of three separate religious traditions: Hindu, yogic, and Muslim. Other Gorakh bani verses, as we will see, also support this division into three general categories of religious identity. More significant, however, is the clear intent of the author to simultaneously identify with all three traditions. He is born a Hindu, later also becomes a yogi, and intellectually adopts, in unfortunately unspecified fashion, the stance of a Muslim.

The second line of the text seems to negate some of the implications of the first line since it implies a rejection of Islam, but I take this to imply a rejection of Islam in terms of ritual practice and exclusiveness, not in terms of philosophical and metaphysical speculations.

Another *Gorakh-bānī* verse makes a somewhat different argument for superseding religious boundaries, one that is similar to a view that, as we shall see, is often argued by Kabir. Here is Gorakh's verse (*sabadī* 182):

daraves soi jo dar kī jāṃṇaiṃ | paṃce pavan apūṭhāṃ āṃṇai |
sadā sucet rahai din rāti | so daraves alah kī jāti ||
A true Dervish is one who knows [how to find the divine] gate,
Who inverts the five breaths,
Who stays conscious day and night,
That Dervish truly belongs to the caste of Allah.

Here Gorakh implicitly juxtaposes the ordinary dervish who knows nothing of yogic meditation and breath control with the dervish who does practice yoga. The latter dervish is the one who truly belongs to the caste of Allah (*alah kī jāti*). Somewhat like Kabir, Gorakh here claims that one can remain a Muslim and nonetheless reach enlightenment. Kabir, however, in a direct comment on this verse, argues that it is not through yoga, but through moral conduct and inner meditation that Muslims, yogis, Hindus, and sants can all attain the enlightenment of spontaneous mystical consciousness (see below).

Several verses from the *Gorakh-bānī* suggest a somewhat sharper rejection of both Muslim and Hindu traditions, at least in terms of ritual practice, and the affirmation of a superior and separate yoga tradition. These verses are quite similar to many verses attributed to Kabir that will be discussed shortly. Here is the most striking of these verses (*sabadī* 68–69):

hindū dhyāvai dehurā musalamāna masīta /
jogī dhyāvai paramapada jahāṃ dehurā na masīta //
The Hindu meditates in the temple, the Muslim in the mosque.
The Yogi meditates on the supreme goal, where there is neither temple nor mosque.

The following two verses, also similar to many verses by Kabir, reject Hindu and Islamic traditions in terms of the uselessness of both the Vedas and the Koran (*sabadī* 4 and 6):

veda kateba na ṣāṃṇīṃ bāṃṇīṃ / saba ḍhaṃkī tali āṃṇīṃ /
gagani siṣara mahi sabada prakāsyā / tahaṃ būjhai alaṣa bināṃṇīṃ //
Neither the Vedas nor the [Muslim] books, neither the *khānīs* nor the *bānīs*. All these appear as a cover [of the truth].[2]
The [true] word is manifested in the mountain peak in the sky [i.e., the Brahmarandhra]. There one perceives knowledge of the Ineffable.
vede na sāstre katebe na kurāṃṇe pustake na baṃcyā jāī /
te pad jāṃṇāṃ biralā jogī aura dunī saba dhaṃdhai lāī //

Neither the Vedas not the Shastras, neither the [Muslim] books nor the Koran, [the goal] is not read about in books.

Only the exceptional Yogi knows that goal. All others are absorbed in their daily tasks.

In these verses, the religion associated with haṭha yoga, the religion of the Nath yogis, is clearly preferred to the religions associated with the Vedas and the Koran, namely the Hindu religion and Islam. As in the verses of Kabir discussed below, there is a clear attempt to move in an independent direction, to establish a religious tradition partly separate from the two dominant traditions. Guru Nanak of course did the same, but his followers institutionalized the move toward independence in a way that the followers of Gorakh and Kabir did not. My argument here is that the reluctance of the Nath Panthis and Kabir Panthis to establish a path clearly separate from Hindu religion and Islam owes at least in part to ambiguities in the ideas of the founder gurus themselves. Since the early works attributed to Kabir are much more numerous than the Gorakh bani and treat the topic in more detail, I will turn now to Kabir.

KABIR, HINDUS, TURKS, AND YOGIS

There are three main early collections that contain Kabir's songs and verses: the Sikh *Ādi Granth,* the Dadu Panthi *Pañca-vāṇī* (the relevant section is usually called the *Kabīr-granthāvalī*), and the Kabir Panthi *Kabīr-bījak.* Other early songs and verses of Kabir are found in the Surdas manuscript of 1582 from Fatehpur, in Rajjab's *Sarvāṅgī,* and in Gopaldas's *Sarvāṅgī.*[3] A combined edition giving most versions of the early songs (without those from the *Kabīr-bījak*) has recently been published by Callewaert (Kabir 2000). There is much overlap of Kabir's compositions in these early collections, particularly between the *Ādi Granth* and the *Pañca-vāṇī,* but even discounting this overlap the total number of songs and verses in quite large. Later collections add many more compositions that they attribute to Kabir, but these collections will not be considered here.

Many of Kabir's verses and songs criticize Muslim and Hindu religious practices quite sharply. Quite a few songs single out the Nath yogis for criticism. Best known are those songs that criticize both Muslims and Hindus. The major older collections contain a dozen or more songs of this type. These dual-criticism songs are somewhat less numerous in the *Ādi Granth,* however, where Hindus and Muslims are usually criticized in separate songs. In the dual-criticism songs, Kabir typically describes the foolish and immoral practices of the Hindus (usually called simply "Hindus" but sometimes "pandits" or "Brahmins") and the Muslims (usually called "Turks" or "Musalamans" but sometimes "kazis" or "mullahs"), one after the other, and then concludes with an exhortation for us either to seek the divine spirit that dwells within all our bodies or to meditate on Ram (sometimes called Govind, Hari, Murari, etc.) or to repeat Ram's name.

As an example, here is a *ramaini* that appears both in the *Kabīr-bījak* and in the *Kabīr-granthāvalī*:[4]

> He who taught the Muslim creed (*kalamāṃ*) in the Kali age
> Was unable to seek out the power of the creation.
> According to karma, the actor performs his actions.
> The Vedas and Muslim books are all worthless.
> According to karma, one became an avatar in the world.
> According to karma, one fixed the Muslim prayers.
> According to karma, circumcision or the sacred thread.
> Neither the Hindu nor the Turk knows the secret.
> Water and air were joined together,
> All this turmoil was created.
> When *surati* is absorbed in the Void,
> On what basis can our caste be told?

Here the words *surati* and *the Void* merit some discussion. *Surati* is a word frequently used by Kabir and other Nirguni poets, but its sense is not always clear. In this and many other passages it seems to refer to individual consciousness inspired or pervaded by the presence of divine spirit. In other words it is a concept similar to *ātman* in Advaita metaphysics and to various other terms used by Nath and Nirguni poets, most notably the word *unman.* Although *the Void* is a term ultimately borrowed from Madhyamika Buddhism, here it seems to represent an inchoate reality into which the surati is absorbed either after death or in mystic illumination. Perhaps it would be more appropriate to compare Kabir's "void" to either the Yogacara

Buddhist *ālaya-vijñāna* (repository consciousness) or to the Advaita interpretation of *brahman* (the ground of being). What Kabir seems to mean is that when individual consciousness is absorbed back into the ground of being, when we lose our individual consciousness and individual attributes, there is essentially nothing for karma to work on. Distinctions of caste and sex no longer operate.

KABIR AND GURU ARJAN

Another song of this type that is found in several different early collections and manuscripts—including the *Kabīr-granthāvalī,* Gopaldas's *Sarvāṅgī,* Rajjab's *Sarvāṅgī,* and the *Kabīr-bījak,* but not in the *Ādi Granth*—is the following:[5]

> These differences are full of confusions:
> Vedas and Muslim books, religion and the world,
> Who is male, who female?
> Semen is one, piss and shit are one,
> skin one, flesh one.
> All arose from one light.
> Who then is a Brahmin? Who a Shudra?
> This body sprang from clay, spontaneously.
> In it sound and semen joined together.
> When it dies, what name will you bear?
> You study and cogitate, but never learn the secret.
> Brahma is red creation, Shiva black destruction.
> And Hari is filled with white virtue.
> Kabir says: Worship the one Ram.
> Nobody is Hindu, nobody Turk.

What makes this song particularly interesting is the final phrase, "Nobody is Hindu, nobody Turk" (*hindū turka na koī).* This phrase is remarkably similar, in wording and sense, to the one that Guru Nanak (1469–1539) is said to have uttered when he emerged from the river after his trance of enlightenment, namely "Nobody is Hindu, nobody Muslim" (*nā koī hindū hai nā koi musalamān*). This statement, well known to all Sikhs, is found first not among Nanak's compositions in the *Ādi Granth,* but rather in an early legendary account of his life, the B40 *janam-sākhī* (see McLeod 1980a, 255; McLeod 1980b, 21).

A similar phrase does occur in the *Ādi Granth,* however, in a song of the fifth Sikh guru, Guru Arjan (1563–1606). In this song, Arjan says: "We are [*or* I am] neither Hindu nor Muslim" (*nā ham hiṃdū na musalamān*). What is particularly interesting about this song is that Guru Arjan gives it Kabir's signature (*kahu Kabīr*). As Pashaura Singh (2003, 16–17, 101–109) has pointed out, Guru Arjan several times quotes Kabir or uses his signature. Arjan does this either to show that the theme of his song or verse is associated with Kabir or to directly cite one or more verses from one of Kabir's compositions. Guru Arjan sometimes uses the occasion to suggest some criticism or modification of Kabir's point of view.

In this case, the first three verses of Arjan's song and the refrain appear to be a direct quote from a song of Kabir that is found only in the *Kabīr-granthāvalī* and in Gopaldas's *Sarvāṅgī* among the early collections.[6] The last two verses are apparently written by Guru Arjan himself, although the first of these two verses includes the *nā ham hiṃdū na musalamān* phrase that, as we have seen, is probably an allusion to Kabir's phrase *hindū turka na koī*. Paradoxically, the final verse that begins "Kabir says" (*kahu Kabīr*) is evidently the verse that most clearly represents Guru Arjan's own words. Here is Guru Arjan's song:[7]

> I don't keep [Hindu] vows, nor [fast] in Ramadan.
> I serve Him who protects me when life is done.
> *For me the [Hindu] Lord and Allah are one.*
> *I have separated from both the Hindu and the Turk.*
> I don't go on Hajj to the Kaba nor offer *pūjā* at [Hindu] holy sites.
> I serve the One [God] and no other.
> I don't do *pūjā* and don't offer *namāz.*
> I welcome in my heart the one Formless God (*niraṃkār*)
> I am neither Hindu nor Musalman.
> Body and breath belong to Allah-Ram.
> Kabir says: I made this declaration.
> Meeting with pir and guru, I recognized the potential in myself.

The final verse in Kabir's song (*Kabīr-granthāvalī,* no. 338)—the only verse of the song that Guru Arjan does not quote—reads: "Kabir says: All error has fled, my mind is attached to the one Niranjan."

These texts of Kabir, Nanak, and Arjan embody two overlapping senses. First, the key phrases can be taken to claim that all external markers of religious identity, all particular beliefs and practices, are essentially meaningless in the light of direct mystical consciousness. Second, these phrases can be taken to indicate that Kabir, Nanak, and Arjan all tended to reject a personal religious identity as either Hindus or Muslims and were moving in the direction of building an independent religious identity, separate from both Muslim and Hindu traditions. The change in pronominal reference from "no one is" (*nā koī*) in Kabir and Nanak, to "we are not" (*nā ham*) in Arjan also suggests a shift in the direction of the second sense that fits well within the overall course of Sikh history.

KABIR'S CRITICISMS OF HINDUS AND MUSLIMS

Kabir's rejection of the ritual practices and exclusivity of Hindus and Muslims more often takes the form of songs that criticize either the Hindu or the Muslim traditions. In general, we can say that the songs that criticize Hindus are more frequent, but the criticisms of Muslims are often expressed in harsher terms. Often he especially attacks the Hindu practice of animal sacrifice and the Muslim practices of killing (and eating) cows and other animals. Here is a pair of *ramainīs* found in the *Kabīr-granthāvalī* that seems to be purposely juxtaposed, one following the other in this collection:

The first *ramainī* criticizes, in rather lurid fashion, the killing of cows by Muslims:[8]

> We have searched the Turk's religion (*turakī dharam*).
> These teachers throw many thunderbolts.
> Recklessly they display boundless pride.
> While explaining their own aims, they kill cows.
> How can they kill the mother
> Whose milk they drink like that of a wet nurse?
> The young and the old drink milk pudding,
> But these fools eat the cow's body.
> *These morons know nothing. They wander about in ignorance.*
> *Without looking into one's heart, how can one reach paradise?*

The *ramainī* that follows is directed against the Hindus, especially the Vedic pandits:[9]

> The pandits have gone astray studying and pondering the Vedas,
> Lost in many secrets they do not find their own selves.
> Absorbed in their daily prayers, sacrificial libations,
> And the six ritual acts, they stay in their ashrams.
> They have imparted the Gayatri mantra throughout the four ages,
> But go and ask if any have attained salvation.
> Ram is found immanent in everyone, but they purify themselves.

Tell me who is lower than these?
So virtuous, they display excessive pride.
But excessive pride is not good.
The Lord who is the destroyer of pride,
How can he endure such pride?
Abandon all thought of arrogance and search for nirvana.
When the seed and seedling [of pride] are destroyed,
Then one finds the place of bodiless being.

In the early collections, Kabir mentions several specific titles that can refer only to Muslims. Using Callewaert and Op de Beeck's word index to the *Kabīr-bījak* and to P. N. Tiwari's edition of the *Kabīr-granthāvalī,* we find the following frequencies:[10] pir (*pīr, pīran,* twenty-three), kazi (*kajī,* nine), Sufi sheikh (*seṣ,* seven), mullah (*mulā, mullā,* seven), prophet (*paigaṃbar. paigaṃbhar,* three), saint (*auliyā,* two), sayyid (*saiyad,* two), sultan (*sulatāṃna,* two), dervish (*daravesā,* one), *badshah* (*bādasāh,* one). He does not mention or distinguish specific Sufi schools (*tariqas*), nor does he mention or distinguish Sunnis and Shias. The words Kabir uses for Muslims in general are Turk (*turakā, turakin, turuk, turka, taruk,* etc., thirty-six) and Musalman (*musalamān, muusalamāṃna,* etc., five). The context in which these titles and the words *Turk* and *Musalma*n occur is virtually always a religious one. Kabir never uses the word *Turk* in a principally ethnic sense and he clearly uses Turk and Musalman as synonyms. In the *Gorakh-bānī* the word *Turk* does not occur and the word *Musalman* occurs only twice.

The Kabir song with the greatest variety of Muslim titles is *ramainī* 49 of the *Kabīr-bījak.* This song, like the song quoted above, is directed against the Muslims' slaughter of animals:[11]

Tell me, Dervish, [how to find the divine] gate.
What does the Badshah [i.e. Allah] wear?
Where does His army assemble?
Where does it camp?
I'm asking you, Muslim.
What color are His robes?
Red, yellow, or multicolored?
To what divine presence (*surati*)
do you offer homage?
Kazi, what are you doing?
In every house you have buffaloes killed.
Who ordered you to kill goats and chickens?

Who told you to wield a knife?
You know no pity, but are called a Pir.
Reciting verse, you lead the world astray.
Kabir says: You declare yourself a Sayyid,
  And persuade everyone to be like you.
  They fast all day. At night they kill cows.
  Blood from one, a greeting for the other.
  How can this please God?

What is particularly interesting about this song is that it begins with an obvious reference to the *Gorakh-bānī* verse quoted before that praises the dervish who attains the "caste of Allah" by yogic breath control and meditation.[12] Here, Kabir is claiming that such yogic practices are not enough if the dervish continues to kill animals.

In the case of Hindus, Kabir sometimes mentions specific religious groups including Vaishnavas, yogis, and Shaktas. He often directs his songs and verses to Brahmins, to Pandits, and to Pandas as the principal sponsors of the Hindu practices he criticizes such as animal sacrifice, empty Vedic recitation, the rules of caste purity and untouchability, and the worship of idols. The yogis or jogis are also criticized for the uselessness of their penances and exercises. They are mentioned by name more often than any other group. Gorakh himself is also often named. Using the same word index we find the following word frequencies:[13] Hindu (*hiṃdū, hindū, hiṃduini,* thirty), Brahmin (*babhanīṃ, bāṃmhan, bāṃhman, bābhan, brāhman, bhāmini,* etc. thirty-seven), Pandit (*paṃḍit, paṃḍitā,* sixty-three), Panda (*paṃḍā, paṃḍiā, pāṃḍe,* twelve), Shakta (*sākat,* seventeen), yogi (*jogini, jogiyā, jogī, yogī,* etc. fifty-two), Gorakh (*goraṣ, goraṣanāth,* fifteen), Vaishnava (*vaiṣnav, baisanauṃ,* three).

The use of the word *Hindu* merits special comment. Kabir virtually always uses it in a religious context and never in a noticeably ethnic sense. For Kabir a Hindu is a person who follows Hindu religious beliefs and practices, not a native of the Indian subcontinent. For Kabir Hindus are usually those who worship idols, worship Shiva and Vishnu, sacrifice animals, recite the Vedas, practice untouchability. They are often identified as Pandits and Brahmins, or at least these are taken as their leading representatives (as is, of course, quite appropriate). The yogis and Saktas, however, are set somewhat apart by Kabir, and it is not clear whether he regards them as Hindus or as separate groups. As we have seen, Gorakh's own Hindi bani also tend to set the yogis apart from Hindus and Muslims. In the *Gorakh-bānī* the word *Hindu* occurs three times, the word *pandita* nine times, and the word *Brahmin* only once. Like Kabir, Gorakh always uses the word *Hindu* in a primarily religious sense, not in an ethnic or geographical sense.

Kabir's references to Shaktas (*sākata*), the worshippers of the Goddess (Shakti), may reflect an aspect of his own life history. The earliest legendary biography of Kabir is the *Kabīr-paracāī* by Anantadas, written toward the end of the sixteenth century. At the beginning of this text, Anantadas says: "There was a Julaha living in Kashi who followed the customs of the devotees of Hari. Earlier he spent many days among the Shaktas. Afterwards he lived by praising the virtues of Hari."[14] In other words, Kabir is said to have first been a Shakta and then became a follower of Vishnu. If true, he should have known something about the Shaktas. What we find, however, is that the Shaktas are never mentioned directly in the *Kabīr-bījak*. They are mentioned often in the early Western collections of Kabir's songs and verses (the *Adi-granth* and the *Kabīr-granthāvalī*), but these texts say very little about what the Shaktas believed or practiced.

In his translation of Kabir's songs in the *Ādi Granth,* Nirmal Dass translates Shakta (*sākat*) as simply "non-believer" or "the godless." Although this may be a traditional interpretation of Sikh commentators, it seems to me to go too far. Even if Kabir does not say who exactly the Shaktas were, the etymology and normal use of the term is clear enough. It refers to the worshippers of the Goddess. Whatever they may lack in specifics, Kabir's comments about the Shaktas are all extremely critical. Here is one such song found in many early Western collections:[15]

> Keep to Ram, Ram, Ram, but
> Don't say Ram while
> going astray with Shaktas.
> What can come from reciting scripture (sumṛt) to a dog?
> What from singing the praises of Hari for Shaktas?
> What from feeding camphor to a crow?
> What from having a snake drink milk?
> Shaktas and dogs are brothers,
> Both snarl and bark.
> They drink nectar, and spit vinegar.
> Kabir says: Don't take to their ways.

Kabir's references to Gorakh and his yogi followers are more frequent and more specific. They are found in both the *Kabīr-bījak* and in early Western collections. The modern scholars P. D. Barthwal (1946) and H. Dvivedi (1971) long ago noted that Kabir's songs and verses are filled with vocabulary and imagery borrowed from the Nath yogis. In addition both the Naths and Kabir can be broadly classed as Nirgunis, in the sense that they worship a largely formless God, although the Nath names for this God are mostly associated with Shiva and those of Kabir with Vishnu.

Kabir's use of Nath terminology led H. Dvivedi to speculate that Kabir's family may have belonged to a caste of Nath yogis turned householders who had been recently, and incompletely, converted to Islam and taken the caste name of Julahas. Dvivedi wrote: "Several things make one think that the Julaha family (*vaṃśa*) in which Kabir-das was raised was the Muslim form of a family of householder Yogis who followed the Nath doctrine." More recently the French scholar, Charlotte Vaudeville (1974, 89), although she criticized aspects of Dvivedi's argument, came to a similar conclusion:

> Circumcised or not, Kabir was officially a *musalman,* though it appears likely that some form of 'Nathism' was his ancestral tradition. This alone would explain his relative ignorance of Islamic tenets, his remarkable acquaintance with Tantric-yoga practices and his lavish used of its esoteric jargon. The fact is that, though Kabir is not himself a Nath-panthi, though he ridicules the Gorakhnathis' paraphernalia and even more their pretensions to immortality, he appears far more conversant with their basic attitudes and philosophy than with the Islamic orthodox tradition.

This hypothesis of Kabir's family having had a Nath background does seem to be a reasonable one, although it remains highly speculative. Vaudeville's claim that Kabir had a "remarkable acquaintance with Tantric-yoga practices" and that he made lavish use "of its esoteric jargon," however, represents a considerable exaggeration. Although Kabir does make use of some of the mystic and yogic vocabulary associated with the *Gorakh-bānī*, for the most part he employs this vocabulary in a loose way without giving much evidence of a clear understanding of the technical details of yogic anatomy. Nor does Kabir give any clear evidence that he himself engaged in yogic practices such as breath control, semen retention, and yogic postures. The extent to which Gorakh and the Naths can be classed as tantrik is also debatable.[16]

What the Gorakh and Kabir bani do share is a fascination with a state of mystical consciousness associated with the "sky" (*gagan*)—the tenth "door" (*dvār*), located in the top of the head or just above it. This mystical consciousness has many names. Four important synonyms often found in the Gorakh and Kabir bani are *surati, unman,* the experience of the "unstruck" (*anāhad*) sound, and the "spontaneous" (*sahaja*) experience. The term *samādhi,* the term most often used for mystical consciousness in classical Pātañjala or rāja yoga, appears seven or eight times in early Kabir but only four times in the Gorakh bani. The *Haṭha-yoga-pradīpikā,* an important Sanskrit text of haṭha yoga from about the seventeenth century, claims that all the following terms are essentially synonyms:[17]

> Raja-yoga, Samadhi, Unmani, Manomani, Amaratva (immortality), Laya (absorption), Tattva (Truth), Sunyasunya (void and yet not-void) Parama-pada (the supreme state), Amanaska (transcending the mind), Advaita (non-duality), Niralamba (without support), Niranjana (pure), Jivanmukti (liberation while in the body), Sahaja (natural state) and Turya, all of these are synonymous (*ity eka-vācakāḥ*).

The strong overlap between the Gorakh and Kabir bani can be easily seen in a comparison of key words relating to yoga found in both traditions. Callewaert and Op de Beeck's word index to Barthwal's *Gorakh-bānī,* to the *Kabīr-bījak,* and to P. N. Tiwari's somewhat abridged edition of the *Kabīr-granthāvalī* provides the following examples.

Word	*Gorakh-bānī*	*Kabīr-bījak*	*Kabīr-granthāvalī*	Total Number of Occurrences
sahaja, etc.	50	12	21	83
gagan, etc.	35	10	25	70
unaman, etc.	19	1	12	32
anahad, etc.	20	7	10	37
surati	5	7	15	27
āsana, etc.	12	5	5	22
cakra and kamal	4	7	5	16
nāḍī, etc.	11	0	0	11
suṣamana, etc.	5	0	3	8
kuṇḍalinī	0	0	0	0
prāṇāyāma	0	0	0	0

Some of these words may have possibly overlooked spellings and some can have multiple senses. Also, other synonyms for these words have not been listed here. Nonetheless, the general pattern is quite clear. The *Gorakh-bānī,* as expected, has a greater frequency of yogic words although the Kabir collections also make ample use of this vocabulary. Less expected is the low frequency of explicit references to yogic *cakras* and *nāḍīs* (including *suṣumnā*) and the complete absence, in both Kabir and Gorakh, of the words *kuṇḍalinī* and *prāṇāyāma* and of explicit references to specific haṭha yoga practices such as the Vajroli and Khecari *mudrās.* This low frequency and absence is true both of the *Gorakh-bānī* and Kabir's songs and verses. It is also interesting that the eastern *Kabīr-bījak* has a lower frequency of yogic terminology than the western *Kabīr-granthāvalī*, possibly reflecting the fact that Nath influence was stronger in the West.

From the point of view of an outside observer, this data shows more or less what one expects. Although there is considerable overlap between Gorakh's Nath yoga tradition and Kabir's nirguni sant tradition, there is nonetheless a fairly clear difference of emphasis between the two. As noted, however, it is somewhat surprising that the *Gorakh-bānī* includes such a small number of explicit references to the yogic anatomy of the various cakras (although the Brahmarandhra is often mentioned) and the principal nadis (*iḍā, piṅgalā,* and *suṣumṇā*). Nor are there any explicit references to the associated snake goddess Kundalini.

It is, nonetheless, also true that even Svātmarāma's later and authoritative Sanskrit text, the *Haṭha-yoga-pradīpikā* (Svātmarāma 1975), contains no clear description of the system of cakras, although it does mention various "lotuses" (i.e. cakras) and does describe Kundalini and her progress up the sushumna (*Haṭha-yoga-pradīpikā*, chapter 3). The history of Kundalini and the various systems of cakras is a subject that needs further research. The presence of the snake-goddess Kundalini and the sexual activities of vajrolī-mudrā in texts such as the *Haṭha-yoga-pradīpikā* written considerably later than the Gorakh bani at least partly contradict Gorakhnath's legendary rejection of the Shakta and Kaula traditions associated with his guru, Matsyendranath. Apparently, some sexual practices, mostly those concerned with the control of sexual fluids, eventually infiltrated back into haṭha yoga, or perhaps they had always been present.

Still more surprising is the *Gorakh-bānī*'s almost complete lack of references to yogic techniques such as pranayama, vajroli-mudra, and the bandhas. The word *āsana* does appear twelve times, but no specific asanas are ever named. There is no doubt that the early Nath yogis practiced haṭha yoga. These techniques are explained in detail in many Nath yogi texts, many written in Sanskrit like the *Haṭha-yoga-pradīpikā* and the *Gorakṣa-śataka.* The only partly satisfactory explanation I can make for the absence of any mention of such techniques in the *Gorakh-bānī* is that the mystical songs and verses of this collection were not considered to be a suitable place to engage in didactic explanations about yogic anatomy and yogic techniques.

The same argument could also be used to claim that Kabir may also have adopted yogic practices. In a few songs, however, Kabir sharply criticizes the paraphernalia and practices of the yogis. Here is one such song from the *Ādi Granth*:[18]

> Brother, even dressed up with your staff,
> earrings, patchwork cloak, and arm rest,
> you have gone astray.

Madman, give up yogic postures (āsanu) and breath-[control] (pavanu).
Madman, give up trickery and always worship Hari.
What you want is He who enjoys the three worlds.
Kabir says: Keshav is the Yogi of the universe.

In the present context, it is important to note that the early songs and verses attributed to Kabir generally distinguish four major religious traditions in India: those of the Hindus, the Muslims, the yogis, and rather less prominently, the Shaktas. A few times Kabir also mentions the Vaishnavas, the Shaivas, and the Jainas. He also makes it clear that he considers his own religious position to be, in some respects, independent of all these traditions. It is not clear to what extent Kabir classified the Shaktas, the Vaishnavas, and the Shaivas as different kinds of Hindus. Nor is it clear if he classified the Jainas as non-Hindus. My own impression is that he did include Vaishnavas and Shaivas, and probably the Shaktas, as Hindus, but the evidence is not definitive. When Kabir refers to Hindus, he usually emphasizes the caste and ritual pollution obsessions of the Brahmins or pandits, their blind reliance on the Vedas, the Hindus' foolish worship of idols, and their evil fondness for animal sacrifice. He also sometimes criticizes the avatars and their improper behavior.

What is clear and somewhat surprising is that Kabir clearly regards the yogis as an independent religious tradition, neither Hindu nor Muslim. As we have noted, roughly the same point of view is found in the *Gorakh-bānī.* Here is stanza from a Kabir song found in most of the early Western collections:[19]

The Yogis say "Gorakh, Gorakh."
The Hindus proclaim the Name Ram.
The Muslims have their one God (*ek ṣudāī*).
Kabir's Lord is present in every body.

Another example is the *Kabīr-granthāvalī* version of the *Ādi Granth* song translated above:[20]

You stay fixed on yogic postures and breath-[control].
But, madman, it is mental impurity you should renounce.
What's the use of going about with horns and earrings?
What the use of smearing all your body with ashes?
He whose creed (*īmāṃna*) is fit and proper,
He is a Hindu, he is a Muslim.
He who preaches knowledge of Brahman,
He is a Brahmin

He who knows Rahim,
He is a kazi.
Kabir says: Don't do anything else.
Just repeat the Name Ram,
and you'll get what you want.

What is evident in both these two passages is that Kabir is arguing that true religion comes from the heart or inner spirituality. He recognizes the basic differences among the yogis, the Hindus and the Muslims, but also claims that in some sense all are true if one follows them with a pure heart. Kabir is neither an opponent of Hinduism, Islam, and haṭha yoga nor an "apostle of Hindu-Muslim unity." Rather, he is a radical pluralist. He opposes these three religious traditions *as practiced*, but does not advocate conversion from one tradition to another. If a person rejects the hypocrisy and exclusionary politics of these existing religious traditions, and also rejects their misguided rituals, he can, Kabir implicitly claims, find an inner spiritual enlightenment while continuing to follow any one of these traditions. Whether such a soteriological strategy has in fact any chance of success, depends on how intrinsic the social and political ideologies of religious traditions are to their existence. Can the Hindu religion exist without ascribed social hierarchy? Can Islam exist without an exclusionary social identity? Can either exist without ritual display? Can either exist without the hypocrisy intrinsic to any ideology, religious or secular, that attempts to legitimize social, political, and economic institutions?

In the end, Kabir's own arguments suggest, I think, that his vision of the spiritual transformation of existing religious tradition was not practical, or maybe not even a logical possibility. His vision of religion devoid of hypocrisy and ritual could not plausibly be incorporated within the actually existing Hindu religion, or Islam, or Nath yoga. In terms of its internal logic, Kabir's vision is so radical and individualistic that it is not really compatible with the creation of any organized religious community. Purushottam Agrawal (2004, 215) expresses the incompatibility of Kabir's radical religious stance and institution building in stark terms: "Kabir's poetry does not stop at criticizing the religious practices prevalent in his time; it bears enough testimony of Kabir's dissatisfaction with the very *raison d'être* of religion itself. To hold the view that establishing 'an independent religious tradition' was the aim of Kabir is a great mistake."

Already in the earliest legendary biography of Kabir, Anantadas's *Kabīr paracāī*, doubts are expressed that Kabir's vision could be reconciled with existing realities. When the Hindus and Muslims of Benares came to the visiting sultan, Sikandar Lodi, to complain about Kabir's behavior, Sikandar asks them, "What has Kabir done?" They reply:[21]

> He has done an unconventional thing. He has abandoned the customs of the Muslims and has broken the touchability rules of the Hindus. He has scorned the sacred bathing places and the Vedas. . . . He has scorned the rites of the eleventh day of the fortnight, the offerings to the sacred fire and the ceremonies for the dead. He has scorned the Brahmins, whom the whole world worships. . . . He has scorned the hope of all religion. . . . He respects neither the Hindus nor the Turks. In this way he has corrupted everyone. He has put both the Hindus and the Turks in the same situation. As long as this low-caste weaver stays in Benares, no one will respect us.

It is, I think, nonetheless at least possible that Kabir established a group of followers or allowed such a group to assemble around him for more practical, human reasons. Whenever the Kabir Panth was first created, in Kabir's lifetime or years later, it never separated itself from Hindu religion in the way that the Sikhs did. Most Kabir Panthis today claim to be Hindu, and since Hindu religion is generally tolerant of a wide range of beliefs and practices most Hindus accept this claim.

GORAKH AND KABIR

Whatever Kabir's ultimate intentions may have been with regard to the religious allegiance of himself and his followers, and we will never know for certain, his relation with Gorakhnath's tradition is a key to much of his religious and social ideology, precisely because his and Gorakh's overall views are so similar. One way to deal with the responsibilities, dilemmas, and moral compromises of everyday life, is to retreat into the life of an ascetic. This is the path that Gorakhnath and the Nath yogis chose. Their rejection of the householder's life is clear from the central legend that tells how Gorakhnath rescued his guru, Matsyendranath, from the woman's kingdom (or queendom) where Matsyendra lived as the consort of Queen Mainakini. This legend also indicates a clear rejection of tantric or Kaula rites that involve sexual union between the male adept and his female partner. The rejection of ritual sexual activity was never complete among the Nath yogis, however, as is evident from the vajroli mudra, a technique of sexual control, described in the *Haṭha-yoga-pradīpikā* (1975, chapter 3).

The extent to which Kabir rejected the life of a householder is not clear.[22] Some of his songs in the *Ādi-granth* mention his wife, but these references have sometimes been interpreted as being purely metaphorical. Both legends about Kabir and one of his verses also mention his son Kamal. Legends also mention a daughter Kamali. According to modern Kabir Panthi tradition, Kabir was never married and his children were both adopted. Even assuming that Kabir was married, however, several of his songs and verses express hostile attitudes to women, although these references can also be taken in a primarily metaphorical sense as references to Maya and the distractions of everyday life.

The opening two verses of a Kabir song in the *Ādi Granth* feature a complaint by Kabir's mother that he has abandoned his trade as a weaver in order to follow Ram:[23]

> Kabir's mother sulks about and cries,
> "O Ram, how will this boy live?
> *Kabir has left aside his weaving*
> *And has written Hari's name on his body.*"

Quite possibly Kabir at some point in his life gave up his profession as a weaver to dedicate himself full time to his religious calling. This would, however, not necessarily imply that he completely abandoned family life to become an ascetic. Guru Nanak, for example, abandoned his life as an accountant to dedicate himself full time to religion without completely giving up his life as a married householder. Even if we assume that Kabir became an ascetic, however, there still is a quite clear difference between Kabir's and Gorakh's attitudes toward the human body.

GORAKH'S SONG

To illustrate this difference between Gorakh and Kabir, I will examine a song by Gorakh that is answered and commented on in a similar song by Kabir. These two songs are particularly apt examples in the present context since they each criticize several other religious traditions. Gorakh's song in particular also raises an interesting question about the religious identity of the Yekamkaris he mentions in it. Gorakh's song is as follows:[24]

> O pandit, there are no debates among the devotees.
> He who does not speak is a [true] Avadhut.
>
> The god Brahma is in the leaf, Vishnu is in the flower, Rudra is in the fruit. [With your offerings] you have done harm (*ched*) to these three gods. To whom do you offer your service?
>
> The Ekadandi, the Dvidandi, and the Tridandi became Bhagavatas. Those of Vishnu did not get to the other shore. Wandering from tirtha to tirtha they died.

> The one with the Black Face (*kāla muhāṃ*) who wears his hair in a *jaṭā* became a worshipper of the linga. Those of Mahadeva did not get to the other shore. Smearing themselves with ashes they died. (3)
>
> The four Mahadhars and the twelve disciples became Yekamkaris. Those of the *kāyam* did not get to the other shore. Lighting lamps/lights they died.
>
> The fourteen *pūnamiyā* became those who follow the vow of the Jainas. Those of the Arhats did not get to the other shore. Pulling out their hair (by the roots) they died.
>
> The one mullah (*mulāṃnam*) and two Korans (*kurāṃnam*) became the eleven Khorasanis. Those of Allah did not get to the other shore. Giving the call to prayer, they died.
>
> The nine Naths and the 84 Siddhas became Asanadharis. Those of Yoga did not get to the other shore. Wandering in the forests they died.
>
> The body of five elements will be destroyed. No one is able to preserve it. Death runs away (*davan*) only when knowledge appears. Thus says Gorakh.

In many respects this could also be a song by Kabir. Its emphasis on the inevitable death of the body is a favorite theme of Kabir, as is the insistence on the moral and spiritual emptiness of religious ritual. The verse criticizing the Asanadharis, including the nine Nathas and eighty-four Siddhas, could even suggest that this may not be a song of Gorakh, but rather a song of Kabir himself that somehow got interpolated into the *Gorakh-bānī*. The language of the song, however, is typical of most of the *Gorakh-bānī*, and the mention of the Kalamukhas (*kāla muhāṃ*) also suggests a date earlier than Kabir since the Shaiva sect of this name had largely died out by about 1300. Also, as I will attempt to show below, the quite similar song by Kabir that appears in the early Western collections contains a key criticism of Gorakh's attitude to the human body.

THE YEKAMKARIS AND OTHERS

Before turning to Kabir's song, however, I want to discuss the possible religious identity of the Yekamkaris (*yekaṃkārī*) and others who appear in verse four of Gorakh's song. Gorakh's song is in fact full of confusing details. In verse six, for instance, who is the one mullah (*mulāṃnam*) and the eleven Khorasanis (*surasāṇī*) and what are the two "Korans" (*kurāṃnam*)? Whatever the answer may be, it is clear that it is the Muslims who are referred to in this verse. Likewise, in the fifth verse, it is not certain who or what the fourteen *pūnamiyā* are, but it is clear that the verse refers to the Jainas. The Yekamkaris are more mysterious.

Considering that the other religious groups mentioned—the Bhagavatas, the Kalamukha Shaivas, the Jainas, the Muslims, the 84 Buddhist Mahasiddhas, and the Nath yogis themselves—are all important and well-known religious groups, one has to assume that the Yekamkaris were also a prominent group. But who could they be? My first guess was that they might be the Sikhs, since "*ekoaṃkār*" is the principal, or *mūl,* mantra of the Sikhs, a mantra recited every day by pious Sikhs. After consulting with several Sikh scholars, however, I had to abandon this idea. They pointed out the obvious fact that the verse is probably pre-Sikh and also the fact that it was not easy to identity the four Mahadhars and twelve disciples within Sikh tradition, nor to make much sense of the word *kāyam,* nor to account for the Yekamkaris fondness for lighting lamps. I had suggested that the four Mahadhars might be the first four Sikh gurus and the *kāyam* might be a corruption of the word *qaum* ("community" or "nation"), which at some point (unfortunately, probably somewhat later) came to refer to the Sikh community.

Another possibility is that these Yekamkaris might be Christians. The Christians do have four gospels and Jesus had twelve disciples. Both Roman and Orthodox Christians also have a fondness for lighting lamps or candles. But this still leaves the problem of the *kāyam,* and it also seems unlikely that a poet writing in Hindi sometime between about 1200 and 1500 would have had much contact with the Christians, since in India at this time most Indian Christians lived in the deep South.

When I put this question to Aditya Behl, he immediately suggested that these Yekamkaris might be Muslims, more specifically some sort of Sufis. He pointed out that the word *ekoṃkāra* appears in the first verse of the Manjhan's Sufi romance entitled *Madhumālatī,* written in 1545 in a Hindi-related language usually called Hindavi. In the notes to their translation of this romance, Behl and Simon Weightman (Manjhan 2000, 243) comment that "the term *ekoṃkāra,* the one sound, is a reference to the *Qur'anic* account of creation, in which God said 'Be' and 'It was.' " Behl also noted that the word *ēkaṃkāra* appears as an epithet of God twice in another Sufi romance, Shaikh Qutban's *Mirigāvatī* (see Plukker 1981, 3, 57). Behl takes both *ekoṃkāra* and *ēkaṃkāra,* as they appear in these Sufi sources, as equivalent terms and considers the former to be the more correct form. As explained below, I have some doubts about this.

Like the Yekamkaris, the Sufis also make much use of lamps. Behl commented that Muslims regularly engage in "the practice of lighting a lamp and reciting the Sura al-Fatiha from the Qur'an over the grave of a deceased loved one on a Thursday night. This gets extended, in the Sufi context, to a major public *qawwali* session, with lamps, etc., over the tomb of a Sufi pir every Thursday night, called *jume'rat* in Urdu."[25]

The meanings and origins of the related terms *ekaṃkār(a), oaṃkār(a), oṃkār(a), ekoṃkār(a),* and *ekoaṃkār(a)* are in fact more complex than they might first appear. The Sanskrit word *kāra* means "sound." The Hindi word *ekaṃkār* could possibly be derived from a more Sanskritic *ekam-kāra* (the sound *eka* or *ekam*). The words *oaṃkār* and *ekoaṃkār,* however, suggest that the word *ekaṃkār* should be divided as *ek-aṃkār.* The word *aṃkār* in the compounds *ekaṃkār* and *ekoaṃkār* thus seems to be simply equivalent to *kāra* (sound), although it must be admitted that the word *aṃkār* does not appear in modern Hindi dictionaries. In the Hindi word *nir-aṃkār* (without form), on the other hand, *aṃkār* seems to be equivalent to Sanskrit *ākāra* (form). The word *ek* (or *aik* or *yek* or *ik*) simply means "one," and the word *om* is the famous mystic syllable going back to the ancient Vedas. Literally, the word *ek-aṃkār* most likely means "the sound *ek* (one)." The words *oaṃkār* and *oṃkār* similarly mean "the sound *o* (or *om*)."

What makes these distinctions important in the present context is the fact that Gorakh elsewhere makes a clear distinction between *ek-aṃkār* and *o-aṃkār,* between "the sound *ek*" and "the sound *o* or *om.*" Two *Gorakh-bānī* verses need to be cited here. The first is a *sabadī* or dohā:[26]

> *nirati na surati jogaṃ na bhogaṃ, jurā maraṇ nahīṃ tahāṃ rogaṃ |*
> *goraṣ bolaiṃ ekaṃkār, nahiṃ tahaṃ bācā oaṃkār ||*
>
> [In the highest meditative state] there is neither nirati nor surati, neither yoga nor enjoyment. In this [state] there is neither old age, death nor sickness.
>
> Gorakh says "ek-aṃkār." In this [state] there is no word "o-aṃkār."

The second verse is from a *Gorakh-bānī* song:[27]

> *ek aṣīrī ekaṃkār japīlā suṃni asthūl doi vāṃṇī /*
> *pyaṃḍa brahmāṃḍa sami tuli byāpīle ek aṣirī ham guramuṣi jāṃṇīṃ*
>
> The one-syllable ek-aṃkār is [to be] repeated. The Void and the Material [world are] two-[syllable] sounds. The [individual] body [and] the universe, weighing the same, are pervaded [by the one syllable]. This one syllable we learned from the mouth of the guru.

In this direct contrast between the mantras *EK* and *OM,* Gorakh clearly prefers *ek-aṃkār* over *o-aṃkār.* He also prefers *ek-aṃkār* over other mantras of two (or more) syllables. What seems to be implicit in this contrast is a distinction between a traditional Vedic mantra, namely OM, and a more explicitly monotheist mantra associated with the Nirgunis (and possibly the Muslims), namely the mantra EK (One). God's epithet *ēkaṃkāra* as used by Shaikh Qutban in his *Mirigāvatī* may thus be identical to Gorakh's *ek-aṃkār* and not, as Aditya Behl prefers, simply a variant version of Maulana Da'ud's *ekoṃkāra.*

If this is true, then the combined mantra *ik-o-aṃkār* used by the Sikhs in their Mul Mantra and the *ekoṃkāra* that appears in Da'ud's *Cāndayāna* would similarly be linguistic equivalents. In the Sikh context, this term may well represent an attempt to combine both a nirguni (and possibly Muslim) monotheist mantra (EK) with a more traditional Vedic mantra (OM). This combination is semantically quite appropriate for Guru Nanak but less so for a Sufi such as Maulana Da'ud.

This discussion has carried us somewhat far from the Yekamkaris. Nonetheless, we can conclude that, whoever they were, the Yekamkaris were literally "those who have (or use) the sound *yek* or *ek.* Since they apparently preferred not to use the mantras *oṃkār* or *ek-oṃ-kār,* they might have been some now forgotten strictly monotheist Nirguni group, or as Aditya Behl suggests, perhaps the Sufis.

KABIR'S SONG

Now, we should move on to a discussion of the song that Kabir uses to extend and comment on the song by Gorakh. Here is a complete translation of Kabir's song in its *Kabīr-granthāvalī* version:[28]

> Without Ram this world is dark dust and fog,
> And Death's noose hangs over your head.
> Making his offerings to God, the Hindu dies.
> The Turk dies going on hajj.
> The Yogi dies tying up his matted locks.
> None of them gets [to Ram].
> The poet dies composing his verses,
> The Kāpaṛī going to Kedar mountain,
> The penitent [Jain] tearing out his hair.
> None of them gets [to Ram].
> Amassing riches, the king dies,
> And others take away all his gold.
> The Pandit dies studying the Vedas,

The woman dies deceived by beauty.
Men who make logic their Yoga and understand,
these search [for Ram] in their own bodies.
For them, says the Julaha Kabir, salvation is certain.

Although this song is not simply another version of Gorakh's song, the close relation between the two is clear. In the case of their respective phrases referring to the Jains, the two texts are virtually identical:

kes laumci laumci mūvā (Gorakh)
kes lūmci lūmci mūye baratiyā (Kabir)

Nonetheless, the different groups of people that Gorakh and Kabir criticize are somewhat different. Gorakh mentions the Bhagavata Vaishnavas, the Kalamukha Shaivas, the Yekamkaris, the Jainas, the Muslims, and the Asanadhari yogis. Kabir mentions the Hindus, the Turks (i.e., Muslims), the poets, the Kāpaṛīs (presumably Shaivas since Kedar mountain is a Shaiva site), the penitents (Jainas), greedy kings, Vedic pandits, and vain women. The name *Kāpaṛī* is unusual, but it may be equivalent to *khāpaṛī* (one who has a skull [bowl]), and hence it may be another name of the well-known Kapalikas. Many commentators suggest that Kāpaṛī may be derived from *kapaṛe* meaning "clothes," but this seems less likely. By adding references to greedy kings and vain women, Kabir has expanded the range of people heedlessly caught up in worldly affairs beyond those absorbed in religious rituals. Any worldly concern can keep us from finding Ram.

The most significant contrast between the two songs appears at the end, with two statements that highlight Kabir's and Gorakh's quite different stances toward the human body. Gorakh says: "The body of five elements will be destroyed. No one is able to preserve it. Death runs away (*davan*) only when knowledge appears." Kabir says: "Men who make logic their yoga and who understand, these men search [for Ram] in their own bodies. For them, says the Julaha Kabir, salvation is certain."[29]] Kabir's statement can also be interpreted to suggest that he is advocating some form of yoga ("Men who make Yoga the means and understand"), but even in this case the message about the body is quite different.

For Gorakh and haṭha yoga in general, the body is something to be controlled and purified. It is a source of mortality and decay. By means of yoga one can master the body, purify it, and make it adamantine and immortal. The haṭha-yoga adept practices breath control (*prāṇāyāma*), control over the ejaculation of semen (*vajrolī-mudrā*), and control over the flow of "nectar" falling from the moon in his head. He smears his body with ashes and wears little or no clothes, even in extreme cold. He may sit in the middle of "five fires" or practice vows of silence. He eats little and may even experiment with the consumption of noxious substances and alchemical potions (including mercurial compounds). The goal can be to acquire magical powers (*siddhis*), or it can simply be to reach beyond the body and to transform it into what it is not, into something deathless and immutable.

Kabir, as might be expected, has little use for any of this. For him, the central truth is that Ram dwells within the body. He is always with us. A person need only look within his body to find him. The body is not something only to be controlled and transformed. The body, as it is, is the key to salvation. As God himself says in one of Kabir's most popular modern songs: "Where will you find me, my friend? I'm always near. . . . Look and you'll find me quick as the wink of an eye" (Lorenzen 1996, 213). In song after song, verse after verse, Kabir argues that salvation is easy. The body is Ram's vessel. To find Him, we need only look within.

Another Kabir song may also be intended as a commentary on *Gorakh-bānī pad* 38. This song is found in all the older Western collections.[30] Most versions begin with this refrain: "Therefore serve Narayan. My Lord, compassionate to the poor, offers his compassion." In this case, however, the resemblance to Gorakh's song is only in terms of content, not linguistic structure. As in the previous song, various religious adepts—including pandits, yogis, yatis, tapis, sannyasis, those who pluck out or shave their hair, those who keep a vow of silence, those who wear matted locks, and also pleasure-loving kings—are all said to be destined in the end to die, even if they diligently follow their callings. The only solution, according to Kabir, is to go to the Lord for refuge.

RAM AND MYSTICAL CONSCIOUSNESS

Ram, for Kabir, often appears to be synonymous with mystical experience itself. Ram is the experience of Ram. Ram becomes the *unman* (the higher mind); the hearing of the *anāhad-nād* (the unstruck sound), the *sahajāvasthā,* (the spontaneous state), or simply *surati* (great bliss). As has been noted, the *Gorakh-bānī* also resort to these same terms. It is the means that are different. The experience of mystical illumination, we must assume, is roughly the same. For Gorakh, however, the body must first be overcome. For Kabir, the experience of Ram is there for the taking, without the need to first do more than reject hypocrisy and deceit.

What can a contemporary scholar looking at these movements from the outside make of such claims? What exactly are Gorakh and Kabir talking about? Most

History of Religion scholars would insist that all we can do is examine such statements and descriptions and interpret them in the light of their own consistency and internal logic. Other scholars would argue that no matter how exactly they are described, such mystical experiences must have a physiological basis and should be physically roughly the same.

Most philosophers—even those as far apart as John Searle and Daniel Dennett—and most psychologists and evolutionary biologists now agree that mind or consciousness is in some way dependent on, or a reflex of, brain activity. Mind or consciousness, whatever it is, cannot exist without the brain. Mind is, in some sense, an illusion created by brain activity. The upper-mind, or unman, invoked by Gorakh and Kabir appears to be some special type of consciousness, a consciousness that is perceived to lie behind or beyond ordinary consciousness. The best I can make out from the references to unman in Nath and nirguni texts is that the unman is a consciousness that gives a person the feeling of being at one with other human beings or at one with the entire universe. This does not, however, make the unman any less dependent on brain activity than the *man* is.

The geneticist Dean Hamer (2004, 90–118) has argued that such a feeling of being at one with the universe is a fairly common experience among people who consider themselves to be religiously or spiritually inclined. Hamer found that a particular form, or polymorphism, of the gene identified as VMAT2, was particularly common in people who from time to time had these-being-at-one-with-the-universe feeling and were religious according to the rating-system questionnaire that Hauser used as a means of rating levels of religiosity. This research is still in its initial stages, and Hauser admits that the particular polymorphism of VMAT2 is not the sole determinant of religiosity and the being-at-one-with-the-universe feeling, but he does argue that he has proved that there is a definite correlation between the level of religiosity and the presence or absence of the gene.

My own guess is that the *unman*—and also the *unstruck sound* and other equivalents—are terms used to describe just this sort of feeling. Haṭha-yoga practices like breath control and Nirguni practices like repeating the Name evidently help induce the experience of this feeling. Nonetheless, this must be a biologically-based feeling that can only partly be modified by the religious ideologies and worldviews held by those who experience the feeling. The intertwined history of the Nath and Nirguni movements does, however, go a long way to explaining how this experience is integrated into the larger religious ideologies and world views of these movements. Most important, this intertwined history explains how and why these movements came to regard unman, the Guru, and the Guru's bani, as being equivalent to each other and as together being the tangible manifestations of the ineffable God, whether this God is called the Sat-purush, Niranjan, Shiva, or Ram.

CONCLUSIONS

In his recent study, *Identity and Violence,* the economist and philosopher Amartya Sen (2006) has argued brilliantly for a conception of identity that emphasizes the fact that each of us has multiple and that, to some extent at least, we choose our own identities and also choose to give one or other of these multiple identities priority in different contexts and situations. Sen thus takes issue with "some specific arguments and claims, beginning with the alleged priority of one's community-based identity which have been forcefully advocated in communitarian philosophy" (Sen 2006, 32–33). One claim he strongly rejects is, in his words, "the thesis of severe perceptual limitation," the idea that a person's "social background, firmly based on 'community and culture,' determines the feasible patterns of reasoning and ethics that are available to her." Sen, of course, has to admit "certain basic cultural attitudes and beliefs may *influence* the nature of our reasoning," but nonetheless claims that "they cannot invariably *determine* it fully." If community totally determined our reasoning and ethics, we would be unable to understand, much less sympathize with, the ethics and cultural norms of people belonging to other cultures.

A related, and even more absolutist, argument that Sen rejects is the idea that community identity is something we simply "discover," not something we create. In this view, as Michael Sandel argues, "community describes not just what they *have* as fellow citizens but also what they *are,* not a relationship they choose (as in voluntary association) but an attachment they discover, not merely an attribute but a constituent of their identity."[31] The objection to this view is much the same. In the end, it makes even understanding other communities and cultures virtually impossible. Culture is destiny. Even more unfortunately, with regard to international politics, it leads to the claim of an inevitable "clash of civilizations" as famously espoused by Samuel Huntington (1997).

In this debate, I feel side strongly with Sen and his allies such as John Rawls (1993), Brian Barry (2002) and Kwame Appiah (2005) against Michael Sandel (1998), Charles Taylor et al. (1994), Samuel Huntington, and other communitarians. On the other hand there are certain respects in which Sen seems to overemphasize the possibilities of cultural choice and mutual understanding. Note, for instance, Sen's very peculiar use of the word *nonfeasible* in this comment on Sandel's "discovery" argument (2006, 30)

> It is possible that the often repeated belief, common among advocates of singular affiliation, that identity is a matter of 'discovery is encouraged by the fact that the choices we can make are constrained by feasibility (I cannot readily choose the identity of a blue-eyed teenage girl from Lapland

> who is entirely comfortable with six-month-long nights), and these constraints would rule out all kinds of alternatives as being nonfeasible.

Can something that is clearly impossible be called “nonfeasible”? Here Sen seems to be falling into some sort of curious newspeak.

This point is important in the present context because it highlights Sen’s failure to analyze adequately the different sorts of “contrasting” identities. He sensibly notes (2006, 28) that “different groups may belong to the same category, dealing with the same kind of membership (such as citizenship), or to different categories (such as citizenship, profession, class, or gender).” Obviously one person can be simultaneously a lawyer, an Indian citizen, and a woman. Equally obviously, it is more difficult to occupy two or more identities within the same category. It is, for instance, difficult to be simultaneously a citizen of various countries. In this case, however, as Sen also notes, it is not in fact impossible to have passports from more than one country, although not all countries may permit this.

But not all contrasting identities share this fuzzy, ambiguous border area. Some categories of personal identities are logical opposites and cannot logically coexist. One cannot, for instance, choose to be both a vegetarian and a meat eater at the same time. Nor can one choose simultaneously to be an atheist and a believer in one or more gods. Other identities cannot be chosen because they are biologically given. One cannot choose to be young or old (except of course in a metaphorical way). Nor can one choose to change the biological and genetic component of one’s race or sex (“racial passing” and “sex-change operations” notwithstanding). An easy to arrange DNA test can tell you who your ancestors were, biologically speaking, without any reasonable doubt. It is only when we get to more cultural categories that identity choice has any role to play, and even here certain further distinctions should also be drawn.

One such distinction is between cultural identities that are “imprinted” on our brains between the ages of about five and seventeen and those that are acquired more gradually at a more mature age. Our religions, languages, and communities (or nations) are identities that are commonly acquired in the crucial age five-to-seventeen age bracket. In my case, for instance, I was raised in the United States, but left the country in 1962 at age twenty-two. After living in England, India and Australia, and a couple of years back in the States, I moved in 1970 to Mexico, where I still live. Since this date, I have spoken and heard more Spanish than English, but still often make small grammatical, pronunciation, and vocabulary mistakes when speaking Spanish that I would never make in English. Spanish is still, after almost forty years, not my native tongue in the same sense that English is. My younger two children were born in Mexico and are equally comfortable in either of these languages, although the size of their vocabulary in each may be slightly inferior to that of persons raised in monolingual environments. Much the same can be said of my and my children's national and religious identities. I still feel American, as opposed to Mexican, in a way that they do not, although they have American as well as Mexican passports.

Religiously, my mother and father came from Christian families (Catholic and Protestant respectively) but were not religious. As far back as I can remember, I have been an atheist. Nonetheless, the culture in which I was raised—New England in the 1940s and 1950s—was heavily imbued with Protestant values, including the Protestant Ethic, and I still can act against these values only with the help of introspection and conscious effort. A person undoubtedly can choose to reject such values imprinted in childhood, but to do so requires him or her to wage an uphill struggle.

Identities acquired after puberty are much easier to alter by conscious choice. At the least, the obstacles to such changes are more practical than internal. One can, for instance, change one's profession with relative ease—become a baker, a teacher, or a candlestick maker—presuming that one has the mental or physical aptitude for the new profession and the time and money for the necessary training. It is easier still to voluntarily change one's hobby, one's social club, one's friends, one's favorite football or cricket team, or even one's political party. What makes such changes relatively easy is the fact that such late-acquired identities are not imprinted on our psyches the way our childhood language, nation, and religion are.

This does not mean, however, that linguistic, national, and religious identities are primordial or absolute in the sense that communitarian theorists such as Sandel and Huntington suggest. One can, in demonstrable fact, understand and form reasonably objective opinions about other languages, nations, cultures, societies, economic systems, and religions. For various reasons, many persons decide, as adults, to become professional experts in the history, language, culture, sociology, economy, and religions of societies in which they were not raised. Some persons even decide to change their original language, nation, or religion. What is much more difficult, perhaps impossible, is for persons who make such choices to feel completely and unequivocally at home in these other languages, nations, and religions. This does not necessarily make such persons significantly inferior as language speakers, citizens, or religious adepts. It can even be said that their former outsider status may bring with it some advantages as well as the obvious disadvantages.

What has all this got to do with Gorakh and Kabir? Although we know very little about Kabir as a historical person, and hardly anything about Gorakh, both were evidently religious converts. Kabir was raised in a Muslim family and also may have experimented with, or been exposed to, Nath and Shakta religious traditions before striking out on his own religious path of austere devotion to a formless Ram. Legendary accounts of Gorakh's life, and hints found in the *Gorakh-bānī*, strongly suggest that Gorakh reformed a religious tradition associated with the Kaula Tantrism of his guru, Matsyendranath. Gorakh rejected married life, the worship of all deities except Shiva (especially the female deities of Kaula tradition), and most of Hindu ritualism.

The new religious identities forged by Kabir, Gorakh, and their respective followers were not syncretic in the sense of a simple incoherent lumping together of elements taken from two or more existing traditions. Both Kabir and Gorakh created religious traditions that do carry forward certain elements taken from Shakta tantrism (in the case of Gorakh) and Islam and haṭha yoga (in the case of Kabir), but in the process they reject many aspects of these same elements in a effort to create a logically coherent new tradition and identity. Although both these new traditions do have much in common, their respective strategies and aims are different.

As noted, the extent to which Kabir borrowed elements from Islam is controversial. Most recent scholars have argued that he simply rejected Islam and took almost all his ideas and beliefs from Hindu tradition. Contemporary Kabir Panth sadhus make roughly the same argument. Most of the vocabulary used in his songs and verses is borrowed directly from Hindu tradition. Nonetheless, it is hard not to see the influence of Islam in his insistence on devotion to a single God without form, a god Kabir most often calls "Ram." In fact, however, Kabir carries this one step further and also makes his formless God a God without even a clearly defined personality.

As many scholars, particularly those within the contemporary Kabir Panth, have argued this aspect of Kabir's God clearly reflects his debt to the idea of nirgun Brahman associated with Shankaracarya's Advaita Vedanta. Nonetheless, Kabir's Ram is not simply nirgun Brahman. Kabir's Ram somehow remains a God in a way that Sankara's Brahman is not. For instance, the idea that repeating the name "Brahman" can lead to a mystical experience makes no sense, while Kabir insists that repeating the name "Ram" does in fact lead to such an experience. Evidently Kabir's God does retain at least some agency, something akin to the power to offer grace to his devotees. In general, however, the concept of grace is not well-developed in Kabir's texts. In contrast, God's grace does become a central concern in the thought of Guru Nanak and the Sikh gurus—whose religion is much more theistic than that of Kabir, while still retaining much of Kabir's insistence on a nirgun deity.

Kabir's rejection of ritual, particularly blood sacrifice, also seems to have a composite origin. Much of this rejection probably comes through Gorakh's Nath tradition, but Kabir explicitly rejects even Gorakh's earrings, patched cloak, breath control, and yogic postures. Kabir's Islamic background must also have played some role in his rejection of ritual, but Kabir rejected even pilgrimage and circumcision. Kabir's radical position against all ritual was eventually modified by his followers, but this remains an explosive issue within the Kabir Panth. The current head of the Kabir Chaura branch of the Panth has launched a campaign against the Dharamdasi branch with the claim that the Dharamdasis have betrayed Kabir's message by creating the Chauka ritual and considering Kabir to be an avatar.

In the *Gorakh-bānī,* Gorakh claims that Hindu religion, Islam, and his own yoga tradition can somehow coexist in the life of one person. He claims, as we have seen, the possibility of maintaining a composite religious identity: "By birth I am a Hindu, in maturity a Yogi, and by intellect a Muslim." To the extent to which haṭha yoga is principally a set of techniques to aid body control and meditation, it was in fact adopted by both Hindus and Muslims. It is difficult to see, however, how Islam and Hindu religion can be made mutually compatible in terms of theology and ritual. Gorakh's own relative tolerance for ritual and his devotion to Shiva (even if in a semi-Nirgun form) makes him much more a Hindu than a Muslim or anything else.

Rather than create a composite religious identity, Kabir attempted to rise above both Islam and the Hindu religion. He accepted them as legitimate paths to enlightenment only if their followers abandoned all ritual and purified their hearts. He also rejected the techniques of body control advocated by haṭha yoga. In his theology, Kabir constructed an idea of God that combined elements of the conceptions of both Islam and Advaita Vedanta. In the end, however, he claimed that Ram was virtually identical with the mystical experience of the higher consciousness found within every person's own body. In this respect, his position is perhaps not so different from that of Gorakh. To find this Ram, however, Kabir claims that we have no need of ritual, the physical discipline of haṭha yoga, or even theology. Just open your heart and mind, and He is there.

CHAPTER THREE

Different Drums in Gwalior

Maharashtrian Nath Heritage in a North Indian City

Daniel Gold

Traditions of Nath yogis are found throughout the Indian subcontinent but have developed regional styles that are sometimes most distinct from one another. Throughout India, Naths were generally understood to look to salvation through hatha yoga practices that might bestow powers that could produce material results. Peasants sought Naths' assistance for everyday problems and natural disasters, while kings could find them useful allies of the state.[1] For a king, Naths could be of service in a number of ways: a great Nath yogi could use his esoteric powers to the benefit of an ambitious prince seeking to establish or expand his rule, but less exalted Naths could also be helpful—as fighters, tax-collectors, and enforcers. Thus, in North India, many ordinary Naths cultivated a tough image: one as a hardened Shaiva with some mastery of esoteric powers—able, when necessary, to project a hint of occult menace. In Maharashtra, too, Nath power could stand behind state authority as well as everyday magical practice, but there their image was softened, diffused through a regional culture where Shaiva ways might mix more easily with Vaishnava ones, and sometimes with those of Sufi saints, too.[2] These different Northern and Maharashtrian Nath styles extended to their musical traditions. Although some rural Northern Naths used folk tunes to sing esoteric hymns and relate legendary lore, musical performances in Maharashtrian traditions were often more refined and elaborate, affected by classically-influenced

Vaishnava performance genres. Certainly, the genealogies of Northern and Maharashtrian Naths might ultimately converge, but the styles of religion that they practiced could contrast greatly.

What happens, then, when the course of early modern political history establishes lineages looking to Maharashtrian Nath tradition in a city situated firmly in the North Indian heartland? What roles might these lineages find for themselves in their new environment? How do the local inhabitants respond? When examining two such lineages in Gwalior, Madhya Pradesh, we find them each carving out a niche for themselves that has no obvious socioreligious parallel within their immediate region. In part because of this, these lineages appeal to the city's broad North Indian population much more than other Maharashtrian religious institutions that history has brought in Gwalior. And even though the two Nath-oriented institutions are most different from one another and from regional Nath traditions, in each case, aspects of their collective Nath heritage seem central to their popularity.

TWO MAHARASHTRIAN NATH HERITAGES IN GWALIOR

Gwalior stands at the northernmost thrust of the eighteenth-century expansion of the Maratha empire. On a modern map of India, the city and its hinterlands jut up out of the Central Indian state of Madhya Pradesh, surrounded by Rajasthan on the west and Uttar Pradesh to the east—each with its own mix of characteristically North Indian cultures. The area's political orientation toward the Central Indian territories to the south began in the second half of the eighteenth century, when the Maratha chieftain Mahadji Scindia (r.1768–1794) set his sights on the strategically valuable Gwalior fort and established a base at the city below it. Mahadji's successors in the Scindia dynasty would then flourish in Gwalior, maharajas of an important princely state during British times and remaining wealthy and politically influential today. With them grew a thriving Maharashtrian community—a small but generally privileged group adapting comfortably in this Hindi-speaking, North Indian cultural area, just seventy-six miles south of Agra.

Substantial Maharashtrian settlement at Gwalior began with Mahadji's successor Daulat Rao (r. 1794–1827). A camp for Maratha soldiers was built to the southeast of the fort, their chiefs constructed manors for themselves in this new area of the city—called Lashkar, "the camp"—and administrators were brought in from Maharashtra. In the wake of these officials came their family and retainers together with other professionals. Among the immigrants, sometimes actively encouraged by the new aristocracy, were religious personages of different sorts, some of whom started lasting institutions in the city. These include two institutions with roots in

Maharashtrian Nath traditions: the lineage of Dholi Buwa and the organized worship of Raja Bakshar.

The founder of Gwalior's Dholi Buwa lineage—Mahipati Nath—came, they say, at the request of his highness Maharaja Daulat Rao, who wanted to learn raja yoga from him. Although Mahipati Nath himself was a celibate yogi, his spiritual lineage was eventually continued by Kashi Nath Purandare, a nephew on his mother's side, who was a family man. Since then, the religious lineage has continued within the Purandare family at a large compound on the western edge of Lashkar. Known as the Dholi Buwa math, it grew up around the site of Mahipati Nath's samadh.

Dholi derives from dhol, a big drum, and *Buwa* is a Maharashtrian honorific. While still maintaining a Nath lineage and talking, privately at least, about yogic practice, members of the extended Dholi Buwa lineage are known in town primarily as religious performers, presenting a Maharashtrian-style story and song program that features a signature introductory drumbeat. In addition to presentations at their own math, other temples, and private religious events, they also perform frequently at public fora—at a major Sufi celebration in the main bazaar (Gold 2005, 141), say, or at an annual public worship of the Scindia dynasty's patron saint. The continuing association of the lineage with the Scindias can give its reigning head, himself called Dholi Buwa Maharaj, an exalted civic religious position.

Raja Bakshar, by contrast, presents a humbler image, an object of worship at three smallish shrines in town—not all especially well known to the general populace, and with no obviously high-class clientele. Raja Bakshar's own religious identity is decidedly ambivalent. The worship at the two main shrines is strongly reminiscent of practices at Sufi tombs, but the main priests there suggest—one most emphatically—that the saint is actually a Hindu named Chaitanya Nath, with a spiritual lineage traceable to legendary Naths. What is clear is that the Gwalior Raja Bakshar shrines have antecedents around Maharashtra,[3] and that the two main families of shrine attendants are Maharashtrian. There has also been continuing patronage of Raja Bakshar from the Scindias themselves: the smallest of the three shrines is actually on the main palace grounds, and at least one of the larger ones still receives an annual stipend from the court. Not increased for inflation over the years, though, the stipend these days functions mostly as a visible token of continuing Scindia support.

Indeed, in independent India, the Gwalior Maharashtrian community has lost much of its privileged status. Certainly, the old noble families that remain are rich by local standards, and the Scindias themselves, with their palace and much of their wealth intact, are active in politics and have tremendous local cachet. But with the court no longer the active center of government and patronage, members of the

Maharashtrian community have to compete on an equal footing with others and are not all very well equipped to do so. Although the old administrative families have a heritage of education that keeps them mostly middle class, they have not generally cultivated the business acumen at a premium in twenty-first century India. Demographically, too, the Maharashtrian population counts for less. Branches of some old families have left the city, often for more economically advanced areas in Maharashtra, while the city itself has seen much growth, in good part through immigration from the immediate North Indian hinterlands. Considerably more so than in the past, it makes sense for Gwalior religious institutions with Maharashtrian roots to look for support from non-Maharashtrian sources. Both the Dholi Buwa lineage and the Raja Bakshar shrines have done so successfully, developing different parts of a shared Nath heritage.

Dholi Buwa and the Gwalior Elite

The Dholi Buwa lineage presents itself as a charismatic family, with links to the old Gwalior court and aristocracy, and offers a decorous Vaishnava-laced Nath performance tradition with a broad appeal that reaches well into the middle and upper classes. In a five-page Hindi article in an unpaginated 1980 pamphlet commemorating the twenty-fifth year of the late Dholi Buwa Vasudev Nath's reign, the latter's youngest brother, Shrikant Gopalnath, gives a history of the lineage.[4] His account briefly describes the transmission of authority from Mahipati Nath, the celibate spiritual source of the lineage, to the householder Kashi Nath Purandare and the transformations of the latter's family lineage over eight generations. I will summarize some of its salient points.

The crucial spiritual succession from Mahipati Nath to Kashi Nath, we are told, even though it took place a number of years after the celibate guru's death, came through the guru's own divine will. Mahipati Nath, apparently, had his eye on his nephew Kashi Nath early on, while they were all still living in Maharashtra. Like others in his family, Kashi Nath had been initiated by Mahipati Nath, but outshone all the others in his devotion. Mahipati Nath, seeing this, asked Kashi Nath's father to let him have the boy as a disciple—but was met with a blunt refusal: Kashi Nath's father didn't want his son going around begging from door to door as a mendicant yogi. Thus, Kashi Nath stayed home in Pune, while some of Mahipati Nath's other disciples accompanied him to Gwalior. About a year after his arrival, Mahipati Nath, having taught Maharaja Daulat Rao, expired, and one of his disciples, Narayan Nath, took charge of the establishment that had begun to take shape around his guru's memorial tomb. After seven or eight years, however, Narayan

Nath's health began to fail, and in despair, he asked his guru's spirit what to do. Suddenly a voice came out of the samadhi: "Send for Kashi Nath in Pune; he'll be able to take care of everything."

The divine voice, moreover, was supplemented by clear instructions from Narayan Nath, the incumbent caretaker—who, having sent for his successor, left for Jodhpur, critically ill. Kashi Nath, on getting the message from Gwalior, set out from Pune with his brother—an episode related with allusions to Ram and Lakshman—stopping first at Jodhpur to pay his respects to the ailing Narayan Nath. After accepting Kashi Nath's obeisances, Narayan Nath affirmed to Kashi Nath that he had now been chosen by their guru to carry on their tradition and ceremoniously entrusted everything to him. Sending Kashi Nath off to Gwalior, Narayan Nath closed his eyes in meditation and addressed his guru's spirit: "As per your order, Kashi Nath is here to serve you; please give him a place at your feet."

Through the divine will of the lineage founder and the explicit actions of its incumbent head, then, the transition from a lineage of celibate yogis to a family of householder Naths was effected. This is not, however, quite the end of the story. Some people believe, our author tells us, that Mahipati Nath was so impressed with Kashi Nath's devotion that he himself incarnated as Kashi Nath's youngest son, Gangadhar Nath, the next great guru produced by the family.[5] That belief was further elaborated to me by Santosh Purandare, the son of the currently reigning Dholi Buwa and a gifted performer who also teaches Indian classical music at a local music college. Wondering why so many people born into his extended family are so apt for the family occupation, he suggests that the same souls keep being reborn into it. "They leave us, but then where else would they come back to but here? The same water continues to flow. . . . One leaves and another comes back—it's like that."[6] I've never heard this belief from anyone else, and don't expect it has wide currency in the general public. But this understanding of a perpetually reincarnating family does offer a potent self-conception; it is obviously shared with those interested in the lineage, and may well be an idea to which close devotees give some credence.

Active links with the royal house, which seem to have become tenuous after Mahipati Nath's passing, were renewed with Balkrishna Nath, Gangadhar Nath's successor as the oldest surviving son in the next generation of Purandare cousins. Reigning for twenty-four years, Balkrishna seems to have cut a particularly charismatic figure, gifted at kirtan. He impressed the reigning Scindia monarch, Madhav Rao II (r. 1886–1925)—known as the father of modern Gwalior—to such an extent that the maharaja had his first wife, Chinku Raje, initiated by Balkrishna. A guru-disciple relationship established with the royal house made it easy for Balkrishna to strengthen religious relationships with many of the noble families of the era. Marriage alliances between these families and the Purandares soon followed. By the beginning of the twentieth century, then, the extended family of Dholi Buwa was nicely enmeshed with the local aristocracy.

The performance style cultivated in the Dholi Buwa lineage thus developed to suit Gwalior's more refined classes, drawing on Maharashtrian conventions that were greatly influenced by Vaishnava kirtan styles, with stately circumambulations and occasional formulaic dance poses.[7] Indeed, in Maharashtra, Nath tradition is generally not seen to be strictly Shaiva, as it usually is in the North. Maharashtrian Naths instead are liable to trace a lineage from Nivritti Nath to Sant Jnaneshwar and, through him, also to the broader Maharashtrian sant tradition—which included a number of poet saints such as Tukaram who were strongly pulled toward the Vaishnava worship of Vitthala at Pandharpur.[8] Individual religious personages in the Maharashtrian lineages may be regularly seen as both implicitly Shaiva Naths and more or less Vaishnava sants, an identity reflected in their official titles. Thus, the commemoration pamphlet, from which I have been drawing, shows a picture of its honoree below that of Jnaneshwar with their respective captions using *sant* as an honorific for a religious personage explicitly classed as a Nath: Sant Shri Vasudev Nath and Sant Jnan Nath. Santosh Purandare affirms the dual allegiance matter-of-factly: "We are Naths and Vaishnavas both."[9]

Raja Bakshar and Sufi Tradition

If the Dholi Buwa lineage shows a relaxed sense of sectarian identification within the Hindu traditions of Maharashtra, the worship of Raja Bakshar shows the occasional transcendence of Hindu and Islamic identities in relation to holy persons there—a transcendence seen today in the very widely revered figure of Sai Baba of Shirdi (see Rigopoulos 1993). To some extent, this sort of transcendence is preserved at Gwalior's Raja Bakshar shrines, although much more in one of the main shrines than in the other. Indeed, the two shrines' self-images present an interesting contrast.

At both places, the main worship is accompanied by a fast, pulsing drum beat that is more reminiscent of Sufi styles than anything in the Hindu liturgical repertoire. As at Sufi shrines, the main worship takes place on Thursday evenings, around the replica of a tomb—with the drumming, like Sufi qawwali, sometimes inducing a trance-like state in participants. The participants here, however, are mostly Hindu (at one shrine almost exclusively so) and use the Hindu term arati to refer to the worship, itself presided over by hereditary lineages of Maharashtrian Hindu priests. Although the priests at both shrines admit aspects of the shrines'

Hindu/Muslim provenance, only one seems particularly proud of it. For the other, Raja Bakshar was very firmly identified as Baba Chaitanya Nath.

On Thursday evenings, the Raja Bakshar shrine run by the Suryavanshi family off Gwalior's Daulat Ganj is an exciting place. The drummers here are especially skilled—sometimes professional musicians—and many of the worshippers, packed into the shrine's small area, seem drawn inward, lost in the drumbeat. Inside, there are smells of sweat and incense. From the courtyard outside, the overflow crowd (including all the women) peers in intently. Until the drums reach their climax, the place could easily be mistaken for a straightforward Sufi shrine. But, as the service concludes, it winds down with Sanskrit chants, and the shrine priests, with Hindu forehead markings, come to the fore. One of the Suryavanshi sons, who had looked particularly absorbed during the drumming, performs healing rituals for children brought to him by anxious parents. The healer's father, the head of the family, looks on benignly and mills with members of the dispersing crowd—which is mostly non-Maharashtrian and almost exclusively Hindu. Here, Raja Bakshar, too, is without doubt really a Hindu. In conversations with the Suryavanshi family, I was told that "Baba Chaitanya Nath is a Hindu name" that was later changed to Raja Bakshar.[10] The old Nath, it seems, had the foresight to anticipate the famous temple plundering of the Mughal emperor Aurangzeb, so asked his disciples to build not a Hindu-style samādhi (tumulus) for him but a Muslim-style dargah (tomb). As a Hindu Nath baba disguised as a Muslim, I was told, his tradition was able to survive.

Raja Bakshar has a decidedly more ambivalent identity at his temple over in Jinsi Nala, about a ten minute walk away. The signboard over the lane leading into it from the street indicates in parentheses that it is also a dargah, and two names adorn the freshly renovated shrine itself. One, engraved in the new marble, calls it a temple to Satguru Chaitanya Nath Raja Bakshar. Above that is a professionally made plaque in green calling it a dargah to Shri Pir Saheb Raje Vali. With its renovations, the shrine is larger than the one at Daulat Ganj, and the Thursday night worship seems less packed. The people there also seems less excited, sitting on the floor, while the drum plays a fast but less complex rhythm. The priest himself is clearly worked up during the arati, but most of the rest don't seem too absorbed, some looking around to appreciate the obviously mixed Hindu and Muslim crowd. Here, too, the crowd is mostly North Indian, with a few Hindus and Muslims sporting religio-culturally distinctive dress.

Devotees I talked to were proud of the shrine's dual identity: "At this shrine, Hindus and Muslims pray together, in other places they fight."[11] But still, the togetherness could sometimes be complicated. The shrine's 'urs—its annual festival—is a three-day affair with three separate feasts. On the first day is a special meal for Brahmins, with Maharashtrian food, and on the second, a large event for everyone with the usual vegetarian banquet fare of fried bread and vegetables. The feast on the third day, however—for the Muslim fakirs—is decidedly non-vegetarian, with the sacrifice of a goat and blood offering at the shrine, followed by qawwali into the night. The shrine thus accommodates everyone—often together, but sometimes separately, especially at events featuring activities such as communal eating that are crucial to orthodox sensibilities.[12]

The Sufi dimensions of the shrine are undeniable and even suggested by its Hindu name. To Urdu speakers, the name Raja Bakshar can suggest a vernacularization of a compounded term such as raj (or raja)-baksh: the familiar Hindi-Urdu raj can refer to anything royal (including a kingdom) and baksh is an Urdu compounding suffix meaning giver.[13] The saint of the shrine may have once been lauded in Urdu as a "giver of kingdoms"—a perfectly appropriate epithet for a Sufi. For in the South Asian tradition, fabled Sufis were often seen as kingmakers, able to help aspiring chiefs without their own domains.[14] Indeed, the Scindias themselves, they say, were favored by such a Sufi, a figure named Mansoor who is still worshipped annually by the reigning Scindia monarch (Gold 2005, 132). Morevoer, both Sufi and royal associations recur in the distinctive style of drumming at Raja Bakshar, where they find a form readily amenable to popular participation.

The characteristic style of drumming at the Raja Bakshar shrines—even though it bears some similarity to drumming heard during rituals of possession in village India—is quite unlike anything in the Hindu liturgical repertoire commonly heard in the city of Gwalior. Its lack of consistent rhythmic structure, moreover, while perhaps demonstrating an improvisational ebullience, makes it musically distinct from the drumming heard within established Sufi lineages, which generally follows regular patterns emulating traditional repetitive chants.[15] Still, to the musically naive urban listener, the drums at Raja Bakshar may sooner recall rhythms sometimes heard at Sufi gatherings than those heard anywhere else: similarly evocative rhythms sometimes occur when instrumental preludes to qawwali sessions quicken their pace, and at longer sessions at major shrines, where they are sometimes accompanied by whirling dance. For some devotees, no doubt, the dargah-like surroundings, in which the drumming at Raja Bakshar is heard, reinforces the impression of its similarity to traditional Sufi styles. Differences between the two, however, remain telling.

While the rhythms at Sufi establishments are usually played on small drums of different sorts, designed to let trained musicians demonstrate their artistry, the rhythms at Raja Bakshar resonate on large kettle drums, which have their own practical as well as cultural implications. Practically, compared to small drums—on which a credible performance usually entails some mastery of manual techniques—kettle drums, hit with a stick, are relatively easy to play and so can invite wide participation by spiritually enthused amateurs. These drums are thus sometimes also found at Muharram ceremonies in the subcontinent, where, as at the Raja Bakshar shrines, different individuals in turn can express themselves rhythmically without close attention to traditional patterns.[16] At the same time, culturally, kettle drums suggest an air of royalty and grandeur: they have traditionally been played slowly to mark the arrival of a king or other stately person and have long been found at royal courts. At the shrines of Raja Bakshar, then, the Sufi giver of kingdoms can thus appear himself as a Hindu monarch—one, moreover, who can be evoked with a popular, exciting musical performance in which a number of untrained but enthusiastic devotees can participate.

As Raja Bakshar, the saint of the Gwalior shrines presents experiences to Hindus normally unavailable even at local Sufi establishments, which regularly offer qawwali singers, but no intense solo drumming. At the Daulat Ganj shrine, this experience takes place in an atmosphere that is particularly Hinduized—not only are there Sanskrit chants and the lack of any allusion to the saint's possible identity as Pir Raje Vali, but the brahminic exclusions of leather belts and bags is also enforced. The experience there is, moreover, particularly intense: devotees are attracted by an extremely exciting form of popular worship, with some hoping to benefit from the healing powers it can be bestowed by the shrine priest. If the experience at the Jinsi Nala shrine seems somewhat less impassioned, the intercommunal idea it projects is itself attractive to some, at once liberal and slightly transgressive in what is still largely a conservative provincial milieu. Hindus—and a few Muslims—can mix religiously and revel in their open-mindedness, while still easily maintaining their most sensitive cultural boundaries.

MAHARASHTRIAN NATH HERITAGE IN URBAN NORTH INDIA: A COMFORTABLE FIT

The obvious Sufi dimensions of the Raja Bakshar shrines notwithstanding, the intense, sometimes even transgressive nature of the experience there resonates with some characteristic popular images of Naths—who, with their cut ears and hard practice, were often seen as different and extreme, at the margins of Hindu society. No matter how spurious the story of Baba Chaitanya Nath might turn out to be, the fact that Raja Bakshar's adherents look for his Hindu origins in Nath tradition is suggestive of the way in which that tradition can be perceived as at once extreme and marginal. The image of a legendary Nath and the practices at the Raja Bakshar shrines might thus find congruent places toward the furthest reaches of the socioreligious imagination of someone who knows them both. In practice, however, Gwalior's middle classes are not, for the most part, open to anything *too* radical. It is the tamer, Maharashtrian variants of Nath heritage that flourish in the city, not the more rugged versions that have a place in most residents' broad North Indian cultural taxonomies but not in their everyday practice.

In general, split-eared Naths of legendary visage—still found in rural India—are not major presences in urban areas of the subcontinent beyond monastic centers such as Gorakhpur or Jalor. Contemporary urban Indian religion, without much use for the Naths' earlier royal and popular socioreligious functions, doesn't offer them a ready place: the tough ascetic style that once made the Naths useful to kings is not one attractive to most spiritually-minded modern urbanites, whose gurus tend to cultivate a more nurturing—and often more learned—manner; and while many in the city may seek supernatural help with personal affairs, they tend to favor less the occult powers that a Nath might offer than the theistic approaches of saints and shrines. Although individual split-eared Nath ascetics from the North Indian countryside may find support in urban areas and settle there, they don't seem to play major institutional roles.

In the more relaxed Maharashtrian Nath heritage represented by Dholi Buwa and Raja Bakshar, however, the characteristic royal and popular roles of Nath yogis are transformed into viable urban institutions. In Dholi Buwa, the royal Nath morphs into a sort of civic guru—a religious dignitary called on to perform at major public occasions, gracing them with the authority of an inherited family charisma and an idealized old regime. With Raja Bakshar, the visage of the awe-inspiring Nath yogi, whose exceptional practical power derives in part from his unconventional ways, turns into an unconventional shrine that offers intense experience and magical power. Although Hindu shrines with curing priests—sometimes householder Naths—are common in rural India, they are not very frequent in the cities. Their place often seems subsumed by Sufi shrines—whose attendants may perform similar curing functions, which Hindus also frequent. Raja Bakshar offers Gwalior Hindus a communally ambivalent alternative to conventional Sufi shrines together with a type of intense experience that these shrines don't regularly offer.

The particular institutional roles these two variants of Maharashtrian religion fulfill may explain why North Indian Hindus are attracted to them. In fact, local North Indians don't normally frequent most other Maharashtrian religious institutions in town. Certainly, some of those institutions—an old math (Hindu Cloister) linked to a predecessor of Mahipati Math, say, or a newer one to Sant Ram Das—function largely in Marathi and for Maharashtrians. But the old aristocracy also sponsored a number of temples to Hindu deities popular in Maharashtra but not common in the North—in Dattatreya, Vithoba, and Khandoba—some elaborately built, well-maintained, and open to all. But, given the many other temples in town, few North Indians find any compelling reason to visit them: the version of familiar Hindu worship they offer is not particularly extraordinary and the divinities installed in them exert no special pull. Dholi Buwa and Raja Bakshar, by contrast, are institutions that find no simple counterparts in other religious establishments in the city. They are popular because they are different from others in town, finding unfilled niches toward opposite extremes of the urban socioreligious world, but in neither case exceeding the religious comfort zone of most urban Hindus. Although awe-inspiring, split-eared Nath yogis have a place in the imaginations of North Indian city dwellers, adapted Maharashtrian versions of Nath traditions may be better suited for everyday urban practice.

CHAPTER FOUR

The Influence of the Naths on Bhima Bhoi and Mahima Dharma

Ishita Banerjee-Dube

The considerable overlap between the traditions of the Naths and the Nirgunis (followers of sects that worship a formless God) and between yoga and tantra has been noted by various scholars. It is also generally accepted that all these trends had a pervasive influence over new religious orders in all regions of India. This is not surprising: "traditions" in real lives and societies actually mingle and overlap; their separation into self-contained, tidy categories is a function of academic analysis. Yoga and tantra, linked to practices that relate directly to control over the body, had common origins, although they developed different trajectories in distinct trends through the centuries. What we now consider to be "classical yoga" with "traditions that involve meditation, breath control and postures" arose from trends that are neither ancient nor classical (White 2009a, 105). Early traditions of yoga referred to practices of dying as a yogic event: "of a warrior's departure for the heavens, the sun and the world of Brahman beyond," or of a recluse's practice of yoking one body to another (White 2009a, 97–98). It is this practice of yoking which permitted Gorakhnath, the legendary founder of the Nath yogis, "to leave a myriad of burial tumuli (*samadhis*), scattered across South Asia, tumuli said to house the bodies he left behind, when he chose to inhabit other younger, fresher bodies" (White 2009a, 104). This was how a yogi conquered his own death.

At a different level, yoga was considered to be the union or contact of the individual soul with God, which enabled the human practitioner to attain the eight supernatural powers (siddhis) of the God Mahesvara or Shiva. In this trend also, the yogi imitated Shiva by entering the body of a corpse on a cremation ground (White 2009a, 100). Similarly, a tantric yogi haunted cremation grounds in imitation of his god Bhairava, a horrific form of Shiva, and conquered death by yoking another body to his. Moreover, the yogi could also multiply himself like his god Bhairava in order to combat the demonic forces that would otherwise invade the citadel of the worshipper's body. These ideas took different forms and meanings in diverse trends over the centuries, but the notion of the body as the receptacle of divine energy remained.

With this discussion in mind, let us turn to the interface of such ideas in later religious orders. The focus will be on Mahima Dharma, a radical religious formation of nineteenth century Orissa. My analysis will proceed along two lines. First, it will examine the influence of Nath ideas and practices on Mahima Dharma, and second, it will unpack the palpable presence of yoga/tantra in the religious poetry of Bhima Bhoi, the poet-philosopher of the Dharma, underlining in the process the tensions and confusions that are found in the traditions of the Naths and tantra.

INTERSECTING INFLUENCES

Mahima Dharma was founded in the 1860s by an abstemious, wandering ascetic who came to be known as Mahima Swami. It advocated devotion to an all-pervasive, formless Absolute—equally accessible to all—as the only way of salvation. This seemingly simple message rendered redundant worship of idols, including that of Jagannath, the central deity of Hinduism in Orissa and the state deity for centuries, and questioned complex hierarchies of caste and kingship, and the role of the Brahman as a mediator between gods and men. The radical message was worked out in practices that contravened the rules of caste and norms of commensality. Mahima Swami asked for cooked rice as alms for all households irrespective of the castes of the householders, and later he and his disciples together ate this rice from the same pot.

This brief sketch of the basic tenets and practices of the faith makes it evident that it pertained to the Nirguna tradition although it also absorbed elements from the rich heritage of religious ideas current in the region. Let me pause here to offer a glimpse of the religious panorama of Orissa. The regional identity of present Orissa turns around its language that again distinguishes itself by virtue of its religious/devotional poetry. This is because Orissa has been home to almost all the important currents of religious thought—Buddhist, Nath, tantric, Shakta, Shaiva, and bhakti. The most prominent manifestation of Vaishnavite bhakti is the cult of Jagannath, the Lord of the Universe. In the course of its long and colorful evolution, this cult has drawn upon, assimilated, or suppressed these different trends. Jagannath is at once a *savara-devata* (god of the *adivasis,* or aboriginals), and Buddha-Jagannath, the ninth incarnation of Vishnu. Jagannath is the Great Lord of all but the personal god of none. All his numerous ritual servants, beginning with the Raja of Puri, the first servitor, worship the Devi in her different forms, as their *ista-devata* (personal god). The enclosure where the food offerings to Jagannath are kept within the inner sanctum of the temple is in the shape of a *yoni* (vagina), a clear indication of the influence of tantra and Shakta worship on the cult.

Mahima Dharma imbibed this vibrant heritage of thought and practice although it openly contested rituals and idol worship. Let me cite the first report on the founder of Mahima Dharma, published in the Oriya newspaper *Utkala Deepika* on June 1, 1867, to illustrate my point:

> A new faith was spreading in the princely states bordering Cuttack. It had been founded by a *phalahari sanyasi* (an ascetic who ate only fruits) who lived on Kapilas hill in Dhenkanal. The ascetic had initially subsisted on fruits alone, later on milk and, in the end, only on water. He worshipped Siva. One day, on the directions of *sunya* (the great void), he cut off his matted locks and gave up his vocation as a mere renouncer. He began wearing the bark of a tree and spread a dharma that disregarded caste distinctions, forbade idol worship and rituals—for example, *sraddha* (death rites)—and advocated a belief in one *isvara* (god). The *sanyasi* was described as *ati nirlobh* (completely free of greed) and praised for his efforts to feed people at a time of scarcity. He had constructed large temporary houses where he fed forty to fifty thousand people. He then burnt these houses and moved on to somewhere else. The ascetic was said to command great respect.[1]

This report was given greater flourishes in the reports of local officials in the early 1880s.[2] Colonial administrators organized varied references to a *dhulia babaji*, a *pahalahari sanyasi*, and a *khsira-nira payee* into an orderly sequence of distinct phases in the same person's life. The founder of Mahima Dharma, they stated, was initially an "achari boishnab" (practicing Vaishnava) who at the same time covered his body with ashes like Shaiva ascetics. Hence, he was called "dhulia babaji." During the next phase of his long stay at Kapilas, which lasted twenty-four years, he lived the first twelve years on fruit (*phalahari*) and the next twelve years on milk and water (*khsira-nira payee*). Moreover, although he worshipped Shiva at Kapilas, he continued to wear a *kaupin* (loincloth) and *kanthi* (necklace of wooden beads): "the two distinctive features in the raiment of a Vaishnava."[3] It was only after he had finished his experiments with Hindu asceticism and decided to preach his own faith that he gave up the kaupin and kanthi and wore *kumbhipat* (the bark of the *kumbhi* tree). This symbolic act snapped his links with Hinduism and set him off on his own as the founder of a new dharma.

The play of different motifs and symbols in these reports is significant. He is described as an ascetic who practices Vaishnavism but covers his body with ashes, an ascetic who then becomes a worshipper of Shiva but continues with the garb of a Vaishnava. Shiva and Vishnu are not just two prominent deities of Hinduism. Shiva, the primordial guru of yoga, is identified as the god of the Naths and all Siddha schools (Dasgupta 1976, 195, 197) and the Nirguni *sants* (followers of the Nirguni sects), on the other hand, are notionally related to Vishnu (Lorenzen 1995, 2). Moreover, Shiva and Vishnu represent different notions of sexuality. Shiva is an erotic ascetic, a phallic god, whose asceticism does not entail sexual abstinence (Doniger 1973, 5). The extant mythology of Shiva emphasizes the apparently opposing strands of Shiva's nature, at times offering mutual resolutions between them and at times accepting them as aspects of one single nature.

Vishnu, on the other hand, represents the ideal householder. He—together with his wife Lakshmi, the goddess of beauty and prosperity—assures the conservation and well-being of the universe. At the same time, Vishnu and Lakshmi defy a key norm of domestic sex within marriage, the aim of procreation: the divine couple has no children. Shiva and his consort Parvati, on the other hand, have children. This contradictory situation questions the clear separation between the ascetic and the householder and the related idea of denial of sex (based upon avoidance of all contact with women), and acceptance of sexual relations with women. This has occasioned different understandings of asceticism in different Indian traditions and caused considerable tension between conflicting notions of self-restraint and indulgence. Shiva is the guru both of yoga and of tantra, trends that have distinguished themselves on grounds of distinct emphases on austere asceticism and sexual relations. Yoga is widely associated with austere asceticism and tantra with sexual excess; myths regarding Matsyendranath and his disciple Gorakshanatha (Gorakhnath) graphically represent the tension within the tradition on the issue of association with women (Muñoz 2010).[4]

Mahima Swami, the founder of Mahima Dharma, alternated between and combined elements of the worship of Shiva and Vishnu before preaching his own faith. In popular perceptions, he symbolizes the self-restrained, detached ascetic, a divine incarnation whose death shocked his followers. His disciple Bhima Bhoi, the poet-philosopher of the faith, took the life of a householder, cohabited with four women and fathered two children. Mahima Swami and Bhima Bhoi represent Matsyendra and Gorakh in reverse order: Gorakh saved his guru from the "degradation" he had suffered by falling into the temptation of female company. Bhima Bhoi, on the other hand, deviated from the path of his preceptor and lived with women. His poems justify his householder status on grounds that it was ordained both by fate and by his guru.

Mahima Swami's link to the Nath yogis was reflected not only in his asceticism, but also in the other practices he adopted. Like the Nath yogis, Mahima Swami lit the *dhuni* (a sacred fire), in places of his temporary residence. Although the literature on Naths almost always mentions dhuni, it never properly explains what it signified. The use of dhunis is common among several ascetic orders and sects. Brigg's early work on Gorakhnath and the Kanpatha yogis contains an important reference to the dhuni. Speaking of the necessary "accessories" of the Kanphatas, Briggs describes the dhuni as a "fire, consisting of a smouldering log of wood (or more than one), sometimes in a hollow pit." Briggs goes on to mention that whenever "a Kanphata yogi takes up his abode he lights his fire, provided there is not one already at the place. At all important shrines and monasteries such fires are found, some of which have been kept burning for long periods of time. The dhuni at Dhinodhar, and those at Gorakhpur, Tilla and Pae Dhuni in Bombay are famous because of associations with Dharamnath, Gorakhnath and others. These have been kept burning for centuries" (Briggs 2001, 21).[5] Indeed, the importance of the dhuni among the Kanphatas was such that even the householder followers kept a dhuni lit in their houses (ibid.).

Briggs links the dhuni with the practice of Shaiva ascetics covering themselves with ashes; he also notes that this practice is very old and is not limited only to Shaiva ascetics. This is borne out by the fact that the Udasi Sikhs also use the dhuni. The Shaiva ascetics usually cover themselves with ashes from the dhuni, in the same way that "Shiva, as the Yogi par excellence, covers his body with ashes from the burning grounds" (ibid., 16). Veronique Bouillier makes the same connection of ashes and the dhuni with cremation grounds and physical death, arguing that they also represent the "transition from mundane to secret realms, dissolution of ego-consciousness and destruction of worldly attachments." The ashes on Shiva's body, according to Bouillier, are those of "cosmic conflagration and symbolize Shiva's transformative powers" (Bouillier 2004, 36–37).[6]

All this is significant for our purposes. Early reports on the founder of Mahima Dharma call him "dhulia babaji" and state that he covered his body with ashes but make no mention of the dhuni. It is only after he started preaching the Mahima Dharma that the dhuni became associated with him. The Swami, as we have noted, was a worshipper of Shiva, although he wore the kaupin and kanthi of the Vaishnavas. It is very probable that dhulia babaji got the ashes from his own sacred fire at a time when his links with Shiva and the Nath tradition were more intimate. The new faith he propounded and particularly the mutations in it over time made this connection distant and tenuous to the point of being almost unrecognizable.

The dhuni, one of the markers of Mahima Dharma since its inception, is meant to clear away sin and darkness. The first report on Mahima Swami refers to the sacred fire and a later report corroborates that the first semi-permanent structure that the founder set-up was a *dhuni-ghar* (a room where the fire was kept lit) at Malbeharpur, which he left in charge of one of his disciples before coming back and destroying it.[7] At Joranda in Dhenkanal, the site of the memorial of Mahima Swami, the *akhandabati* (eternal flame) has been a root of contention between two groups of ascetics. The dhuni is an integral part of all Mahima Dharmi rituals; it is said to help the faith usher in the well-being of humankind.

My queries with regard to the origin and the significance of the dhuni often caught the lay followers without an answer, while the ascetics offered a host of responses. Kasinath Baba, leader of a rival group within the dharma, argued that *agni* (fire) has been worshipped since the age of the Vedas and Mahima Dharma, as a "true" Vedic religion, had adopted it.[8] This response is intriguing. Kasinath Baba claims to follow Bhima Bhoi who had advocated *nirveda sadhana* (mediation without the Vedas). I will come to this shortly. For the sadhus of Jamusara ashram (monastic settlement), yet another dissident group, the dhuni lit with ghee (clarified butter) and incense purified the air. It has no other special meaning or purpose.[9] It was Biswanath Baba, a prominent ascetic who steered the evolution of Mahima Dharma in the twentieth century, who traced the practice of lighting the dhuni to Gorakhnath, the earliest yogi, implying thereby the importance of the yogic tradition within the dharma. This is remarkable since Biswanath Baba induced several changes within the faith by aligning Mahima Dharma closely with the Advaita Vedanta tradition of Hinduism. The dhuni also serves practical purposes, according to Biswanath Baba. It gives warmth to the sadhus who sleep in the open, eliminates darkness, and keeps the ascetics *sachetan* (conscious). The dhuni is also lit with a prayer to Alekh Brahma for the welfare of the world.[10]

Perhaps the greatest influence of the Naths and the nirgunis on Mahima Dharma lies in its conception of the Absolute. Despite links to Shiva and Vishnu, the Naths and nirgunis emphasize an "ineffable" god beyond form and attributes and underplay the *saguna* ("with-attributes" or theistic) manifestations of the deity. The god of the Naths, in particular, is stated to be Alakh, which is derived from the Sanskrit *alakshya* (imperceptible, beyond perception). The all-powerful Absolute, which Mahima Swami advocated as the only object of devotion, was also Alakh or Alekh, which the Mahima Dharmis translate as "a God who is beyond writing, indescribable/inexplicable." The world is creation of the *mahima* (radiance/glory) of this Alekh. Indeed, the constant invocation of Alekh by Mahima Swami and his followers meant that in the early phase of its evolution the faith came to be known as Alekh Dharma. As mentioned before, the first detailed report on the dharma published in the *Proceedings of the Asiatic Society of Bengal, 1882* was titled "On a sect of Hindu dissenters who profess to be the followers of Alekh." In describing the Absolute as Alekh, beyond sense perception, Mahima Dharma moved back to the conception of the Naths and away from the Ultimate as *Shunya* propounded in the writings of the Panchasakhas, the Five Friends, and famous medieval mystics.[11] Mahima Dharma is generally believed to bear the closest resemblance to the Panchasakhas in thought and theology.

The third term and practice borrowed from the Naths is that of *avadhuta* (or *abadhut*). Although avadhuta has different connotations and prevalence among diverse traditions, it generally refers to an ascetic who has risen above bodily consciousness and worldly concerns. The Nath Panth, as is well known, is an Avadhuta Panth which regards Gorakh Nath to be the ideal avadhuta and highlights the role of the guru and the practice of yoga. Mahima Dharma does not follow the Nath tradition of a *guru-sishya parampara* (a continuous lineage of preceptor and disciple). But for the followers of Mahima Dharma, as well as for Biswanath Baba, Mahima Swami was an ideal abadhut, the guru of the world, who restored the tradition to its pure form and earlier glory.

TANTRIC TRANSITION

Let me now leave Mahima Swami and turn to Bhima Bhoi, a direct disciple of the Swami and the poet philosopher of the faith. It bears pointing out here that the founder left no compositions or written records of his own. His figure is constructed out of stray features in newspapers and legends, which were given coherence in reports of colonial administrators drawn up in the early 1880s following an incident that brought the faith to the notice of the colonial state. For this reason, what we know of the theology of Mahima Dharma comes from Bhima Bhoi's verses and later interpretations of the tenets of the faith offered by scholar ascetics like Biswanath Baba. The tension between two groups—the dominant one that seeks to marginalize Bhima Bhoi as a householder devotee, and the rival faction that hold his works to be the canons of the faith—has had a long history, including prolonged legal suits over control of the memorial of the guru.[12] Consequently, my use of the term *transition* in this section is only in the sense that followers do not associate Mahima Swami with tantric practices. The dominant image is that of a celibate ascetic, reinforced further by his description as the ideal avadhuta by Biswanath Baba. At the same time, members of the rival group define him as Yogesvara (The

Lord of Yoga), which can be taken as an indication of his knowledge of yoga and his identification with Shiva.

According to legends, Bhima Bhoi was blind and was born to or raised by Khonds, a group of *adivasis* (original inhabitants). Mahima Swami initiated him and conferred on him the "eye of knowledge." Bhima Bhoi had grown up with no formal education but had absorbed and apprehended various traditions of religious and popular literature current in Orissa by the time he was initiated into Mahima Dharma. His imaginative and creative mind combined these received ideas with the teachings of Mahima Swami to produce original compositions. Consequently, his works represent a rich assortment of elements from Vaishnavism, Buddhism, tantra, mysticism, and bhakti. Indeed, one scholar finds in Bhima Bhoi's compositions the culmination of the *nirguna dhara* (line of Nirguna thought) in Oriya religious literature, which began with the Nath yogis and was enriched by the Vaishnavas and the Panchsakhas. Mahima Dharma granted widest circulation to the concept of a Nirguna supreme (Pradhan 1986, 235).

This blend of diverse ideas makes it difficult to place Bhima Bhoi within one particular tradition, a fact that has caused serious disagreement among scholars on his possible genealogy.[13] Rather than go into this debate, I will focus on the influence of yoga and tantra in his compositions, elements often relegated to the background in analyses of his works. As Bettina Bäumer has noted, this relegation is the result of the Vedantization of Mahima Dharma by Bishwanath Baba and his followers of the Joranda branch: "The more philosophical and *bhakti* aspects of his work are generally accepted, but the strong tantric current of his spirituality has been suppressed" (Bäumer 2008, 159).

It is in order here, as Bäumer reminds us, to ask the difficult question: what is tantric? *Tantra* is a diffuse term that signifies a wide range of beliefs and practices across varied traditions. David Gordon White, in his introduction to *Tantra in Practice*, broadly defines tantra as "that Asian body of beliefs and practices which, working from the principle that the universe we experience is nothing other than the concrete manifestation of the divine energy of the Godhead that creates and maintains that universe, seeks to ritually appropriate and channel that energy, within the human microcosm, in creative and emancipatory ways" (White 2000, 9).[14] Since there is no singular, well-defined way to channel divine energy within the human body, tantric ideas and ritual practices remain elusive and pervasive.

It is true, however, that tantra has come to acquire a negative significance because of its close association with *shakti*—woman considered to be manifestation of divine energy—as a mode of emancipation. This concept, introduced in the *Guhyasamaja Tantra* of Buddhism in the fourth century CE, lent itself to diverse apprehensions over centuries—resulting in an amalgamation, in the conception of the Absolute, of the figures of the tantric goddess Tara with the goddess Kali of the Shakta trend of Hinduism (Das 1988, 27–28). Indeed, according to Paritosh Das, the Naths also derived their inspiration from the Vajrayana branch of Buddhism, although "they Hinduized the teachings of the Buddhist Tantras" (ibid., 29). The myths related to Gorakh and Matsyendra, as indicated above, highlight the contrary pull of celibacy and sexual pleasure caused by the "Hinduization" of Buddhist tantra. Of course, not all currents of tantra advocate sexual intercourse with a ritual partner, but the association of tantra with sex has caused its negative association, the reason Bäumer cites for the "suppression" of its influence on Bhima Bhoi.

Bengal and Orissa, we need to remember, were home to all the schools of Buddhist and Hindu tantra and the worship of Shakti (the Goddess). Moreover, the prominence of different strands of Vaishnavism in the region meant that in Western Orissa, Bhima Bhoi was perceived as the *nityasthali* (eternal) Radha (the lover of Krishna) and a range of Dalakahai and Rasarakeli songs, which spoke of the love of Radha and Krishna, were ascribed to him. These songs have nothing in common with the precepts of the faith he followed. Yet they are widely held to be his creations.[15] Lay disciples find no inconsistency in the identification of Bhima Bhoi, the ideal devotee, with Radha. For scholars, of course, it is a contradiction that requires explanation. Artaballabh Mahanti cited works believed to have been composed by Achyutanada, one of the Panchasakhas, which prophesied the birth of Radha as a blind poet in Orissa. This blind poet was to propagate the teachings of the Sunya Purusha (Void Lord), who was to appear as an abadhut.[16] Yet another scholar argued that Bhima Bhoi composed the love songs in "first flush of his youth," before his initiation into Mahima Dharma: "Here is no restriction of Mahima religion, no control of the senses, no mystery of the Brahman. Drawing Radha and Krishna into the vortex of earthly life, the poet expresses his hunger for flesh in the most naked, provocative, sensuous language" (Nayak 1984, 135–36).

Thus, Bhima Bhoi is a figure who eludes classification. His emotive chants are difficult to be contained by the dictates of any one faith, and his association with women confounds the moral norm of a celibate, ascetic preacher. While the *bhajans, stutis,* and *janans* (eulogies of and prayers to the Absolute) composed after initiation into Mahima Dharma imbued the teachings of the founder with new meanings, his life as a householder preacher generated a host of legends which led to his deification in Western Orissa. A detailed discussion of the huge corpus of Bhima Bhoi's compositions is beyond the scope of this paper. I will provide a rough idea of the key elements in order to highlight the presence of Nath, Nirgun, and yogic-tantric ideas in them.

Bhima Bhoi's verses speak of an Absolute (Brahman), omnipresent and omniscient, who created the world out of his *mahima* (radiance, glory), but who is beyond attributes—formless and indescribable. He is the Lord of Lords, the one and only guru who had taken form and come down to earth to redeem humanity by establishing *satya dharma* (true religion). This guru is accessible to all through devotion. His worship does not require priests, temples, or pilgrimage. The pilgrim sites are located in the body: indeed, the *pinda* (body) is a replica of the *brahmanda* (universe). Through proper concentration and control, one can find the Absolute in oneself. The worship of images, the mediation of priests, and rituals thus become totally redundant in the path to salvation.

According to the German scholar, Anncharlott Eschmann, Bhima Bhoi had drawn three crucial elements from the thought of the Panchasakhas. These were: "the worship of the sunya, the theory of Pinda Brahmanda, and the idea of a future redeemer who will come and openly establish what is for the time being a secret doctrine" (Eschmann 2008, 38). Let us pause here to reflect on the importance of the notion of pinda-brahmanda. It is clear from our brief discussions above, that the idea of the body, either as the microcosm, of the universe, or, following White, the body as the internalized representation of the universe, is derived from yoga and tantra. The basic implication here is that the body is the prime mode of realization of the Supreme Reality. This implies a further interiorization not only of the external world, but also of the mythical and religious world (Bäumer 2008, 162). Later schools understood this idea in different ways and worked it out through varied practices. The Buddhist Sahajiyas and the Naths, for instance, explain the state of *sahaja* (spontaneity, illumination) as a state of perfect equilibrium in which the yogi becomes one with the whole universe. In such a state, he himself is the disciple and the preceptor (Dasgupta 1995, 196).

Many of Bhima Bhoi's works evoke the sense of a journey in which the disciple moves closer and closer to complete identification with the preceptor. The *Stuti Chintamoni*, taken to be an intensely personal, autobiographical text, takes the reader along the course of Bhima Bhoi's journey, which begins with complete ignorance of the guru, passes through his initiation, and ends with his realization—by dint of devotion, meditation and contemplation—of identity with his Lord. He comes to recognize the mutuality in the relationship between the guru and the *sishya* (pupil), the incompleteness of the one without the other. The all-knowing, all-pervading and all-powerful *ananta purusha* (infinite spirit, or lord) has created the *bhakta* (devotee) out of his limitless mahima to act as an instrument for the spread of true faith. The devotee complements the master; the bhakta and the guru are inseparable and interdependent, neither being superior to the other. This idea finds expression in several *padas* (couplets) of *bolis* (sayings) 35, 36, and 37:

> It is not important who is the Guru and who the disciple.
> Remember that *bhakta* and *bhagabana* form one body and eat together at the same place (*boli* 35, *pada* 19).
> Know that the master and the disciple are one and the same
> The disciple worships the feet of the Lord; the Guru worships the disciple (*boli* 36, *pada* 11).
> As the *jiba* and *parama* lie undifferentiated in the body
> So are the minds of Guru and disciple inextricably intertwined (*boli* 37, *pada* 1).

It is difficult to ascertain whether this identification is linked to the sahaja state that the disciple has attained and whether the poet's journey included only practices dedicated toward spiritual advancement, or whether he also engaged in yogic practices that aimed at attaining an immutable body. What is clear, however, is Bhima Bhoi's interest in yogic practices evident in the use of yogic-and-tantric metaphors in many of his verses that underline the concept of pinda-brahmanda. These verses offer detailed descriptions of the internal landscape of the body, the ideal *tirtha* (pilgrimage site). This fits in perfectly with Bhima Bhoi's (and Mahima Dharma's) criticism of the external practices of pilgrimages and temple worship. Bettina Bäumer sees in this internal integration achieved through the identification of pinda and brahmanda a close resemblance with tantric sadhana (religious practice) which aims at such an integration of the outer and the inner through the mediation of the body (Bäumer 2008, 162).

The move away from the Vedic path is reflected in the title of another important composition, the *Nirveda sadhana*. This text closely resembles those of the Panchasakhas in language and style and is composed in the famous *dandi matra* (a special meter) of the Oriya *Bhagabata*; it narrates the story of Anadi Prabhu (the Absolute) and his first disciple, Govinda Das, who is none other than Lord Jagannath of Puri. Indeed, Jagannath is the first to recognize Anadi Prabhu once he appears on earth as an avadhuta. Jagannath, as Govinda Das, leaves Nilachal (Puri) to become Anadi's disciple and rid himself of the sins he had acquired in his different incarnations. Govinda then goes to Bolasingha, performs *sharan* (prostration) to Anadi and begs him to show the way, to give him *jñana-mantra* (the formulas of wisdom) and teach him the path of nirveda sadhana. The steps of this sadhana are replete with metaphors of the yogic-tantric sadhana.

The first step for a true disciple is to become aware of Arupa Brahma (Formless God) as the supreme object of the world. This Brahma is eternal. He is free from good and evil, action and non-action. Like air, he fills the universe and permeates all objects. Brahma jñana-mantra (incantation of the knowledge of Brahma) is present in both Veda and in *nirveda* (non-Vedic) traditions. To acquire the mantra, the bhakta has to concentrate on the name of Brahma while infusing his mind with air and placing *jñana* (knowledge) and its five companions—*satya* (truth), *kshama* (forgiveness), *shila* (good conduct), *daya* (kindness) and *daksha* (skill)—in his heart.

> The name is an invaluable asset
>
> It is completely free of sins.
> Sit in meditation of that name,
> Blend mind and air and place the six companions in your lotus-heart.[17]

The path is difficult and Govinda falters. His mind is troubled. He realizes that he has spent twelve years following the dictates of the guru that has made him suffer at the hands of gods and men, but Anadi Prabhu has not appeared again to give him further instructions. He decides to move toward the east, toward Kapilas, in search of his master. The guru comes to know of the doubts in the pupil's mind. Anadi Prabhu leaves his place, comes and meets Govinda midway, and reprimands him. He makes the disciple go through a trial.

Govinda Das is locked inside a temple. The guru claps three times from outside and tells Govinda that he will be able to come out only if he is a proper *yogi-putra* (son of a yogi). Govinda realizes his mistake; he sits in meditation of *ekakshara* (non-dual letter). He mixes his mind and air and concentrates solely on Arupa. His body becomes the ground, and the navel becomes the *dhunikunda* (a metal pot in which the sacred fire is lit)—Govinda lights the sacred dhuni in his navel. Anadi is pleased. He comes to the temple, releases Govinda and takes him to a mountain cave, an idyllic place on which Mother Nature has lavished all her bounties. It is here that Govinda's doubts and queries are answered, and the theory of creation explained.[18]

The recurrent suggestion of yogic practice runs all through the text, although the poet does not make it explicit. Perhaps he deliberately couched his compositions in the '*sandhya bhasha*' (enigmatic or "twilight" language), which bore different meanings for ascetic initiates and the lay followers. At the same time, he revealed his knowledge of the Naths and Sahajiyas by mentioning Matsyendra Nath and Gorakh Nath, and Tantipa and Haripa in the *Nirveda sadhana*.

The *Brahma nirupana gita*, a difficult text of Bhima Bhoi, one that is admittedly addressed principally to the initiated ascetics, gives further indication of his knowledge and practice of yoga tantra:

> The indescribable, incomprehensible Supreme resides in a place which is inaccessible to all; it is *nigama bhubana*, where there is no light nor dark-

ness, neither day nor night, neither sound nor color, neither hunger nor thirst, neither creation nor destruction. There is complete cessation of all activities. It is a temple of soundlessness. Not action, nor prowess nor speech can find entry there. Even water or air cannot reach that place, which is why I call it *agamya* (a place which cannot be reached). There is no creation, maintenance or destruction; it is devoid of dreams and desires. (*Brahma Nirupana Gita* (Bhoi 1925), chapter 1, *padas* 43–46)

This Supreme, at the same time, belongs to all; he dwells in all human bodies. The poet divides the body into several sections (cakras) from the feet up to the brain, and tries to feel the presence of the Brahma in all the parts separately.[19]

The clearest indication of Bhima Bhoi's knowledge of yogic-tantric practices appears in his *Adi Anta Gita*, a composition hardly ever recited or quoted by the followers of the faith. The text deals principally with the body as the instrument of sadhana, the repository of all the eighteen siddhis or spiritual perfections. It shows a clear influence of the *kaya sadhana* (bodily practice) of the Nath, yogis which also aimed at making the body immortal (Dasgupta 1995, 218, 219, 228, 234). At one place in the text, Bhima Bhoi states clearly: "The birth is difficult to attain. The body will not be destroyed. It is called indestructible and immortal."[20]

As Bäumer notes: "Obviously, this knowledge is the very secret of micro-macrocosmic relationship or pinda-brahmanda, which only the saints can realize" (Bäumer 2008, 163–64). As mentioned before, Bhima Bhoi's description of the cakras and the yogic body and mixing of ascent and descent through the cakras do not conform to standard yogic descriptions. A careful and systematic analysis of the relevant passages and allusions is required, affirms Bäumer, in order to decide whether this "apparently unsystematic treatment corresponds to his personal experience or it is just an expression of his poetic freedom." At the same time, his familiarity with the yogic path is unquestionable. The *Adi Anta Gita* describes the path leading to the formless Absolute as *asadhana marga* (a path without any means, a pathless path). This is very much in tune with the highest means described in the *advayavada* (non-dualism) of Kashmir Saivism. In his *Bhajanamala* and *Brahmanirupana Gita,* Bhima Bhoi defines the road to illumination as *anupaya* (ibid.).

Let me now turn to another feature of the *Adi anta gita*, one that relates to the use of sexual symbolism. Like most of Bhima Bhoi's other compositions, the verses here recount a dialogue between *jiva* and *parama*, the soul and the Supreme. What is interesting is that the jiva here is represented as a *yuvati* (a young girl), and parama as a male. At the same time, jiva is also the disciple, Bhima Bhoi, and parama his guru, Mahima Swami. Apart from the fact that the assumption of the female voice is a practice prevalent among the nirguni sants and Vaishnavas, Bhima

Bhoi's representation of himself, the devotee, as a yuvati, goes perfectly well with the belief that he was eternal Radha. The union of the jiva and the parama, thus, has to be understood as a union on three different planes: the union of man and woman; the soul and the Supreme, and the disciple and the preceptor. Once again, we come back to the use of the sandhya-bhasa, the multi-layered language common in tantric texts.

Finally, let us link this use of tantric metaphors and sexual symbolism with Bhima Bhoi's life of a householder where he cohabited with four women.[21] One is widely regarded as his spiritual consort, while he fathered children with two others. The tension these relations caused among the renouncers of Mahima Dharma occasioned a division between the ascetics and Bhima Bhoi, and later, between two groups of ascetics. The dominant group attempted to suppress the tantric elements in Bhima Bhoi's poetry and marginalize him as a householder devotee, not a preacher. But the confusions continued and found expression in the wide variety of legends around Bhima Bhoi.

To conclude, this paper has attempted to highlight not only the common origins of yoga and tantra and their very close association with the Naths, but also the persistence of their mixed expressions in a wide range of later traditions coming down to the nineteenth and twentieth centuries. Through a focus on Mahima Dharma and its founder and poet philosopher, I have tried to show that the tensions reflected in the legends around Matsyendra and Gorakh with regard to association with women are replicated in the stories of Bhima Bhoi and Mahima Swami. In other words, despite repeated efforts at upholding celibacy as a key element of asceticism within dominant Hinduism, and the marking off of yoga from tantra on grounds of yoga's distance from women and sexual practices, the separation between yoga and tantra has neither been final nor complete. The continued expression of their separation finds new significance in the different ways they are understood, appropriated, and worked out in practices of varied religious orders. It is time perhaps to pay greater attention to these combined articulations in order to understand the great hold of the overlapping yoga-tantra traditions rather than to look at them as deviations or distortions from the norm.

PART 2

Theology and Folklore

CHAPTER FIVE

On the Magnitude of the Yogic Body[1]

David Gordon White

A work attributed to Gorakṣanātha, the twelfth- to thirteenth-century founder of the Nāth Siddhas, the *Siddhasiddhāntapaddhati* (SSP),[2] the "Step by Step Guide to the Principles of the Perfected Ones," was composed some time between the late twelfth century and the sixteenth century (Gorakhnath 1954).[3] While we cannot be certain that this is the work of a single hand rather than a compilation composed over several hundred years, the dates of many of the identifiable sources, which it directly quotes, do in fact support a terminus ad quem of the twelfth century. These include the *Vāmakeśvara Tantra* (eleventh century), the *Pratyabhijñahṛdaya* of Kṣemarāja (eleventh century), and the *Svacchanda Tantra* (seventh to eleventh century), all three of which are seminal Kashmirian works of the Śākta-Śaiva tantric tradition, whose terminology the SSP frequently adopts. This is a work in six chapters, all of which are devoted to the body (piṇḍa), the perennial focus of Nāth Siddha doctrine and practice. Of these, the third (SSP 3.1–14), entitled "Knowledge of the Body," presents the most complete and detailed identification of human body with the universe of the "Puranic" cosmic egg.[4]

This is not the standard Nāth Siddha description of the subtle or yogic body, with its sixteen supports (*ādhāras*), five voids (*vyomas*), nine *cakras*, and ten channels (*nāḍīs*); these are detailed in the SSP's second chapter (SSP 2.1–38). Rather, it is a point-for-point identification of the various parts and organs of the human body with worlds, regions, landforms, heavenly bodies, and living creatures, as well as abstract qualities and human emotions, within the Egg of Brahmā (*brahmāṇḍa*). As such, it constitutes a bridge of sorts between the great volume of vernacular poetry attributed to Gorakhnāth—the *Gorakh bānī* (GB)[5]—and the Sanskrit works attributed to Gorakṣanātha. For whereas the latter are generally dry discursive technical guides to the theory and practice of haṭha yoga, the former tend to emphasize the experience of the haṭhayogin, and often resort to metaphorical or allegorical depictions of the subtle or yogic body of the practitioner, after the fashion of the pre-twelfth-century Old Bengali *Caryā* songs.[6] In these poems, the constituent parts and processes of the yogic body are compared, for example, to a goldsmith's workshop,[7] a polo match,[8] a hunting expedition,[9] a city,[10] a liquor shop,[11] the four *yugas*,[12] the Doab,[13] net-fishing,[14] caste relations,[15] a city of thirsty animals,[16] etc. A vernacular verse work entitled the *Gorakh bodh* (GBo), which is cast as a dialogue between Gorakhnāth and his "guru" Matsyendranāth, presents a wide range of such comparisons, which bring the nine planets, five elements, subtle channels, cakras, etc. into play.[17] The Nāth Siddha work that most closely resembles the SSP 3.1–14, however, is attributed to another figure, named Caurangīnāth, whose *Prāṇ sāṅkalī* (PS) is likely a fourteenth-century work (in Dvivedi 1980, 19–28). Here, the yogic body is described as containing the eight serpent clans, the eight underworlds, seven continents, seven oceans, seven rivers, seven heavens, fourteen worlds, five elements, twenty-five metaphysical principles (*tattvas*), five fields, 92,000 (the standard number is 72,000) subtle channels, the 8,400,000 creatures, seven days of the week, fifteen days of the lunar fortnight, twelve signs of the zodiac, the gods and lesser deities, and the four ages—which it details in ways similar to the SSP (PS 22–135). In both, for example, the seven bodily constituents (*dhātus*) are identified with the seven days of the week, the nine planets with the nine bodily orifices; and the four Vedas with the navel, heart, throat, and mouth (PS 96–98).

1. PIṆḌA-SAṂVITTI

What follows is a translation of the discussion of the construction of the body that comprises Chapter 3 of the SSP: "Comprehensive Knowledge of the Body":[18]

> Comprehensive knowledge of the body (*piṇḍa-saṃvitti*) is discussed herewith. He who cognizes the mobile and the immobile [universe as existing] inside of his body becomes a yogin possessed of comprehensive knowledge of his body. (3.1)
>
> The tortoise[19] is situated in the sole of the foot; Pātāla in the big toe, Talātala above the big toe, Mahātala in the heel, Rasātala in the ankle, Sutala in the calf, Vitala in the knees,[20] and Atala in the thighs. Thus, the seven-fold underworld submits to the supremacy of the Rudra deities.[21]

Within the body, Bhāva in his wrathful form is none other than Rudra, the Destroyer of the Fire of Time.[22] (3.2)

The earth is [located] in the anus, the atmosphere in the genital region, [and] heaven in the region of the navel. Thus, the god Indra [abides] in the triple world within the body. The controller of all the senses (*indriya*), he is none other than Indra. (3.3)

The World of Magnificence (*maharloka*) is in the "sprout" of the spinal column, the World of Generation (*jana-loka*)[23] in the hollow of the spinal column, World of Asceticism (*tapoloka*) in the stem of the spinal cord, [and] the World of the Real (*satyaloka*) in the lotus flower of the root-[*cakra*].[24] Thus the divinities beginning with Brahmā dwell in this four-fold world, in the midst of the body, as the embodiments of every sort of pride and self-assertiveness. (3.4)

The world of Viṣṇu is situated in the belly. The god Viṣṇu who engages in a variety of activities is there, in the midst of the body. The world of Rudra is in the heart. There, the god Rudra dwells in the midst of the body, embodying terror. The world of Īśvara is in the breast region. There the god Īśvara dwells in the midst of the body, embodying satisfaction. Blue-Throat (*nīlakaṇṭha*) is in the throat. The god Nīlakaṇṭha dwells eternally in the midst of the body. The world of Śiva is in the uvula. The god Śiva dwells in the midst of the body in his incomparable form. The world of Bhairava is in the base of the epiglottis. There the god Bhairava dwells in the midst of the body in his unsurpassed form. In the middle of the forehead is the World of Him Who Has No Beginning (*anādiloka*). There, the god Anādi, who embodies ego-transcending bliss, dwells in the midst of the body. At the peak[25] [of the forehead] is the world of the Clan (*kulaloka*). There. the god [named] the Lord of the Clan (*kuleśvara*), whose innate form is bliss, dwells in the midst of the body. Inside the [left] temple, in the region of the heavenly Ganges, the god [named] the Lord of the Clanless (*akuleśvara*) dwells in the midst of the body, in an attitude of humility. In the fontanelle is the World of the Supreme Brahman (*parabrahmaloka*). There the god named Supreme Brahman abides in the midst of the body, in the condition of plenitude. In the uppermost lotus is the World of the Transcendent and Non-transcendent (*parāparaloka*). There the Supreme Lord (*parameśvara*) dwells in the midst of the body, in a transcendent and non-transcendent state. In the region of the triple-peak (*trikuṭi*) is the World of Feminine Energy (*śaktiloka*). There, the transcendent goddess (*parā*) Śakti dwells in the midst of the body, as the totality of the creative powers of every [individual *śakti*]. Thus [concludes] the examination of the twenty-one[26] regions of the Egg of Brahma, together with the seven underworlds, [situated] in the midst of the body. (3.5)

The Brāhmaṇas dwell [within the body] in the principle of righteous activity, the Kṣatriyas in valor, the Vaiśyas in resolve, the Śūdras in the attitude of service, and the sixty-four socio-religious classes (*varṇas*) in the [body's] sixty-four constituent parts (*kalā*).[27] (3.6)

Now the seven seas and the seven island-continents are considered. Rose-apple Island (*jambudvīpa*) is in the marrow, Śakti Island (*śaktidvīpa*) in the bones, Subtle Island (*sūkṣmadvīpa*) in the head, Curlew Island (*krauñcadvīpa*) in the skin, Cow-dung Island (*gomāyadvīpa*) in the pores, White Island (*śvetadvīpa*) in the nails, and Fig Island (*plakṣadvīpa*) in the flesh. Such are the seven island-continents.[28] (3.7)

In the urine is the salt sea, in the saliva is the milky sea, in phlegm is the sea of curd, in the fat [of the body] is the sea of clarified butter, in the serum is the sea of honey, in the blood the sea of sugarcane juice, and in the semen is the sea of nectar. Such are the seven seas. (3.8)

The nine divisions (*khaṇḍas*)[29] [of the central island-continent of *jambudvīpa*] dwell in the nine bodily orifices. The Bhārata division, the Kāśmīra division, the Karairpara division, the Śrī division, the Śaṅkha division, the Ekapāda division, the Gāndhāra division, the Kaivartaka division and the Mahāmeru division: such are the nine divisions. (3.9)

[Mount] Meru dwells in the spinal column. Kailāsa dwells in the fontanel, Himālaya in the back, Malaya in the left shoulder, Mandara in the right shoulder, Vindhya in the right ear, Mainaka in the left ear, Śrīparvata in the forehead. Such are the eight clan mountains (*kula-parvatas*). The other secondary mountains dwell in all of the fingers and toes. (3.10)

The Pīnasā, Gaṅgā, Yamunā, Candrabhāgā, Sarasvatī, Pipāsā, Śatarūdrā, Śrīrātri and Narmadā are the nine rivers that dwell in the nine [principal] channels (*nāḍīs*). (3.11)

Other secondary rivers, streams, and rivulets are situated in the 72,000 secondary channels. (3.12)

The twenty-seven lunar asterisms (*nakṣatras*), the twelve signs of the zodiac, the nine heavenly bodies (*navagraha*), the fifteen lunar days: contained within the circle of the heavens, these dwell in the 72,000 spaces [enclosed by the lines of] one's own hand. The various constellations dwell in the waves of existence.[30] The 33,000 gods dwell in the pores of the upper body. The primary and secondary mounds (*pīṭhas*) dwell in the pores.[31] The gods, Titans (*dānavas*), Dryads (*yakṣas*), Protectors (*rākṣasas*),

Flesh-Eaters (*piśācas*), Beings (*bhūtas*), and Ghosts (*pretas*) dwell in the joints. The serpent chiefs dwell in thorax. Others among the hermit (*muni*) host, starting with Sanaka, dwell in the pores of the armpits.[32] Other mountains dwell in the hairs of the belly. The Celestial Musicians (*gandhārvas*), Kinnaras, Kiṃpuruṣas, Nymphs (*apsaras*), and Hosts (*gaṇas*) live inside the belly. Others among the Śaktis[33]—the playful sky-faring Mothers—[as well as] terrible deities dwell in the flow of breath. The various storm clouds dwell in the shedding of tears. The various sacred fords (*tīrthas*) dwell in the vital organs. The immortal Siddhas dwell in the light of perception. The sun and moon dwell in the two eyes. The many trees, vines, shrubs, and grasses dwell in the hair that grows on the shanks. The many worms, insects, flying insects, etc. dwell in excrement. (3.13)

Happiness is what heaven is made of; hell is sorrow. Karma is bondage; the absence of false notions is release. Whatever shape or state of mind—sleep, etc.—one may be in, peace resides in being awake to one's true self. Thus the Supreme Lord, who embodies himself as the universe, is present in every one of its bodies. The universal self, who is by nature undivided, abides in the form of consciousness within the vessel of each and every body. Thus comprehensive knowledge of the body becomes [manifest]. (3.14)

2. PIṆḌAS

Many scholars, myself included, have identified Indic discourse of this type as descriptive of the human "microcosm," a miniaturized replica of the universal "macrocosm."[34] This ancient Greek term, which entered into the English language via post-classical Latin and Middle French, of course means "miniature universe."[35] Behind this term lie a number of aphorisms that ground Western religious anthropology: "God created man in his own image," "Man is the measure of all things," and so on. One need not look far to find analogous statements in Indic sources. To cite but one example, the 300 BCE–400 CE *Caraka-saṃhitā* (CS), one of the three textual pillars of Āyurveda, states that, "this world is the measure (*sammita*) of man. However much diversity of corporeal forms and substances there is in the world, that much [diversity] there is in man; however much there is in man, that much there is in the world."[36] But does this make the human being a microcosm? There is no term in the Sanskrit language for microcosm. Monier-Williams's English-Sanskrit dictionary proposes *sūkṣmajagat*, *sūkṣmaloka*, and *sūkṣmasaṃsāra*, but I have yet to find such terminology anywhere else—either in the Sanskrit canon itself, or Sanskrit lexicons, including Monier-Williams's own Sanskrit-English dictionary. In this article, I will suggest that, within the context of the yoga tradition, the human body is not a microcosm of the universal macrocosm.

I begin with the SSP chapter just translated, which opens with the statement "he who cognizes the mobile and the immobile [universe as existing] inside of his body becomes a yogin possessed of comprehensive knowledge of his body." It is an axiom of Indic epistemology that the most reliable of all forms of valid cognition (*pramāṇa*) is "yogic perception" (*yogipratyakṣa*). More than any other type of human being, yogins are able to know things as they truly are, including objects normally invisible to others: the distant quarters of space, past and future time, atoms, wind, the mind, their own souls, the souls of others, and the interior of people's bodies.[37] Therefore, this opening statement constitutes a non-falsifiable truth claim: this is what the inside of the body—or at least a yogin's body—is really like. It also infers that it is this knowledge, of the identity of the interior of his body with that of the universe, which makes one a yogin. Nowhere, however, does this chapter say that the universe a yogin sees inside has been miniaturized to fit inside the contours of his human body.

What, then, is the source of this body, and what was its original relationship to the universe? The answer to this question is the subject of the SSP's opening chapter, which is entitled "Origin of the Body" (*piṇḍotpatti*). The term *piṇḍa*, best known from the context of the Hindu funerary rites and post-mortem offerings to the ancestors, simply means "ball" or "lump." Through the successive offering of rice balls (*piṇḍa*s), a transitional body is constituted for the departed (*preta*), which serves him until his reunion in the world of the ancestors with three generations of forefathers, a reunion concretized in the rite of *sapiṇḍīkaraṇa* (Knipe 1977, 111–24). Whereas the term is employed in *Ṛg-veda* (ṚV) 1.162.19 to signify "lump of flesh," and in *Bṛhadāraṇyaka Upaniṣad* (BṛU 4.2.3) to signify a "clot" of blood, it is only rarely applied in later literature to the human body. One encounters it in two early Vedānta works, the circa sixth-century *Paramārthasāra* (PAS), a work by the philosopher Ādiśeṣa, and a commentary on the BṛU, dating from the same period, by Bhartṛprapañca. In both, piṇḍa (or *piṇḍānta*) is the last in a series of states (*avasthā*s) in the devolution of the transcendent Brahman into the manifest body.[38] The term *piṇḍa* is explicitly identified with the body in the *Mālinīvijayottara Tantra* (MVUT), a foundational eighth- to ninth-century Śākta-Śaiva work from Kashmir (MVUT 20.2).[39] Here, the compound *piṇḍastha*, is used to denote the "embodied" waking state, which, while it is the lowest of a series of "states of lucidity" (*avasthā*s), nonetheless constitutes the first step on the path to comprehensive knowledge (*saṃvitti*) (MVUT 19.30–33; 20.4), culminating in cognizance of the universe as self, after the divine model of Śiva. In his *Tantrāloka* (TĀ), Abhinavagupta duly comments on the MVUT's use of the term, hierarchizing these states on the basis of their objectivization of phenomena. In the lowest of these, the piṇḍasthā waking state, all perceived entities appear to the subject as completely external phenomena. Yet, as Abhinavagupta maintains, the term *piṇḍastha* was taught to yogins in order to facilitate their attainment of siddhis, as well as their achievement of identity with their object of contemplation, through immersion into the objectivized (TĀ 10.237–243).[40] At the end of this progression, the yogin identifies with the entire universe, comprehensively knowing it to be himself—which is Śiva's mode of being and knowing.

Gorakṣanātha—who uses the term *piṇḍa* more extensively than any other Indian author—was clearly influenced by these theories of knowledge. That the semantic range of the term as he uses it extends far beyond the physical body becomes clear in the first verses of the SSP's first chapter. Almost immediately, the reader is given to understand that the piṇḍa whose origin is being described is not a human body, but rather the body of the universe: this is in fact a cosmogonic account, albeit one that is more metaphysical than mythological in character, after the fashion of other tantric cosmogonies. There are, in fact, several piṇḍas in this account, of which the first, called the "Supreme Body" (*para-piṇḍa*), arises from the union of a series of five feminine energies (*śaktis*) that have devolved from a primordial principle called "The Nameless" (*anāma*) (SSP 1.4–13). This "Supreme Body," also termed the "Beginningless Body" (*anādi-piṇḍa*), is identified with Śiva's transcendent self, which, like the śaktis from which it arose, is also fivefold (SSP 1.14–21). This in turn generates another series of five devolutes, which, taken together, comprise the "Primordial Body" (*ādya-piṇḍa*) (SSP 1.22–29). Another set of five devolutes, the supports of the five elements (called "Great Ether," "Great Air," etc.), comprise the "Great Body Having Form" (*mahā-sākāra-piṇḍa*) (SSP 1.30–36). This body is identified with the embodied forms (*mūrtis*) of eight divinities, descending from Śiva down to Brahmā. Brahmā gives rise to the "Body of Materiality" (*prakṛti-piṇḍa*), which is, in turn, the source of the bodies (*śarīras*) of living beings (SSP 1.37–42). The remainder of the chapter enumerates the manifold components that comprise the subtle and gross aspects of human bodies (SSP 1.43–68), and concludes with a detailed description of embryogenesis, called the "arising of the *piṇḍa* in the uterus (*garbholi*)" (SSP 1.69–73).[41]

Apart from the occurrence of the word *śarīra* in verse 37 of this chapter, *piṇḍa* is the sole term that is applied, throughout SSP 1, to denote the body, of the universe as well as of the person.

3. THE BODY OF GOD WHEN GOD IS A YOGIN

With the exception of the body that arises from the uterus, i.e., the biologically given human body, all of the piṇḍas introduced in this chapter may be readily identified with one or another aspect of the universal body, or of the body-as-universe of (a) transcendent being. From the time of the ṚV 10.90 (the "Hymn of the Man") forward, such a universal "Great Man" or "Great Person" has been a standard fixture of Indic cosmological systems, ranging from the Vedic Puruṣa to the Buddhist Mahāpuruṣa to the Jain Lokapuruṣa. Adapted into the sectarian traditions of the new theism of the epic period, the abstract universal man becomes a personalized god whose body is coterminous with the universe—as, for example, the body that Kṛṣṇa displays in the 200–400 CE *Bhagavad-gītā* (BhG) theophany of his Universal Form (*viśvarūpa*) (van Buitenen 1981):

> "Behold," [the god says to Arjuna], "my hundreds and thousands of bodies (*rūpāṇi*)
>
> . . . behold the entire universe with standing and moving creatures here in one place, inside of my body . . . I give you divine sight (*divyam cakṣuḥ*): behold my masterful yoga (*yogam aiśvaram*)!" (BhG 11.5–8).[42] If in the sky the light of a thousand suns were to rise at once, it would be the likeness of that self-magnified self. [Arjuna observes], "I see you with a mouth that is a blazing fire, burning this universe with its flame. All of the space that extends between heaven and earth, all horizons are filled by you alone
>
> . . . you who are brushing the sky . . . There, all of Dhṛtarāṣṭra's sons, together with the amassed kings . . . are rushing as they enter your mouths." (BhG 11.12, 19–20, 24, 26–27)

Also in this chapter, Kṛṣṇa is called a Master of Yoga (*yogeśvara*) and a *mahāyogeśvara* (BhG 11.4, 9); these terms are found nowhere else in the BhG, save for the concluding verses of the entire work, when Sañjaya, the narrator in the text, twice refers to the god as a yogeśvara. In a long hymn of praise to him, found in the *Mahābhārata's* (MBh) thirteenth book, Śiva, too, is termed a Master of Yoga, as well as a Great Master (*maheśvara*), and a Master of the Person (*puruṣeśvara*) who emits the hierarchized samkhyan universe of twenty-six *tattvas* (MBh 13.14.163b, 181b,182b,190b).[43] He emits Brahmā and Viṣṇu, from his right and left sides, respectively (MBh 13.14.183ab), and at the end of a cosmic age (*yuga*), he emits Rudra who destroys the world and all its creatures. "Becoming Time (Kāla), he burns as brightly as the fire of dissolution. [Then] this [same] god Mahādeva emits the world and all its moving and inert beings [once more], and when the eon comes to an end, he [alone] remains, having struck down the memory of every one of them" (MBh 13.14.183c–185b). Similar language is found in the *Īśvara-gītā* portion of the *Kūrma Purāṇa* (KūP) (1972)—inserted by Pāśupata redactors into what had earlier been a Pāñcarātra work, toward the beginning of the eighth century (Hazra 1975, 71)—which identifies Śiva as the guru of yogins, a Master of Yoga, and the Great Master of Masters of Yoga (*mahāyogeśvareśvara*) (KūP 2.4.16, 19, 30, 32). Here, the description of the yogin god, as beheld by yogins capable of perceiving his form, is reminiscent of Kṛṣṇa's theophany as viewed by Arjuna:

> They saw the dancing cosmic creator god, the god with a thousand heads, a thousand shapes, a thousand arms and legs . . . suffusing the entire cosmic egg with his brilliance, blazing with the light of ten million suns, the transcendent being who dwells within the egg and outside of the egg, who is both inside and out, emitting the blazing fire that incinerates the entire universe. (KūP 2.5.3, 8–11)

The final chapter of the KūP returns to the theme of the yogin god Śiva's cosmic destruction, this time linking his yogic appropriation of other bodies to the sun.

> At the end of an eon, the Fire of Time decides to reduce the entire [universe] to ashes. Entering the self with the self, he becomes the Great Master (Maheśvara) and burns the entire cosmic egg, including its gods, titans, and men. Entering into him, the Great God (Mahādeva) puts on a fearsome appearance and carries out the destruction of the worlds. Penetrating the solar disk, he multiplies himself into seven times seven true [solar] forms of himself and incinerates the whole world. . . . Filling the horizons of space . . . the god whose garland and ornaments are made from the skulls of the gods—the great-armed, gape-mouthed . . . god of a thousand eyes, a thousand shapes, a thousand hands and feet and a thousand rays—stands [alone] engaged in masterful yoga (*yogam aiśvaram*). (KūP 2.44.2–5, 8–10)

4. ĪŚVARAS AND MAHĀN ĀTMĀS, DIVINE AND HUMAN

"Over and against the idea of man as 'microcosm,' India postulated, from the very beginning, a 'macranthropic' universe, that is, a universe having a human form.

Since that time, Puruṣa, the sacrificial man, has become a yogin" (Biardeau and Malamoud 1976, 108). These, the words of Madeleine Biardeau, summarize the arguments of the preceding section. In the epic and Puranic canon, Kṛṣṇa and Śiva, the sole deities who are cast as yogins, are specifically called yogins when their bodies are being identified with, or are shown to be coterminous with, the entire universe. In both the BhG and the KūP, the great gods Viṣṇu and Śiva are said to practice yoga precisely when they are in the process of internalizing all external phenomena by either manifesting the entire universe within their cosmic bodies or by swallowing all, as the doomsday sun at the end of an eon, until they are left standing alone. We have also seen that both gods are called Masters of Yoga in this role, and that the universal display of both of these gods is termed their "masterful yoga" (*yogam aiśvaram*). One of the names by which the Puranic Śiva is best known is Maheśvara, the "Great Master," a name taken to be synonymous with Mahādeva, the "Great Divinity." In the context of early yoga theory, the term *īśvara* was not a synonym for the term *deva*. Rather, it denotes a person who has, through his practice, attained "mastery" (*aiśvarya*). A synonym, in the Pāśupata system, for *siddhi* ("supernatural enjoyment") (Bisschop 2005, 552), *aiśvarya*, like the term *īśvara* of which it is the abstract form, is a technical term specific to yoga as it was theorized in these, the earliest theoretical sources on yoga.[44] One of these is the two hundred eighty-ninth chapter of the MBh's twelfth book, which is contained in the epic's 200–400 CE *Mokṣadharma-parvan*. This source states the matter as follows:

> The empowered yogin becomes radiant with glory and very powerful, like the sun at the end of time, which desiccates the entire universe . . . Yogins who are without restraints [and] endowed with the power of yoga (*yogabalānvitāḥ*) are [so many] masters (*īśvarāḥ*), who enter into [the bodies of] the Prajāpatis, the sages, the gods, and the great beings. Yama, the raging Terminator (Antaka), and death of terrible prowess: none of these masters (*īśate*) the yogin who is possessed of immeasurable splendor. . . . A yogin can lay hold of several thousand selves, and having obtained [their] power, he can walk the earth with all of them. He can obtain [for himself] the [realms of the] sense objects. Otherwise, he can undertake terrible austerities, or, again, he can draw those [sense objects] back together [into himself], like the sun [does] its rays of light. (MBh 12.289.21, 24–27)

This epic passage is, I would argue, the original theoretical topos of this usage, with the term *īśvara* (master) specifically denoting a practitioner of yoga who has attained mastery (*aiśvarya*) through his practice (MBh 12.228.14, 21). The forms that that mastery takes include the power to take over the bodies of other creatures, as well as the power of the sun to draw back into oneself all of the matter and energy in the universe, and thereby remain the "last man standing" in a universe that has been fully internalized. In both scenarios, the body of the yogin-as-īśvara becomes possessed of the same power of expansiveness or magnificence (*mahattva*) as those of the yogeśvaras, Kṛṣṇa and Śiva. Such is the explicit conclusion, and the narrative climax of MBh 12.289:

> When his self-magnifying self (*mahān ātmā*) and the magni-ficent (*mahān*) [universe] have fused into one another, a yogin may enter [into] women, men and the assemblies of Gandharvas, the quarters of the sky, the hosts of Yakṣas, the mountains and the serpents, and the clouds together with the forests and all the rivers, and the terrible oceans and all the mountain peaks, and the ancestors and serpents and all the divinities, [and] verily the immaculate overlord of men together with the stars, and the greatly massive firmness [i.e., the earth element], and the whole [circle of] splendor [i.e., the fire element], and [the goddess] Siddhi, the spouse of Varuṇa [i.e., the water element], and supreme Nature [together with] pristine pure being, massive passion and evil darkness (*sattva, rājas, tamas*), and the six high-minded sons of Brahmā and the six-faced one (Kārttikeya) and Dharma and Bhava and the boon-granting Viṣṇu, Brahmā the master and . . . indeed That, the magni-ficent (*mahan*) highest Brahman. He is liberated shortly thereafter. . . . Surpassing all mortal yogis, [the yogi] whose body is the magni-ficent [universe] and whose self is Nārāyaṇa, acts. (MBh 12.289.58–61, 62b)

Here, the use of the term *mahān ātmā* is of signal interest. As the nominative singular of the present active participle of **mah*, a verb root, which from the epic period forward carried the sense of "magnify," *mahān* may be literally translated as "magnifying." Its Indo-European cognates—Greek, Latin and English, respectively—are *mégas, magnus,* and "much."[45] Combined with *ātman*, *mahān* can only be read here as the "(self-) magnifying self," in other words, a self whose quality of expansiveness empowers it to become coterminous with the entire magnified or magni-ficent universe (*mahān*, or *mahat* in the neuter). The term *mahān ātmā* is first introduced in the circa 300–100 CE *Kaṭha Upaniṣad* (KU) as the metaphysical category immediately below the unmanifest (*avyaktam*) and the supreme person (*puruṣa*). This early adumbration of the three highest Sāmkhyan categories is to be juxtaposed with that of the 350–450 CE *Yoga-sūtras* (YS), in which it is *buddhi* and *prakṛti* that precede *puruṣa*. In both the Pātañjala Yoga and classical Sāṃkhya philosophical systems, the buddhi (intellect)—or its analogue mahat—constitutes the ground for all that exists

(Kapani 1993, 413), in the light of which the use in this passage of *mahān* and *mahān ātmā* for both the whole of existence and for the yogi whose self is coterminous with the whole of existence makes perfect sense. In both of these soteriological systems, the goal of practice is to free the intellect or "the magnificent" from the afflictions (*kleśas*) that skew its perception of its true nature as free and limitless, i.e. as the self-magnifying self that "knows," as the 500–400 BCE *Bṛhadāraṇyaka Upaniṣad* puts it, "that 'I am Brahman,' [and thereby] becomes this everything."[46]

Like the Upaniṣads, Hindu tantra is, for the most part, a gnoseological system, in which one becomes what one knows oneself to be. This applies to mainstream tantric yoga as well: the goal of yoga is identity with the divine, the realization of a god's eye view of the universe, in which one sees "that" (*idam*) as "I" (*aham*). This is the purport of the 600–800 CE *Mataṅgapārameśvarāgama* (MPĀ), a work of the mainstream Śaivasiddhānta tradition, which concludes its description of a practitioner's meditation on Rudra, by stating that

> When he has visualized [Rudra in this way] he should immerse himself in him entirely, [thinking] "Without a doubt this is who I am." Meditating [thus] he should wander day and night . . . considering . . . that "the universe is contained in myself" or "I abide in all that moves," and conquering his mind through yoga (*yogatas*).[47]

The SSP draws on this tantric gnoseological system when it defines the yogin as a person capable of fully knowing the manifest universe as existing within his body. This text's fifth chapter describes the process by means of which a practitioner realizes this homogeneity of individual experience with that of the divine (*samarasa*).[48] Here, by fully knowing his own body (*nijapiṇḍa*), the yogin experiences the magnificence (*mahattvam*) of his own body, recognizing it to be a "great mass of [solar] rays (*mahāraśmipuñja*)." After twelve years of practice, the yogin becomes Śiva's equal, the creator and destroyer himself (SSP 5.10, 12, 41). The SSP's sixth and final chapter, a celebration of the fully realized yogin, here called the *avadhūta-yogin*, expands on these themes:

> He who causes the entire [universe] to revolve inside of himself, and who always knows the universe to be himself due to his identity with it, is called an *avadhūta* . . . he is a yogin, a knower, a perfected being, a vow-taker, a master (*īśvara*). . . . (SSP 6.15–21)

CHAPTER SIX

Awakening Generosity in Nath Tales from Rajasthan[1]

Ann Grodzins Gold

"Awakening Generosity" evokes a Rajasthani locution, *alakh jagarno*, common to regional Nath lore. I might literally translate this as "to awaken [to] the imperceptible" or the "Unseen." This phrase occurs frequently in Rajasthani Nath oral traditions. It is used very specifically in cultural performances to describe what Naths, also called Jogis, do to announce their presence when they approach the homes of ordinary people, usually to perform instructional stories and to collect food donations.[2] Jogi minstrels command the attention of their patrons by crying outside their gates and doorways, "*Alakh, Alakh*!" (Unseen, unseen!).[3]

At least a double entendre is embedded in the phrase *to awaken [to] the imperceptible*. First, jogis are waking up their listeners to the existence of invisible realities far more significant than mundane ones. Second, they are subtly advising those listeners that a handful of grain or a piece of bread given to a jogi might be the closest that people enmeshed in worldly affairs may ever get to the imperceptible. A third awakening, implied in both of the small tales I shall consider in this chapter, is a kind of warning: if giving to jogis is meritorious, and may bring blessings, holding out on them is dangerous and could bring disaster. Second chances will not be found easily, so to be on the safe side householders should give unstintingly and without thought of any return or reward.[4]

Nath performers traditionally went from house to house and neighborhood to neighborhood, generally twice a year at harvest time, to perform fragments of epic tales about world renouncers' trials, sorrows, and powers as well as to gather grain.

They refer to this practice as "making rounds" (*pheri lagana*)—a phrase used, at least in the region of Rajasthan where I have worked, solely in connection with Naths. A more encompassing expression applicable to all religious mendicants, to beg for alms (*bhiksha mangna*), is also commonly employed to describe Nath practice. In 2007, I asked Chanda Nath—a householder, farmer, and singer—what the difference was between "making rounds" or "begging" and "alakh jagarno." He replied without hesitation, and with strong conviction, that alakh jagarno was for "supreme truth" (*paramarth*), while the other two actions were for "the stomach" (*pet*). Others agreed with his clear-cut conceptual opposition.

From my outsider perspective, however, it seems that Nath lore conflates practices of demanding and receiving food alms with spiritual instruction and progress in a variety of ways. I may give one example that does not occur in the stories this chapter presents, but rather in the paradigmatic Nath epics of kings who become yogis: Gopi Chand and his mother's brother, Bharthari. In both these epic tales, to receive alms (a crust of stale bread) from a former wife or sister becomes the pivotal action that creates a true renouncer who is fully detached from his former worldly identity and, indeed, accepted as one who has achieved knowledge of the imperceptible (A. Gold 1992). In other words, a good deal more than an empty stomach may be at stake when a Nath comes to the door and, having cried "Alakh alakh," receives food.

HOUSEHOLDER NATHS IN RURAL RAJASTHAN

Members of the Nath *jati* (community or "caste") in rural Rajasthan live as married property owners but claim affinity, both spiritual and genealogical, with world renouncers. This duplex identity, these lived contradictions, play out in legend, history, and the everyday. In earlier publications, both Daniel Gold and I have provided detailed descriptions contexualizing the oral narratives and religious practices of Rajasthan's householder Naths.[5] Here, I offer the bare minimum as requisite background.

In Ghatiyali, the Rajasthan village where I have periodically undertaken ethnographic work on diverse topics for about thirty years, householder Naths identify themselves as a caste group (*jati*) and are well integrated into local society. Naths own land and livestock, and some of them have prospered in various other ways. For example, my friend and occasional assistant, Shambhu Nath—whose uncles included an epic bard as well as a famous magician who meditated in cemeteries and was able to read minds—served as *upasarpanch* (elected assistant to the village head man) for a number of years. In what can be a thankless and suspect role, he was unusually well trusted and well liked, and perhaps for that reason, he found the job exhausting. Shambhu now runs a general store and flour mill in the center of Ghatiyali, having moved there from the somewhat liminal Nath neighborhood, which adjoins the community's burial ground.[6]

As respected religious experts, Naths perform a number of roles in and around Ghatiyali. They serve as worship priests (*pujari*) in many regional Shiva temples and shrines; as repositories of healing and protective knowledge, possessing spells that provide succor for various afflictions; as singers of *nirgun bhajan*s (hymns to a divinity perceived as formless) and officiants at death rituals for members of an esoteric sect associated with their teachings.[7] A very few—either by familial tradition, personal inclination, or most often a combination of both—learn to play the *sarangi* and to sing and perform religious epics. In the Nath repertoire of this region, the two most important and frequently performed pieces are the epic tales of renouncer kings Gopi Chand and Bharthari. Somewhat less in demand but also popular is "Lord Shiva's Wedding Song," the story of how Parvati won the ascetic Shiva for her husband, and married him.[8]

In 1987, I recorded from the aging bard Madhu Nath the two much slighter stories I present here. Madhu gave them to me after he had completed his performance of King Bharthari's epic—the text I had come specifically to elicit—as a kind of "bonus track." Following Nath practice, I refer to these short, sequentially linked episodes, as the "Potters' Tale" and the "Dairymaid's Tale." They sat dormant in my fieldnotes for twenty years. In the summer of 2007, my old friend, Ugma Nathji, a lead Nirgun bhajan singer who earns his living herding goats, told me that many Nath performance practices were radically on the wane. In the face of this discouraging news, I nonetheless set out to learn more about the two stories.

Although Shambhu Nath had been my research assistant in 2003, I had not done any research or writing focused on Nath traditions for over a decade. When I explained to Shambhu that I wanted to find Naths who knew these short tales, he was dubious himself at first. However, with his help and with the new mobile phone network that now covers much of rural Rajasthan, we were able to contact in short order three persons who readily and enthusiastically rehearsed for me the two tales, and were eager to tell me more. None of them lived more than a two-hour ride from Ghatiyali.

In what follows, I shall draw heavily on Madhu Nath's performance of twenty years ago, which was the most leisurely of the four versions I now have in hand. I draw also on all three recordings from 2007 which display fascinating narrative variations. In 2007, moreover, I was able to elicit interpretations from the performers themselves which I had never done with Madhu Nath, as for him I had played the more traditional role of appreciative, passive patron.

The three men whom I recorded in 2007 were: Banna Nath (a former householder and father of a large family who some years ago took up a renouncer's life in a Shiva shrine on a river bridge); Shankar Nath (an initiated renouncer with yogis' earrings who is uncle to my friend Shambhu Nath's daughter's fiancé); and Chanda Nath (a householder and farmer who plays the sarangi and performs Nath tales at fairs and by invitation, but says that he does not "make rounds").[9] Each of the four storytellers was born in a different village in Rajasthan's Banas Basin region. Each tells the stories slightly differently. Although the facts and processes of variation are not my project here, I shall note them when they contribute to an interpretation; equally those elements that do not vary across the four performances are quite significant.[10] In this chapter, however, my main course is charted along the narrative surface of the tales, with occasional dips into their deeper intentional messages.

The single most powerful message in these evidently enduring stories has to do with the significance of giving to jogis—or more specifically of feeding them. It is notably never a question of cash. Rather, everyday foodstuffs—bread in the Potters' Tale and milk in the Dairymaid's—are at stake. Both stories seem to me to spin multiple meanings around the simple generosity of sharing food with jogis as well as its opposite: withholding food from them. These meanings include spiritual teachings as well as comical cultural critique. Spending time with Naths in 2007, after a long interlude, I was struck by the ways their community—however well integrated into the social order—continues to have an edgy relationship to it. The tales that follow seem both in content and style to be permeated with an attitude I might characterize as a refusal to take the pressing concerns of householders too seriously. To put it more precisely, I note an ability to see beyond such concerns even while immersed in them. This would be the specialty of householder Naths with their double identity.

THE STORIES THEMSELVES

The Potter and Dairymaid's Tales are linked sequentially. Gopi Chand and his mother's brother Bharthari first stop at the home of a potter couple in a place identified as Tijara village in Alwar District.[11] After they leave the potters' house, following a conventional period of twelve years, they arrive in a Gujar or herders' hamlet, also in Alwar, where the Dairymaid's story takes place. The Potters' story is always told as a prose story, but the Dairymaid's story is sung, with interspersed prose explanations (*arthav*), just as are the epic tales that are Nath performers' chief bread and butter.[12] This could suggest that the Dairymaid's story is older and more "traditional" than the Potters' story. Another indication of this is that the Dairymaid's story charters events at the Alvar mela or fair where Naths still gather annually. It is thus integral to their community's history and landscape. The former royal identity of the renouncer kings is frequently invoked in the Dairymaid's Tale, although never in the Potters' Tale, another factor suggesting that this episode is more closely linked to Nath epics, as the performative style also indicates. However, according to performative practice as well as narrative sequence, the Potters' story comes first. Thus, we too will begin with it.

The Generous Potter and his Stingy Wife

I offer a full translation of the first portion of Madhu Nath's 1987 rendition of the Potters' Tale, including the words or grunts of the "respondent" (*hunkar*), to convey the oral performance flavor. Then, I lapse into summary mode for the remainder of the tales, with occasional returns to the texts for poetic enhancement or nuanced meanings that are lodged in language.

> Now, Gopi Chand and Bharthari went, where? to Alvar City!
> /to Alvar city/
> They went to Alvar city where they arrived at a potter's doorway.
> /both of them, uncle and nephew/
> Both uncle and nephew, together.
> /yes, yes/
> At this time in their lives they stayed together. So they arrived at a potter's doorway—the doorway of a potter who was a devotee.
> /hmm hmmm/
> The potter was a devotee, and so he undertook to serve them, generously. He gave them marijuana and hashish to smoke, and massaged their feet, and provided facilities for them to bathe, and washed their loincloths.
> /Gopi Chand's and Bharthari's/
> Yes, he washed their loincloths. That Potter, well, he served them.
> /hmm hmmm/
> He kept them with him.
> /hmm hmmm/
> He kept them for one day; he kept them for two days; he kept them for four days; he kept them.

/hmm hmmm/

But now that Potter's wife, she won't give any more bread, My Daughter!

/hmm hmmm/

That Potter's wife . . .

/ . . . to the great kings/

Yes, she won't give to them. She said to her husband, "Why are you keeping these Babajis here, for no reason?"

/yes, yes/

"So, let them go on their way, because I am not able to roll out their bread and I am not able to grind their flour."

He said, "O you slut! We have plenty of grain, and it is the Lord Shankar's own storehouse. Lord Shankar gives us all the wealth we possess, so for you to give a couple of pieces of bread, what trouble is that to you?"

/yes!/

But she answered, "If you want to feed your Babajis then go ahead and feed them, but they won't get their bread from me!"

/yes, yes/

So, my son! She didn't give them any bread.

/hmm hmmm/

But even so the potter would not let them go.

/hmm/

At meals she gave the potter just three pieces of bread to eat.

/ yes, yes /

So she gave him just three pieces of bread, just three, that Potter's wife. Even so, he did not let them go.

/yes/

So he gave each of them one piece of bread, one piece to each sadhu, and the one bread left, he ate that one. He ate only that one.

/the potter/

The potter. The potter ate, and afterwards he sat with them to talk about divine knowledge, and in the evenings they meditated ["did *bhajan*"; could also mean sang hymns, but from the context, I believe it refers here to meditative practice].

/yes, yes/

So in the evening he talked with them about divine knowledge and served them; and in the daytime he made pots. And he kept them with him for twelve years.

/Gopi Chand and Bharthari, both of them/

Yes, Gopi Chand and Bharthari! For twelve years he served them.

/yes, yes/

Now he made pots, he made pots and he began to bake them, in the kiln on that day, when twelve years were complete. On that day he put the pots in the kiln.

/he put them in the kiln/

He put them in the kiln, in the kiln, to bake.

I condense portions of what follows:

> The two great jogis get ready to depart before dawn while the Potters, who are exhausted from a hard night's work preparing their kiln, sleep. The jogis hang up a sign on the kiln, "a great big piece of paper with big thick letters, red ones" on which is written:
>
> alvar bich tijara
> jaha Gopi Chand Bhartari tape varash barah
> baba ka het[13]
> may ka kuhet
> adha kanchan adha ret
> In Alvar's midst lies Tijara
> There Gopi Chand and Bharthari did tapas twelve years.
> The father's devotion,
> The mother's disgust,
> Half gold, half dust!

These rhymed lines appear in every version, although Madhu Nath's is the only one in which they are said to be inscribed on paper. In all the others, they are pronounced, almost like a magical spell that transforms the pots.

After the two jogis have quit the scene, a merchant happens by on his way to the latrine. This detail I might have attributed to Madhu Nath's always earthy style, but I find it is included in all four versions. Perhaps it is simply the most conventional explanation for someone being out and about early in the morning. But it may also work deliberately to degrade, to insult, the merchant. Madhu Nath's tale has perhaps the nastiest portrait of this folklorically despised being, describing in detail just where he goes for his latrine and having him stop at the potters' place on his return—presumably not having yet even properly washed his hands! In his polluted state, he reads the note left by the jogis. In the other versions, he sees the pots glittering through openings in the kiln or overhears the jogis pronouncing the spell.

In all cases, the merchant then is able to swindle the potter's wife into selling him the contents of the kiln before it is opened. Needless to say it is always the wife, perfectly in character, driven by greed, who agrees to the merchant's offer. However, for this piece of the tale, each narrator embellishes the situation with a slightly different arrangement. One explained that the potters were in deep debt because they hadn't sold any pots for twelve years, and the merchant simply offers to cancel their debt. Madhu Nath gives the potters a somewhat better deal: the merchant offers ten thousand rupees for all the pots in the kiln, sight unseen, to which the avaricious potter's wife eagerly agrees.

Disturbingly, in Madhu Nath's tale, the potter—so willing to give away his bread—looses his detachment when it comes to gold.

Here is how this scene unfolds, not to his spiritual credit:

> The pots had become golden, and they were sparkling, and the potter began to beat his chest. He cursed out his wife, "You worthless slut! I did twelve years of service, and gave two breads to the sadhus and I ate only one. For twelve years I did this service, and look! It became bright, and I received the fruits of my twelve years.[14] But you slut, you have made the pipal tree wither with your sin."

While it might seem more natural to blame the conniving merchant, that never happens. Merchants are stock figures of exploitative greed. They appear as a kind of fate-like force, or a force of nature, in their determination and capacity to fleece the poor. One might say it is their folkloric dharma. So this one is only doing what merchants do and the potter curses his wife.

The potter wants to give back the ten thousand in exchange for just one of the many golden pots. The merchant however refuses, saying, "Why should I take ten thousand for a pot worth a hundred-thousand?" Madhu Nath concludes his tale, then, with a realistic reference to local political economy:

> So he took them all, and wouldn't even leave one pot for the Potters. And ever since then Riddhi Siddhi (goddesses who are personifications of Wealth and Fortune) dwell in merchants' homes. That is why merchants have Lakshmi (the goddess of wealth). Wealth left the potters and went to the merchants!

In Banna Nath's much shorter version, everyone loses, and it seems a bit more poetic justice prevails:

A merchant came along, on his way to the latrine, and he saw that half the kiln was glittering. So the merchant didn't go to the latrine, but stopped and said, "O Potter, I'm in need of pots so sell me the entire kiln full."

The potter answered, "No, I ought to give them to the whole city and not only to you."

The merchant said, "But I will give you as much as you ask."

At this time the potter's wife thought to herself, "What bad luck, when we have a customer at our door, to refuse. Why should I have to peddle them through the town?"

So the potter's wife said, "Could you feed us as long as we stay alive? If so, then I'll give you all the pots?"

The potter said, "No no no! Don't sell the whole kiln, give him some but not all."

But the merchant called his accountant to pay the potters for the whole oven-full of pots. He paid the potter's wife. And then all the golden vessels that were there turned back to clay.

At least in Banna Nath's admittedly condensed, impromptu account, the fruits of the potter's hard twelve years of service do not go to the merchant.

In general, however, the Potters' tale has a curiously unsatisfying closure. In spite of his exemplary twelve years of devoted and genuinely self-sacrificing service to the powerful jogis, the potter himself never is able to claim the blessing they attempt to bestow on him. It would be discouraging to conclude that having a stingy, worldly wife ultimately obstructs all spiritual progress—for surely the gold represents something more than wealth. It may be that when the golden pots arouse his lust for worldly gain, and he seems to forget all his former capacity for self-restraint, the poor potter loses the fruits of his service in a stunningly lightening-swift backslide. I must leave this unresolved puzzle behind in Tijara, to follow the two Babajis to a cow herders' hamlet and the next story.

The Arrogant Dairymaid

The famous jogis (one or both) proceed now to the house of a woman who belongs to the Gujar community, traditionally herders and providers of all kinds of dairy products. Here, there is no generous husband to serve as foil to the ungenerous female. The dairymaid speaks of her sons, but no man appears in her story, and she is clearly the sole mistress of her household. The dairymaid is not only prosperous but arrogant and unbending in her prosperity, and that stiff-mindedness is her downfall. Like many of us, she is willing to help others but feels quite justified in setting limits to her charitable practice. When things go badly for her, the dairymaid consults various religious experts and spirit mediums, as many afflicted rural people still do today. They tell her that she has only herself to blame and force her to recollect her arrogant and stingy behavior. Having learned her lesson, she not only regains her prosperity but comes to understand how to be truly generous, as do her descendents for ever after. In this happy outcome, the Dairymaid's Tale diverges from that of the Potters who are left empty-handed and from whom no enduring charitable legacy remains.

To recapitulate the tale, drawing on all versions: Gopi Chand and Bharthari—or sometimes just Bharthari without his nephew—continue their wanderings after departing from the Potter's home in Alwar. They come to a Gujar hamlet, and feel hungry and thirsty. Every one of the four versions mentions their hunger, along with their expectation of being well fed just *because* they are in a Gujar settlement. All four versions describe them doing alakh jagarno outside the home of a dairywoman. They call, "Alakh, Alakh!" followed by, "Give us a cup of milk." The dairymaid, sometimes named as Sav Gujari, refuses them the milk, even though she has a big pot of it.

Here is Banna Nath's spoken version which has Bharthari alone as the chief actor and speaker:

> Sav Gujari was her name, and her village is still there.
>
> Bharthari awoke the imperceptible [that is, cried out "Alakh, Alakh"], and said, "O Mother, I'm hungry. Give me a bowl of milk."
>
> She said, "Ten thousand people come and go, and to whom shall I give milk?
>
> Because my house is right on the road. But I don't even have enough milk for my sons, so how can I give it to you?" So she refused.
>
> He said, "O Dairymaid, don't be proud! You just have a big pot of buttermilk, but there was a day when I had one hundred elephants and I was the king of Ujjain, but that wasn't written in my fate so I became a Jogi. . . . Please give me a bowl of milk, I'm about to die of hunger."
>
> She said, "No, I will give you buttermilk."

The dairymaid is obstinate in her resolve to offer beggars only buttermilk. In one version, they ultimately drink the buttermilk; in the other three, they refuse it. But in all four they first try to reason with her and in the end curse her.

In Chanda Nath's elaboration (arthav) on his sung performance, both Jogis are present, but Bharthari is again the chief speaker. He gives the dairywoman quite a long and compelling sermon on the perils of arrogance. I present portions of this exchange:

> She said, "If you want buttermilk (*cach*) I can fill your gourds."
>
> They replied, "No no no! Give the buttermilk to your husband, your son, your servants, but we will accept only milk."
>
> The dairymaid answered, "No, no! I give them milk because they do things for me, but what are you doing for me that I should give you milk? Who knows where you will go after I give you milk!"
>
> "Hey Mother, never be proud of your sons or your milk! In the way that the sun and moon are joined, in the same way sons and milk are linked and they will both be here tomorrow, but who knows about the saints and whether they will ever come again."

Notice this "seize the moment" approach to giving to Naths which turns upside down the dairymaid's implication that it is useless to give to people who will not stick around to return the favor. The Naths by contrast emphasize that this is exactly why she should take advantage of the rare opportunity their presence offers her to practice meritorious charity.

Notice also that, while ordinary villagers worry enormously and perpetually about the survival of their sons, from the Nath renouncer point of view made explicit here, sons are a dime a dozen![15] Here is the dairymaid's riposte after hearing out her visitors' homily:

> No, my house is on the road, and plenty like you come this way, plenty who are making rounds, plenty who awake the imperceptible [notice how the two ideas are linked here]. Should I give to all of them? If you had such a craving for milk you should have stayed at your own house; why did you become sadhus?

Her argument seems to strike home: after all, the whole point of renunciation is no longer to crave anything.

As the story goes, however, the renouncer and former king immediately dismisses this approach. He grounds his rejection of the dairymaid's statement in his former identity as a king. Of course, ideally a renouncer completely dies to his previous identity at initiation. However, this has never been the case in any of the extensive lore about Gopi Chand and Bharthari who always seem to hover between their former royal persona and their self-realization as yogis.

Here the former king appears to indulge in his own arrogance, claiming superior social status to the woman from whom he is begging. He then goes on to criticize the dairymaid for her pride. I quote at length from Chanda Nath on this clash of wills, and its aftermath:

> Bharthari answered, "Don't think I'm an ordinary person. Mine was a kingdom. I left my kingdom, my Queen Pingala, because it was my fate. People like you used to sweep my floors! Look at the power of time, how things change, I left my brother Vikramaditya, my elephants and horses! And all I ask of you is just a little milk.
>
> "Let me tell you about the fruits of arrogance:
>
> The ocean was full of jewels, and became proud, and God made the water salty.
>
> The demon Ravana was proud, and God turned Golden Lanka into dust.
>
> The wild peacock was proud of his beauty, and God gave him the ugliest feet of all.
>
> Wealth is like a wave, coming and going, you can't hold it!
>
> You may become a water carrier for every house in the village. Your churn might hang on a peg forever! You had better accept what I say as the truth. I will absolutely drink milk."
>
> Still, she would not give him milk.
>
> So Bharthari left her house and went to a Jogis' camp near a village where there was a fair taking place, and from there he sent Bhairuji [an active deity, Shiva's emanation] to destroy everything the dairymaid possessed [instructing Bhairu]: "Go and curse her."
>
> So Bhairuji came to her house and awoke the imperceptible [that is, Bhairu who is a deity arrives at the dairywoman's house in the guise of a wandering Jogi and calls, "Alakh Alakh!"].
>
> She responded [in highly insulting fashion], "One Babaji already came and quarreled with me and now, where have you come from anyway? Here is another one!"
>
> Bhairuji had a very hot temper, so when he heard this he cursed her: "Your churning stick will hang on a peg and your churning pot will lie upside-down. Black crows will sit on your buildings and tigers will attack your livestock; wolves will come too and eat your sheep and goats; your cow will be mooing in the jungle and the calves will be mooing in the cattle pen, but they will not meet one another ever again."
>
> In the evening when the dairymaid started to milk the buffalo she found milk in two udders, but in the other two blood and pus. She

> became distraught, and began to run here and there, and her sheep and goats were eaten by wolves and her cows and buffalos were ruined.

The dairymaid now sought help—in different stories from different diviners. Foolish woman that she was, she did not immediately comprehend the causal relation between her refusal of milk to jogis and all these disasters which followed as quickly as instant karma.

In Madhu Nath's tale the dairymaid runs to consult a spirit medium: a priest who becomes possessed by Bhairuji. The *bhav*—that is, the god speaking through the mouth of the priest—tells her that her troubles will not be cured by him. She begs to know what sin she has committed:

> "What did I do to be such an unfortunate woman, what is my sin?"
>
> He quizzes her then, "So, who came to your door this morning? And what did they ask you for?"
>
> "Alas, alack! Grain-giver, two Jogis came and they each wanted a cup of milk."
>
> "So, did they get it?"
>
> "Alas Alack! I am an ill-fated slut, they didn't get it."
>
> "O you broken-hearted slut, they were Gopi Chand and Bharthari, and if you had given them milk, then it would have been a good day for you, but you are such an ill-fated slut that they turned your female buffalos into males, and your cows into bulls; and wolves and jackals ate your sheep and goats, and your herd-boy got a high fever, and he won't be cured."

Bhairuji, still speaking through the medium, then elaborates on all the other delicacies she should have served to the jogis. As soon as she hears this, the dairymaid sets off to search for them, carrying every kind of delectable preparation of Rajasthani foodstuffs with her, on a tray on her head. She is unable to locate Gopi Chand and Bharthari. Clearly, and just as they had warned her, restitution is not to be so easily enacted. After all, the jogis had told her to seize the opportunity while she had a chance. Now she has plenty of time for remorse. She returns to her devastated home unsuccessful and suffers the absence of milk, the crying of the young, the lack of a "white stream" until the folklorically conventional period of twelve years has elapsed, and the immortal pair happens to arrive once again at her door.

In another version, the one told by the renouncer Shankar Nath, the dairymaid consults not a possessed priest but a Brahmin, who tells her what is more or less the same thing. However, there is a different twist in the resolution:

> She went back and searched for the babajis, and wandered all day, asking the herders and all. All day she was in such great difficulty that she wanted to jump from a hilltop, she was so distraught. She thought to herself, "I didn't give the sadhus any milk; everything is gone; I might as well die."
>
> So she threw herself down from the hilltop, and Gopi Chand and Bharthari told Bhairu, "Run and catch her, because if she dies it will be our sin."
>
> So this place was in Alwar district, the place where Bhairuji caught her. And when he told her who had saved her, she fell at their feet, and they told her, "Go and if you give all the sadhus who come milk, everything will be good, and if any sadhu comes you should never refuse him."
>
> So in this very place—this is where they hold the Bhadva Fair [a major annual gathering of Naths]. This happened in Vikram Samvat 1272. On the eighth there is a fair, on the bright eighth of [the month of] Bhadva.
>
> So this dairywoman made a vow on this day, "I will make rice pudding and pancakes in syrup, and offer feast food. I will distribute blessed leftovers to the public with my own hands."
>
> And for ever after, in this dairywoman's family, in her lineage, they give feast food to all. Many sadhus come; the public comes; the place is near Sariska.[16] The Dairymaid founded the fair and people in her lineage continue it. These things are written on a stone.

Suicide is not a common motif in Rajasthani oral traditions. It is interestingly viewed in this variant as a sin that would blemish anyone who caused another person to seek such a radical route of escape from suffering. The dairymaid is saved from despair and allowed to make restitution. Her tale has a generally more satisfying closure than does the Potters' Tale. Here generosity, learned the hard way, is perpetuated as enduring tradition, and the formerly tight-fisted dairymaid's lineage comes to be honorably identified with ongoing largesse.

REFLECTIONS AND INSTRUCTIONS

I asked Shankar Nath, "What is the instruction in these stories?"

My friend Shambhu immediately broke in before the other could speak, and gave the most straightforward answer possible: "You should do the *seva* (service) of great souls."

Shankar Nath, who was not discomposed by Shambhu's intervention, offered a far more elaborate and thoroughly oblique reply in the form of a spontaneous religious discourse, which I find worth citing at fair length:

> God gives eighty-four *lakh* births and, among these, human life is the most important.[17] Our human life, our bodies, are made of five elements. These things were created by Paramatma. So, think, our body, this form, is given to us by God.
>
> In the eighty-four lakh births, this is the only one in which we can get liberation; otherwise we keep going from one to another. This is the birth in which one is able to think about oneself and to ask, "What should I do and not do?" There is only one birth in which one is capable of reflecting on oneself and one's actions; but the real Doer is Paramatma.
>
> So, it seems as if human beings are the form of god because, like god, they cause things to happen.
>
> We don't come with anything from there. Here in this world we get our mother and family, and wealth. We come without all of these. Whatever we get, we get it here, and the Giver is him. Our body is the soul's house, and the Lord gave it to us.
>
> In the same way, clouds form in the sky and rain is created. Or, snow falls in the mountains, and then it all melts. Human life is like this, like clouds or snow. We don't know from where it came or where it goes.
>
> *Paramatma* (the Great Lord) who made us, we don't know his true form. And often we forget him and do not sing his praises. We forget him after being trapped in this delusion (*moh*) and illusion (*maya*).
>
> When we are so foolish, we have a human birth and we don't even praise god or know who he is, we have to go back into the eighty-four lakh of [non-human] wombs. Back! So we keep wandering as bugs and birds and animals, and we take birth many times and die many times. This is a sorrowful affliction, and we cannot reach Paramatma. . . .
>
> We can't get anywhere without a guru. . . . The guru is such that he can turn us from being a crow to a swan, and then we are liberated from the eighty-four lakh of births.
>
> All the rivers have names, like the Banas River, and then there is the filthy gutter. We can see the difference. But when you get to the ocean, no one can say what the difference is. As long as we are alive we know our form, but after we get liberation we are in the ocean, our deeds are wiped out, and we take the form of god.

In his speech, Shankar Nath made absolutely no explicit connection with the two stories he had just related to us. Nonetheless, this was his direct response to my request for these stories' *shiksha* (their instruction or religious meaning). Naths (both householder and renouncer) often serve as gurus to non-Nath householders in the region, so the reference to the guru's saving grace is not at odds with the immediate cultural milieu.

On first hearing this long speech, I had suspected Shankar Nath of just reciting for me, in simple Hindi, some kind of standard, preachy wisdom. Unlike any of the other storytellers, Shankar Nath had spent some time in the popular pilgrimage and tourism center of Pushkar and had interacted with foreigners there. However, on reflection and discussions with some of my associates in Rajasthan, I am able to perceive direct continuity between his homily and the moral of both stories: give charitably while we have the chance—in our human birth. Do not let the opportunity slip away (as the dairymaid did) or forget what truly matters (as the potter did).

In the two linked stories, both the potter's wife and the dairymaid are willing to give something but both of them set limits—as most of us do with our own charities. Yet the texts urge us to realize that when dealing with the imperceptible, or its representatives on earth, limits are not appropriate. What is appropriate is to surrender what you need most or what is most precious to you without any calculation of reciprocity. In the case of the Potter, this meant to give and go hungry himself. In the case of the dairymaid, it meant to give the best—to give not just what can be spared but what one most desires to keep.

Moreover, the less you have the more you should be willing to give. This theme appears elsewhere in Nath lore. For example, Simon Digby's retranslation of the Gorakh Nath cycle includes a household so poor that the husband and wife stay naked indoors and cannot appear in public together because between them they possess only one piece of clothing. The wife weeps when Gorakh's disciple Pavan Nath comes to beg for milk, because she has nothing to offer. She is ultimately well rewarded for her passionate desire to practice charity even in a state of utter destitution (Digby 2000, 208–11).

Chanda Nath was a consummate performer; he could play proficiently, and he sang and spoke beautifully, movingly. I tried to find out why he did not make rounds—as many householder Naths with talents such as his, or significantly less developed than his, would surely do. He gave me an intimate answer. His was not the answer of an all-powerful jogi, but of a farmer-performer mindful of his own dignity and social standing. He said, "Today we start to play and people chase us away, so we don't make rounds. If I go to some house and ask for something and don't get it, then I feel very badly. That is the reason we are not going out." Thus, he confirmed what Ugma Nathji had told me of a general decline in Nath performative practices—a decline based not on the Naths' reluctance to sing but on the public's giving less value and respect to their performances than had formerly been the case. That shift in audience attitude would effectively transform the valued process of delivering religious instruction or "awakening the imperceptible" into a devalued process of begging, for the sake of the stomach. Because most of Rajasthan's Naths own some agricultural land and thus have other sources of income at their disposal, those who once performed may decide to give up making rounds if they perceive that the practice brings disrespect rather than a welcome reception. In other parts of India where jogis are often identified as "mendicants," the situation may be quite different.

To help me understand his point, Chanda Nath neatly turned the experience of potential rejection around to apply to an ethnographer. He said to me toward the end of our conversation: "For example, you have come and asked me to sing and tell. If I say, 'no, I won't sing,' then you'll feel badly, you'll feel insulted. So, as much as I know, I am telling it to you. I believe it is the work of dharma, and I do it for the sake of Paramarth [supreme truth]."

I gave him 1100 rupees (around $25), which was excessive, more than double what my companion and guide Shambhu Nath thought appropriate. But perceiving my determination, Shambhu did not scold me, as he often would, quite relentlessly, when I paid too much in the market or in a shop. It seems the stories' meanings had sunk in, and awakened our generosity.

CHAPTER SEVEN

Matsyendra's "Golden Legend"

Yogi Tales and Nāth Ideology

Adrián Muñoz

THE THREEFOLD NĀTH CANON

Unlike the Sikhs and other religious traditions in South Asia, the Nāth yogis have made no real attempt at organizing their various texts so as to form a canonical corpus. Their prodigality apart, all of these texts respond to different needs, and the approaches and concepts in them vary greatly. This fact makes it all the more difficult to try to "unify" the Nāth traditions. Among the few exceptions, we may mention the *Gorakṣa-siddhānta-saṃgraha*, a rather late text (circa seventeenth century). As the title shows, this text attempts to convey a "summary of the doctrines of [the school of] Gorakṣa." Other Nāth-related literature comprises texts not directly attributed to Gorakh or other Nāth figures, yet their topics closely deal with Nāth terminology and practices. Here, we should give special mention of the *Ṣaṭ-cakra-nirupaṇa*, the *Haṭhayoga-pradīpikā*, the *Gheraṇḍa-saṃhitā*, the *Śiva-saṃhitā* plus the so-called Yoga Upaniṣads. The Nāth identification of these texts is, however, disputable.

My contention here is that in order to fully understand how Nāth ideology has been transmitted, we ought to look closely at various texts. I will argue that the Nāth tradition is passed on through what I term a "threefold canon". This canon is made up of both written and oral texts. However, I do not mean to say that the Naths themselves had a conscious agenda that this "canon" was intended to propagate and enforce. Rather, I would say that this pseudo-canonical corpus has been gradually constructed through time and today includes both formal texts, mostly written in Sanskrit, and folk texts, mostly written in vernacular languages. All of them have contributed to the creation and continuity of the Nāth tradition. Before I continue, it is important to note that my calling this cluster of texts a "threefold canon" is not a prescriptive device, not even a descriptive one, but rather a means to analytically comprehend them all. For the Naths, there is no such a canon, even if they recognize the authority of compositions such as the *Gorakṣa-śataka* or the *Amanaska-yoga*.

This threefold canon is thus made up of the following classes of texts: Sanskrit texts on haṭha-yoga, vernacular Nāth poetry, and hagiographic narratives. It is worth noting that among these classes of text only the first two are considered direct works of the Naths. For the most part, the allegedly early works in Sanskrit are attributed to Gorakh, whereas the later Sanskrit texts on haṭha yoga are not. The vernacular poems and songs are mostly attributed to either Gorakh or other important Nāth personalities, but the actual identification of their authors is somewhat dubious. In any case, Sanskrit and Hindi Nāth literature attributed to specific authors has become a means of transmission, unofficial yet efficient. The third corpus, the hagiographic narratives, belongs more to folklore and has no identifiable authors. Yet it seems clear that the legends originated in a Nāth milieu and then spread into the culture at large.

These legends of prominent yogis have proved to be of special relevance in spreading Nāth ideals. The Nāth temple at Gorakhpur, for example, periodically publishes compilations of these narratives. Yet we ought to pay attention to the fact that some of the versions of the legends are retold by identifiable people: the authors of Sanskrit or vernacular dramas, editors of compilations of these legends, or bards.[1] Strictly speaking, only the first two corpuses can be labelled as literary compositions—didactic and poetical respectively. The third corpus, hagiography, is to some extent the creation of a collective mind, that is, it belongs to the general category of folktales. By bringing together these variegated texts, we can gain a deep and helpful insight into the Nāth's shifting identities. In this chapter, I will discuss some narratives (folk and literary) that evoke vital aspects of Nāth ideology. I understand *ideology* to be a set of beliefs, ideals, and practices that help define the identity of a given community.

A common mistake in Nāth scholarship is to consider the Nāth Panth to be *only* a by-product of tantric culture, through its Sanskrit literature, or to be *only* a forerunner of medieval vernacular cultures. My argument is that scholarship on the Nāth Panth should equally assess all these three corpuses: Sanskrit texts, vernacular songs, and folktales. Whereas individual studies on the texts of each corpus are undoubtedly necessary, a collective reading of all three together is urgently called for. An attempt to examine these texts from a relational perspective may contribute to widen our understanding of how the Naths articulate their identity, soteriology, and praxis. It could also shed light on how some aspects of the Nāth traditions may have changed through time and geography.

NĀTH LITERATURE

As already hinted above, the *literary* production of the Naths is wide and can basically be divided into two branches: Sanskrit texts and vernacular poetry. The texts relevant to a study of the Nāth Siddhas comprise not only those attributed to Gorakh but also the later texts on haṭha yoga (usually written in Sanskrit) and the various vernacular songs attributed to different Nāth bards. The nature and the style of both genres widely differ, as should be expected. Differences depend not only on the grammatical and semantic differences of the languages in which the texts are written, but also on the particular approach to a topic and the goal of the text itself. Although both categories of text generally describe and teach the attainment of a mystical state, they employ different means in order to accomplish this aim. The Sanskrit texts often resort to a more didactic and dogmatic methodology, whereas the vernacular texts make use of a somewhat more direct and experiential approach.[2]

The Nāth texts in Sanskrit convey a clear tendency to expound the diverse practices associated with haṭha yoga and to elucidate its terminology. In general, they all are relatively short compositions, most of them written in verse (usually *ślokas*). Like most of their tantric relatives, the Nāth texts cannot boast of a very refined and polished style. As with the sūtra tradition, it is likely that their function has been mainly to provide a mnemonic tool that would facilitate the learning of the techniques and key terminology of the sādhana by the adepts.[3]

The main topic of the Sanskrit Nāth texts is the mystical physiology of the yogi. This physiology is organized in several basic categories: a subtle (*sūkṣma*) body superimposed on the material, or gross (*sthūla*), body; energy centers (cakra) vertically situated throughout the subtle body; a subtle "vein"-complex (*nāḍī*) where the vital energy flows in the shape of breath (*prāṇa*), and a source of latent energy usually conceived of as a coiled serpent (*kuṇḍalinī*). A Nāth yogi's sādhana depends to a great extent on haṭha yoga performance—itself aimed at activating, controlling, and channelling the various energies contained within the subtle body.

The most notable Nāth-related texts that deal with haṭha yoga are the following: *Gorakṣa-śataka, Yoga-mārtaṇḍa, Viveka-mārtaṇḍa, Gorakṣa-saṃhitā, Gorakṣa-paddhati, Yoga-bīja, Amanaska-yoga* (AmY), *Amaraugha-śāsana, Yoga-viṣaya,*

Siddha-siddhānta-paddhati, *Gorakṣa-siddhānta-saṃgraha*, *Haṭhayoga-pradīpikā* (HYP), *Gheraṇḍa-saṃhitā* (GhS), and *Śiva-saṃhita*. The last three, as I previously mentioned, are only equivocally circumscribed in a Nāth terrain (I will come back to this later). Although strictly speaking not a direct part of the Nāth literature, other texts such as the *Kaula-jñāna-nirṇaya* (KJN), the *Akula-vīra-tantra*, and the *Matsyendra-saṃhitā* are associated with haṭha yoga ideas and can be of great value in defining the ideology, terminology, and identity of the Nāth Panth. As Kiss shows in his chapter in this volume, there are significant apparent inconsistencies in the *Matsyendra-saṃhitā*'s depiction of yoga. As the title evinces, this texts is at least associated with Matsyendra, a key figure in Nāth lineage. The *Kaula-jñāna-nirṇaya* and the *Akula-vīra-tantra* are also attributed to him.

The Nāth poetry written in the vernaculars is less "scholastic" in many ways. This poetry does not intend to systematically teach yoga techniques and physiology, but rather to express a spontaneous experience of the Absolute—the merging of the human yogi with Śiva, who is seen as the Primeval Nātha. This literature was apparently intended to reach a larger audience than that of the Sanskrit corpus. Thus, vernacular Nāth poetry made use of folk language instead of the language of traditional, learned theology. As an alternative to weighty discursive exegesis, the vernacular Nāth poets made use of everyday items—such as pottery, food, and laundry—to express the mystical goals of the yogis. Evidently, the Sanskrit texts are not expected to be directed at a wide audience. Nāth poetry and songs, on the other hand, aimed to inculcate a deeper and longer-lasting reception of Nāth religion by the people. The listeners could easily relate to the language and could thus respond aesthetically and emotionally to the verses in a more direct fashion. In this regard, it is sensible to suppose that this implied a contest of sorts with other proselytizing religious groups that made use of the vernaculars, especially between the thirteenth and the sixteenth centuries. Religious identities in the medieval literature, as Lorenzen shows in his paper, are rather aware of each other and seek to surmount one another.

So far, only two basic compilations of Nāth poetry and songs have been properly edited and published: the *Gorakh-bānī* attributed to Gorakh and the "Sayings and Songs of the Nāth Siddhas." The first collected, and probably the most important, was edited by P. Barthwal. The temple of Gorakh at Gorakhpur has put out an edition of its own based on Barthwal's. Winand Callewaert and Bart Op de Beeck have included the same *Gorakh-bānī* in their edition of the *Pañc Vānī*. The "Sayings and Songs of the Nāth Siddhas" were edited by H. Dvivedi (1980). This collection contains fewer songs attributed to Gorakh than the one edited by Barthwal. Both collections are basic for any scholarly study of the Naths.

NĀTH HAGIOGRAPHY

As I have previously suggested, the cycles of legends are equally important to a balanced study of the Nāth Panth. Not only do these legend cycles introduce the sect's key teachers, usually in heroic depictions, but also, in subtle ways, convey significant ideological messages. The lives that the legends present are, above all, exemplary lives.

According to the legends, the Nāth Panth does not originate exclusively with Gorakhnāth—although he lies at the core of the sect's imagery and ideology. The legends note that Gorakh's guru was Matsyendranātha, the reputed founder of the wider school called Kula-mārga or Yoginī-kaula, itself related to both the Southern Śrīvidyā school and the Northern Kashmiri Śaivism.[4] Gorakh's symbolic role is to contribute to the preservation of a wider tradition, in itself divided. This continuity notwithstanding, Gorakh's role also entails tensions and serious critiques. At the same time, exchanges with other sects have enhanced the Nāth Panth and vice versa. Think of the various schools of nirguṇī saints and tantric practitioners. Probing into the Nāth world entails an examination of the different ways in which the Naths give shape to their identity both as followers of a specific religious order and as actors within the larger horizon of South Asian religiosity. We need to track the Naths' beliefs and the means of transmission of these beliefs as keys to the group's ideology and identity.[5]

In examining these many texts, one has to face a major problem—namely, the large span of time over which they were composed. The various texts that comprise the Nāth lore were apparently produced starting from the time of Matsyendra and Gorakh (ninth to eleventh century); yet the earliest texts are those attributed to Matsyendra and are not necessarily part of Nāth literature as such. A large quantity of vernacular poetry can understandably be placed some time later, possibly after the fourteenth century. As for the legendary tales, there is simply no way of really knowing when they came into existence, but we can safely state that many have been current for many centuries. Still, some features and concepts found in the Nāth texts overlap despite differences in genres—yoga treatises, vernacular songs, and legends—and also despite differences in the times in which they were written. This is not to say that the Nāth practices have not undergone any changes throughout time. Obviously they have. In this essay, however, I will be mostly concerned with identifying continuities in Nāth beliefs and practices.

In many ways, the hagiographical narratives of Nāth lives resemble the medieval exemplary lives of saints (*exempla*), which became famous and widely spread in Christian Europe. The *exemplum* was a usually brief anecdote, whether real or not, intended to transmit moral and religious teachings; Don Juan Manuel's *El conde Lucanor,* as well as the works of Chaucer, Boccaccio, and Petrarch, are just a few names of authors who made use of the *exempla.* This genre became also popular in the Renaissance. Yet the yogi tales are often longer stories than the exempla and would be perhaps best conceived as a sort of Indian "golden legends." The *Legenda aurea* (circa 1260) was a compilation by Jacobus de Voragine of the (often fanciful) lives of saints, such as St. George. Its original title was *Legenda sanctorum* (Readings of the Saints), and its popularity became even stronger with the development of the printing press. As we can commonly find in Indian religious narratives, the Legenda aurea do not only include accounts of various miracles performed by saintly characters but also display fanciful etymologies of the saints' names. The story of the origin of Matsyendra, for example, is related to the name of the character himself—because he was supposedly born from a fish, he was named Matsyendra, the King of Fish. A similar thing happens with the birth of Gorakh. According to some accounts—e.g., the *Gorakh carit* (GorC1) and the *Gorakhnāth caritra* (GorC2)—he is said to have been born from a heap of cowdung mixed with the consecrated ashes that once the Yogi Matsyendra gave to a pious but child-less woman (GorC1: 14–17; GorC 2: 5–10).[6] Although the name *Gorakh* formally comes from the Sankrit *go* (cow) and *rakṣa* (protector), the vernacular tradition derives the name from *go* and *rākh* (ashes).

Elsewhere (Muñoz 2010), I have tried to deal with these issues in a more comprehensive manner by comparing legends of different yogis and relating these legends to references found in a wide range of vernacular songs as well as to the content of Sanskrit treatises on haṭha yoga. My aim in this chapter is to single out one tale from Nāth hagiography and try to relate it to the other two literary corpuses so as to illustrate how the overlapping functions. I have chosen the tale of Matsyendra's release from the Kingdom of Women by his disciple Gorakh. This tale does not only intimate some basic haṭha yoga principles, but also relates a major ideological dispute with a historical basis. This legend is beyond doubt one of the most popular tales from Nāth hagiography, comparable in this respect to the tale of King Gopīcand.

The story of Matsyendra is told in a number of vernacular works—Vidyāpati's *Gorakṣa-vijay,* Fayjulla's *Gorakṣa-viṣaya,* and Shyamdas' *Mīna-cetana,* to mention a few.[7] Most of the known, relevant hagiographies are post-sixteenth–century works from Bengal and, significantly, by Muslim authors; the reason may be that by this time there was a "tantric reform" taking place in Bengal, i.e., that probably some religious leaders were trying to mould a "sterilized" form of tantra easier to admit by Brahmins and maybe even by Muslims.[8] Significantly, Mādhava's Sanskrit biography of Śaṅkara (ca. sixteenth century) records this story as well, which allows us to suppose that the story of Matsyendra's rescue by Gorakh may be four hundred years old or older. In Mādhava's text, Śaṅkara himself undergoes a similar story to that of Matsyendra; it is one of Śaṅkara's disciples who eventually rescues him from a life of sensual pleasures and brings him back to his ascetic condition. It can be said that the purpose of Mādhava is to criticize the yogis' way, through the exemplum of Matsyendra—that is, that yogis are depraved, lust-driven personages. But interestingly enough, Śaṅkara takes no heed of his disciple and—like Matsyendra in this account—enters the corpse of dead king, stays in the court for some time, and enjoys the delights of sex until his disciples decide to "rescue" him.

Matsyendra's story is also registered in many folk tales, and there are a good number of editions of folk tales containing Matsyendra's rescue by Gorakh, probably deriving from older romances in verse. Published in the form of cheap booklets, these editions are available to a large number of people. Although pertaining to popular culture (modern, cheap compilations), these sources are not to be neglected; actually, their being easily available account for their remaining a distinct source of Nāth lore. Yogīs who wander about singing the deeds of legendary Naths usually include this story as well. These contemporary formulations of Nāth heritage in a way bear a more direct impact on the general audience (sometimes including wandering ascetics as well) than do the Sanskrit works on yoga.

Whereas analyses on single versions can reveal specific intricacies and a definite ground on which to tread, I will be looking for a wider spectrum of possible dialogues. I will sketch a condensed plot of the tale first and then offer some comments on it.[9]

A YOGI IN THE LAND OF WOMEN

It is said that once Matsyendra arrived in the Kingdom of Women, in the Kadali Forest. There, he joined Queen Mainākinī and became her lover. For a long period of time, Matsyendra enjoyed sensual pleasures not only with Mainākinī but with a host of sixteen hundred courtesans as well. Orders from the palace declared that no man, and particularly no yogi, was to be let in into the kingdom. Twelve years passed by.

Meanwhile, Gorakh got to know about his guru's situation and decided to act to save him. Rumors were already spreading that Nāth practices were at great risk.

Gorakh arrived to the borders of Kadali Forest and devised a way to enter the palace and meet his guru. He happened to encounter a group of female musicians heading for Mainākinī's palace. He asked their leader, the dancer Kaliṅgā, to let him join the group. She told him that no man was allowed into the kingdom, but

Gorakh replied that he would take the form of a girl. Kaliṅgā then asked him what his qualifications were as a musician: Gorakh then proceeded to sing verses to the sound of a drum. Kaliṅgā and her companions were delighted.

Still, one more obstacle lay ahead. Hanumān was said to stand guard at the borders of the kingdom in order to prevent any man from entering. To avoid the monkey-faced god was no easy task, she argued. Queen Maināskinī herself had obtained this special favor from Hanumān through her devotion. Hanuman's protection of the kingdom meant that Matsyendra could perform Kaula rites undisturbed. Gorakh replied that he himself was a great siddha and yogi, and no harm could be done to him. No one could stand in his way.

Gorakh waited for nightfall. He then conjured up invisible weapons by means of his mantras. He hurled various weapons against Hanumān, and soon the god lay stunned on the floor. Dazed and abashed, Hanumān called upon his lord, God Rāma. Rāma appeared and told Hanumān what had happened to him, who the perpetrator was, and what reasons lay behind it all. Hanumān protested that he had given his word to Queen Maināskinī that no man would come into the Kingdom; he could not let his word be broken.

Rama and Hanuman both went to speak to Gorakh. But the yogi would not abandon his cause. He had a sacred duty, he said, and would not leave the kingdom unless his guru joined him. Gorakh and Hanumān were about to fight, but in the end Hanumān was convinced that his promise had been kept for a sufficient time. Now, Gorakh could pursue his goal and rescue Matsyendra.

In the morning, Gorakh, along with Kaliṅgā and the other musicians, headed for the capital of the Kingdom of Women. They were welcomed and all arrangements for their stay were duly made. Matsyendra, Queen Maināskinī, and all courtesans took their seats in the hall, and the musicians were ushered in. The performance then began.

Kaliṅgā danced beautifully to the sound of music. Gorakh played a *mṛdaṅga* drum with expertise. Eventually, the drum beat took over, and the audience became enthralled. But Gorakh made the drum emit words the only his guru could understand: "Wake up, Matsyendra; wake up. Gorakh has arrived." The drum beats became more insistent: "Wake up, Matsyendra. You're a great knower of yoga, Guru-ji; it isn´t proper for you to give in to sexual pleasures and be embraced by the net of Māyā." The drum continued: "Stop this behavior. Abandon all Kaula practices. If you continue to cherish the tigress Māyā, you'll dry up the *amṛt* (nectar of immortality). Infatuation with bracelets and anklets will bring about the loss of all the gains of Great Yoga, and your semen will leave your body. I'm here to remind you of the Nāth sādhanā."

Gorakh saw that Matsyendra was being attended by courtesans fanning him and caressing his feet. Gorakh played on: "Wake up, Matsyendra; Gorakh has arrived. Guru-ji, there is no need for the company of women; your body will succumb to Death. Woman is an obstacle to yoga. During the day, she appeals by means of ornaments, sensuous movements, and beautiful garments. At night she dries up the ocean of immortality through embraces and amorous encounters. The woman is a tigress. Just as a tree on a river bank is bound to fall, so man will perish on account of a woman's exertions. When the *amṛt* flows down from Mount Meru through *suṣumṇā-nāḍī*, the body weakens, legs flicker, and old age takes over; then, the hair resembles a heron's tail. You've forgotten the words of the Guru. There is no further truth. You are a *ūrddhva-retas* yogi, so your staying here is most unfit. Meditate on Alakh Nirañjan!"

Matsyendra finally recalled his former condition. He recognized his beloved disciple and embraced him. Still, they continued to stay in the kingdom for some days since Matsyendra had engendered a son called Mīnānātha and both Matsyendra and Mainākinī were deeply fond of the child.

One day, Matsyendra told Gorakh that the child had not had a bath for some days, since he had been ill. He asked Gorakh to go and take the boy to the river and wash him. Gorakh acted accordingly and took the child. Once in the river, Gorakh smashed the boy against a washerman's stone as if he were but a rag of clothes. The boy soon died.

Then, Gorakh scrubbed the skin off the slab and washed away the entire residue. Back in the palace, he hung up the flayed skin on a roof. Matsyendra inquired about his son. "I did as you told me—I washed him up. He's now drying on the roof." Matsyendra and Mainākinī became incensed and cursed Gorakh.

After some discussion, Gorakh agreed to restore the child's life. He took a handful of ashes and scattered them over the boy's skin. One hundred and eight Mīnānāthas sprang forth. Gorakh asked the queen to choose her real son from among them, but she argued that she was not able to do so—they all looked the same. "If you're not able to recognize your own son, how can you call him *yours*?" said Gorakh. The queen conceded the point to the yogi. He then proceeded to produce the real child and asked Mainākinī for her consent for him to leave. She had to agree.

Matsyendra and Gorakh then left the palace and went on pilgrimage.

TOWARD AN INTERPRETIVE READING

The tale is both entertaining and complex. There are implicit and crucial issues here. Unlike the *Śaṅkara-dig-vijaya*, in this version Matsyendra does not resort to a king's corpse but goes in his own body to the Realm of Women in Kadalī Forest. According to various sources, it was precisely while staying in the Kadalī Forest that

Matsyendra devoted himself to Kaula practices. The historical implications of this tale, therefore, are found at this very point. Apparently Gorakh and his school decided to separate from Kaula practices, that is, from tantric rituals involving sexual intercourse. There is much evidence that supports the thesis that Matsyendra's Kaula-yoginī school was definitely tantric, as can be deduced from the *Kaula-jñāna-nirṇaya* attributed to him and from other texts. As the *Amanaska-yoga* says, there are hundreds of gurus, but to find a guru who is not a Kaula is a rather difficult task.[10] This Sanskrit text is attributed to Gorakh, as most Sanskrit Nāth literature is. One aim of the legend of Gorakh's rescue of Matsyendra is thus to draw a line between Nāth yogis and Kaula/tantric practitioners. Once again, we cannot state who the author of the tale was, but we can safely assert that the tale is told from a Nāth, not a Kaula, perspective.

Matsyendra's Kaula-yoginī school clearly belongs to the tantric universe. This is manifest in the divinization of the feminine principle, which is then translated into a ritualization of sexual union. Moreover, Matsyendra's stay in the Kingdom of Women suggests, if only vaguely, the practice of *cakra-pūjā* or *yoni-pūjā* rituals. These are precisely the rites that include sexual contact between men and women practitioners. In this context, the worship of the vagina leads to coitus and the production of bodily fluids. During his stay in Mainākinī's kingdom, Matsyendra is said to have enjoyed the company of all the women in the palace. Matsyendra's *Kaula-jñāna-nirṇaya* explicitly sponsors physical union with ritual partners and the consumption of the five forbidden items known as the five M's (*pañca-makāra*); the KJN here makes a clear allusion to the performance of a typical *kulācāra* ceremony as executed by a ritual "hero," or *vīra* (cf. KJN 7.22; 8.5, 13–15; 18.18–21; 21.5). All of this clearly suggests Matsyendra's role as a tantric practitioner in the tale.

In all versions of the story, the climax occurs when Gorakh's drum sounds "Wake up, Matsyendra; Gorakh has arrived." It is at this point that Matsyendra recognizes his disciple and becomes aware of his own situation. Nevertheless, in some versions Matsyendra still needs some time to fully return to his former ascetic life. In one version (A. Gold 1992), for example, Matsyendra intends to attend the music-and-dance performance until the end, even after having acknowledged Gorakh. Matsyendra is depicted in this narrative as still enmeshed in the snares of Māyā, whereas Gorakh is always lucid. Matsyendra's awakening is ambivalent, as can be implied by the words used in Hindi: either *jāg, Macchandar*; or, *cet, Machendar* ("Wake up, Matsyendra"). *Jāgnā* literally means "to wake from sleep," whereas *cetnā* means "to become aware." Accordingly, Matsyendra not only wakes from the sleep of confusion, but *becomes conscious* of who he really is. Thus, in one rendering of the tale, on listening to the drum Matsyendra utters: "I'm becoming aware now."[11]

We also need to be aware of the fact that music and dance are more than mere adornments to the narrative. In a sense, they contribute to work out a parallel illusion to that which ensnares Matsyendra. Gorakh fights fire with fire, worldly illusion with yogic illusion. We can interpret this passage as the construction of an alternative Māyā, a *prati-māyā*, so to speak. This second, yogi-produced illusion overcomes the first illusion, i.e., the cause of Matsyendra's oblivion. Matsyendra, even if for a moment, forgets his current condition as ruler, husband, and father. Then, he suddenly wakes up from both illusions: the aesthetic experience is gone, and so are his false views about himself. A very good indication that this is but Māyā's influence features tellingly in one version of the tale (A. Gold 1992). Here, the flayed children (two here instead of one)[12] come back to life at the same time that the performance ends. Also, at this moment, dawn breaks, which is to say that the light of truth shines forth (see A. Gold 1992, 287).

Gorakh makes use of his own tools and musical instruments in order to display a show of his own. The sounds from the drum stand for a yogic process, which leads to the awakening of the self, an awakening that puts the yogi in contact with Īśvara or God. The emphasis on the beating of a drum can be related to discussions of sound in yoga treatises such as the *Haṭhayoga-pradīpikā*. According to this text, the path of haṭha yoga leads to the state of *samādhi*, also termed rāja yoga (HYP 1.1, 1.2, 2.77), which comprises four stages, each accompanied by a distinct sound. The HYP says:

> tṛtīyāyāṃ tu vijñeyo vihāyomardadhvaniḥ /
> mahāśūnyaṃ tadā yāti sarvasiddhisamāśrayam //
> cintānandaṃ tadā jitvā sahajānandasaṃbhavaḥ /
> doṣaduḥkhajarāvyādhikṣudhānidrāvivarjitaḥ // (HYP 4.74–75)

Svātmārāma, the author of the HYP, explains that the third stage (*tritīyaṃ*), which is to be known (*vijñeyo*) just before the emergence of the final inner state, is accompanied by the sound of a little drum. According to the HYP, at the same time that the practitioner listens to the drum, his breath goes into *Mahāśūnya* (the Great Void), and he achieves all siddhis as well as spontaneous and mental bliss. This experience makes him invulnerable to both physical and mental diseases, as well as hunger, thirst, sleep, old age, and death. Then, the yogi listens to a *vīṇā* (Indian lute) and can attain full identification with, or absorption (*laya*) in, Śiva (HYP 4.76–78).[13]

Even though there are no clear indications of yogic techniques in the hagiographic narratives, this fact does not preclude the possibility of underlying presuppositions. As we saw in the story, Gorakh says to Matsyendra: "When the amṛt flows down from Mount Meru through *suṣumṇā-nāḍī* the body weakens, legs flicker, and old age takes over; one's hair becomes as white as a heron's tail." These words explicitly borrow from Nāth ideology and yogic conceptions of anatomy. Mount Meru here of course stands for the highest cakra located above the head, the *brahmarandhra* or *sahasrāra-cakra*. This is where a subtle, mystical moon is supposed to lie and where the nectar of immortality flows from. Moreover the amṛt, the moon, and the semen are considered to be intrinsically connected. Men are expected to die when the essence flows out from the Moon near Mount Meru and is consumed by the fire lying at the bottom of the nāḍī and cakra system (HYP 3.52).

In other words, if the yogi is not able to control his semen and preserve it, then he will age, sicken, and die. Semen is correlative with the amṛta within the subtle body, and this latter is believed to drop inwardly downwards. Semen-draining means loss of life; it means to let go the nectar of immortality. Loss of semen, that is ejaculation, evinces a lack of perfection of the technique known as *ūrddhva-retas,* usually translated as "upward-going semen." In fact, it would be more sensible to understand it as "withheld semen," for what really ascends through the subtle body is the kuṇḍalinī, not the semen. Yogis are supposed to be able to retain their semen "even if in contact with beautiful women," provided they resort to the proper haṭha-yogic methods (HYP 3.42–43). The practice of this method—many texts assert—can bestow many perfections, or siddhis, on a yogi.[14]

One problem regarding yogic terminology is a constant overlapping of imagery. On reading the texts, one is likely to become confused about the specific meaning of certain words. Concepts like breath, wind, mind, and thought tend to coincide, just as semen, *bindu* (drop), *amṛita* (nectar of immortality), and *mahārasa* (great juice) do. At the same time, and due to the ambiguous description of internal processes, it is difficult to ascertain whether the ascent of yogic energy means the kuṇḍalinī or the breath, or whether it implies both. It is the kuṇḍalinī that is supposed to go upwards piercing the cakras, but the texts also state that the breath flows upwards through the veins called nāḍīs by means of mudrās and other techniques. So, the serpent power and the breath merge. We may then understand that substances (semen, ambrosia) are to be prevented from draining, whereas energies (breath, kuṇḍalinī) are to be made to go upwards. A verse from the *Gorakh-bānī* that seems to address this issue is *sabdī* 17:

aradhai jātā uradhai kāṃma dagdha je jogī karai /
tajai alyaṃgan kāṭai māyā tākā bisnu pakhālai pāyā //

Forcing up the descending [substance],
The yogi burns up desire.

If [the yogi] gives up the embrace and cuts off Māyā
Even Viṣṇu will wash his feet.

Matsyendra is linked to the ūrddhva-retas technique through the related *matsyodarī* technique. It is worth noting that the name for this technique seems to suggest some association with Matsyendra's name; both the technique and Gorakh's guru imply a fish. The matsyodarī, the "fish-belly method," consists on working a contraction of the diaphragm so as to force an inverted flow of breath, semen, and thought. This is not an easy thing to do, but a rather difficult one; the *Amaraugha-prabodha* explicitly states that the breath is to be controlled by force (*Amaraugha-prabodha* 10; see also White 1996: 222–29, 231–33). Although it is not very clear how this is to be performed, the implications can be safely inferred. This technique is beyond doubt closely linked to the ūrddhva-retas method.

At the same time, the ūrddhva-retas method bears comparison with *ūlṭa-sādhanā* (the regressive progress). This ūlṭa-sādhanā is performed in order to produce a sort of involutive process—which, on the one hand, makes the kuṇḍalinī force lying at the bottom of the yogic body go upwards and, on the other, counteracts the amṛta/semen's tendency of dripping down—once *fallen*, the amṛta is forced upwards by means of the ūlṭa-sādhanā. Through ūrddhva-retas, the yogi is supposed to prevent his semen from coming into the penis and thus to store all inner heat in order to increase his *tapas* (ascetic energy). The methods of retentions and contractions (āsanas, mudrās, prāṇāyāma) prescribed by haṭha yoga are directed toward achieving these involutive, regressive processes (cf. Dasgupta 1995, 229–35).

Nāth poetry does not only deals with this same issue, but apparently refers to this very episode from Nāth hagiography, namely that of Gorakh rescuing Matsyendra. One *pad* from the *Gorakh-bānī* reads:

gurūjī esā karam na kījai, tāthaiṃ amīṃ mahāras chījai
divasai bāghaṇi man mohai rāti sarovar sokhai /
jāṇi būjhi re sūrikh loyā ghari ghari bāghaṇī pokhai //
nadī tīrai[15] birṣā nārī saṅgai puraṣā alap jīvan kī āsā /
manthaiṃ upaj mer khisi paḍaī tāthaiṃ kaṃdh bināsā //
goḍ bhae ḍagmag pept bhayā ḍhīlā sir bagulāṃ kī paṃkhiyā /
amīṃ mahāras bāghaṇīṃ sokhyā ghor mathan jaisī akhiyā //
bāghaṇīṃ kau nidilai bāghaṇīṃ kau biṃdilai bāghaṇīṃ hamārī kāyā /
bāghaṇīṃ ghoṣi ghoṣi sundar khāye bhaṇat gorakh rāyā //

Oh Guru-jī, don't do that, for that destroys the amṛt, the mahāras.
During the day the tigress confuses the mind, in the night she drains the lake.

The idiots intentionally feed the tigress in their own house.
The man attached to a woman is like a tree standing by a river—
Few are its hopes to survive.
Mind-born passion brings about the ruin of the body:
The foot stumbles, the leg weakens;
The hair becomes as white as a heron's tail.
The tigress sucks the amṛt, the mahāras,
And churns it in most terrible ways.
Spurn the tigress; pierce the tigress!
The tigress is our body;
She roars and roars devouring gods and men.
Thus speaks Gorakhnāth.

(*Gorakh-bānī*: pad 43)

In still another verse, we find:

din din bāghinī sīṃyā lāgī rāti sarirai sokhai /
vikhai lubadhī tat na būjhai dhari lai bāghanīṃ pokhai /

Day after day does the tigress sleep and suck the body.
Who is eager for sensations doesn't know the True Essence
And lodges a tigress in his own house.

(*Gorakh-bānī*: pad 48.1a)

In both tale and poetry, Gorakh warns Matsyendra that to give in to sensuality means to perish. Accordingly, the vagina is depicted as an all-consuming demoness (*rākasī*).

Gorakh's behavior is that of a perfect yogi (siddha-yogī) who has cut himself from all secular and family ties; one who has become an avadhūta. If Matsyendra is to regain his status as a perfect renouncer, he is expected to reject all sensuous images and objects: "All forms are mischievous, Gurudev. The tigress is foolish, foolish. Him whose mother shows the world, sleeps placidly in her lap" (pad 49). After warning Matsyendra that Māyā eats life up and up to the very marrow, Gorakh goes on in the same pad to rebuke his gone-astray guru:

You've grown old and acquired a kingdom;
you haven't relinquished illusion and delusion.
Thus speaks Gorakh: listen Machandar, son of Īśvar;
Only he who prevents ejaculation is a [true] *brahmacāri*
and only he is called and *avadhūta*.

The tone of Gorakh is that of utter indignation. He is not to witness his teacher's reputation give in to female ensnares; as a consequence, his attitude toward women is anything but fair. Another pad says (*Gorakh-bānī*: *pad* 44):

> bhogiyā sūte ajahūṃ na jāge / bhog nahīṃ re rog abhāge //
> bhogiyā kahaiṃ bhal bhog hamārā / manasai nāri kiyā tan chārā //
> ek būṃda nar nārī rīdhā / tāhī maiṃ siya sādhik sīdhā //
> bhogiyā soi jo bhagathai nyārā / rājasa tāmasa jharai na dvārā //
> bhaṇat gorakhnāth suṇo nar loī / kathaṇīṃ badaṇīṃ jog na hoī //

> The joyful ones sleep and haven't waked up.
> Oh unfortunate ones, that's not joy but sickness.
> The joyful thinks his joy a good thing:
> By fixing the mind on women, the body becomes ashes.
> The real Bhogin stays away from the vagina. . . .

The depiction of Matsyendra in the tale (and implicitly in the verses) is that of a former ascetic who has confounded worldly enjoyment (*bhoga*) with the practice of yoga. The joy of a true yogi is not to experience sexuality, but to experience union with Alakh Nirañjan, the Absolute. To enjoy the company of women, slaves, and family is equivalent to a life of prostitution, according to Gorakh. So, he says to his guru: "Don't let the gained seed be lost / By giving yourself to a woman and neglecting Nirañjan" (*Gorakh-bānī*: *pad* 55). Gorakh is here echoing his famous *Gorakṣa-śataka* (GorŚ). After duly saluting his teacher Minanatha (GorŚ 1–3), he later recommends all retention of breath and semen: *yāvad bindhuḥ sthito dehe tāvanmṛtyubhayaṁ kutaḥ* (GorŚ 70a), i.e., as long as the semen is fixed within the body, there should be no fear of death.

However, Matsyendra enjoyed sexual delights and aesthetic amusements with Queen Mainākinī and a host of sixteen hundred slave girls. He even engendered a son. He abandoned the way of an avadhūta. Gorakh did everything in his power to prevent this from continuing. He recurred to his powers as a miracle broker and displayed a yogic performance of illusion and overcoming of illusion. The zealous disciple even killed and resuscitated his guru's child.

What remains crucial here is that the legend of Matsyendra's stay in the Kingdom of Women and his eventual "release" by Gorakh reveals some deep ideological anxieties of the Nāth Panth. There is a clear rejection of sex and worldly enjoyment. This rejection seems to have been preserved in all other corpuses of the "threefold Nāth canon," that is, in poetry and yoga treatises. In a more subtle way, there is also a rejection of a specific antagonistic school—Matsyendra's Kaula-yoginī school. This specific enmity against the Kaulas does not appear in Nāth poetry, at least not openly. As we have seen, many verses seem to refer to Matsyendra's stay in Kadalī Woods but do not explicitly call any Kaula school by name.

Some haṭha-yogic practices appear in the tale. In some cases, they are referred to directly; in other cases, they are conveyed through motifs in the narrative. Gorakh symbolically conveys a yogic, inner process through the sound of the drum, and by this means speaks to Matsyendra about the ūrddhva-retas method. Kaula rites can be inferred only indirectly. Since—however, we know from other sources that Matsyendra followed a Kaula-oriented ideology—we can reasonably assume that he performed Kaula rituals while in Kadalī Woods and the Kingdom of Women. This shows that Gorakh was not only trying to rescue his guru, but was also attempting to uproot a set of religious practices that he rejected.

Thus, Nāth poetry and hagiography are more or less consistent with the rejection of rituals involving sexual union, but Nāth literature written in Sanskrit is not. In the haṭha-yoga treatises, there is an extended ambiguity in this point. On the one hand, Gorakh would readily rebuff all contact with women in both verse and tale; on the other, yoga handbooks implicitly accept rituals of sexual union, provided the yogi makes use of different methods in order to control his bodily fluids. This is what we find with the practice called vajrolī-mudrā, for example.

According to Svātmārāma, the yogi should obtain two difficult things to find, namely: milk and a woman.[16] Considering the context, it is possible that milk (*kṣīra*) may here denote semen, although some commentators would not agree. Despite possible interpretations that give this aspect of the text a merely "symbolic reading," the HYP quite clearly states here that a "drawing up" should ensue after sexual intercourse and declares that by practicing vajrolī-mudrā one should obtain success (siddhi).[17] Here, retention of the seed does not seem to mean full suspension of seminal emission, but ejaculation and re-absorption of the semen (HYP 3. 85–88). The discussion on vajrolī-mudrā and kindred techniques (*amarolī* and *sahajolī*) continues for several verses—until HYP 3.103. The fact that these problematic techniques demand so many verses may bear witness to the fact that they represent crucial and important practices. It is sensibly clear that these techniques must include sexual intercourse. A sexual/tantric interpretation is further attested by the allusion to the Kāpālikas, a heterodox tantric Śaiva sect in HYP 3.96. The existence of such different points of view within Nāth tradition may even suggest that this tradition is in fact a whole cluster of traditions, all gathered together under the general label of the Naths. This cluster would include both the Tibetan lineage of the eighty-four Siddhas and the nine Nāthas of the Indian tradition. It is interesting that the HYP (1.4–9), apparently an Indian text, cites a list of reputed teachers of the sect that matches the Tibetan lineage rather than the Indian one.

We cannot find an explicit rejection of the Kaula system in Nāth poetry, yet the rejection of women and sex is indeed a leitmotif in this poetry. It is likely that Nāth poetry and songs had a much wider audience than their Sanskrit counterpart. The vernacular language was a crucial feature that contributed to this presumed popularity, Sanskrit being accessible to a much smaller number of people. Perhaps, the Nāth singers were not interested in advertising the names of sects and teachers from other traditions. They may have been more intent on teaching the basic issues from Nāth ideology through poetic motifs and religious symbols. Sex and women, through the symbol of the tigress, serve to express a clear rejection of female contact, regardless of its religious associations. At the same time, we should also note that this poetry does not attempt to give detailed expositions on haṭha-yoga techniques. These are rather reserved for the Sanskrit texts or to the guru's direct teaching.

As for the controversy on sex, probably sexual practices had always been an integral element of haṭha yoga, on account of the tantric origins of this system. Gorakhnāth (or others after him) apparently tried to expunge these origins, so that eventually sexual practices were exorcised from the Nāth Panth but not necessarily from all of haṭha yoga. At some point, haṭha yoga attained such wide popularity that it was no longer an exclusive Nāth practice—if it ever had been. Thus, non-Nāth practitioners of haṭha yoga were able to retain sexual imagery and praxis, as seems to be true with the Buddhist Mahāsiddhas. This may explain some of the apparent inconsistencies between the *Haṭhayoga-pradīpikā* (HYP) and Gorakh's creed. My feeling is that strictly speaking, the HYP is not a Nāth text, although it is of course related to the Nāth cult. Just remember the list of reputed teachers mentioned by Svātmārāma; he lists Gorakh, Matsyendra, Cauraṅgī, and Kāṇerī (Kānhapā), usual members of the Nine Nāthas constellation, but he also lists Virūpākṣa, Bileśaya, Buddha, and Tiṇṭiṇi, common names among the Tibetan tradition (HYP 1.4–9).[18] It in fact seems as though Nāth yoga more and more was tried to resemble raja-yoga, the classic form developed by Patañjali. The "six-limbed" yoga of Gorakh in some Sanskrit Nāth texts is usually nothing but a version of Patañjali's "eight-limbed" yoga, with the first two limbs (*yama* and *niyama*) taken for granted.[19] In contrast, Matsyendra's yoga is sometimes designated as "vajra-yoga"—a very suggestive appellation—or the yoga aimed at obtaining amṛta and offering it to the Goddess (e.g., KJN 15.20, 18 to 7–9; 21.7–8). Whereas yoga in the KJN explicitly involves erotic measures, the school of Gorakh strongly prevents it, as can be seen in his *Gorakṣa-śataka*.[20]

Imaginative dialogues between conservative, "aseptic" voices and transgressive ones can often be misleading. It is interesting to note that Śaṅkara's intention to enter a king's corpse, according to Mādhava's account, was for the purpose of learning about the science of sex (*kāma-śāstra*). In the *Śaṅkara-dig-vijaya* (ŚaṅDV), the famous *advaitin* pays no heed to Matsyendra's legend and rather praises Śrī Kṛṣṇa's mastering of continence while sporting with the *gopīs*. This continence is called the "yogic practice of vajrolī" (ŚaṅDV 9.90). That here this *vajrolī* entails sex play is evident. In the end, however, Śaṅkara can claim that physical contact was not defiling to him, since it was someone else's body that entertained such amorous indulgences—unlike Matsyendra in the tale discussed in this chapter. It is very likely that Mādhava knew about haṭha yoga, whether from contact with yogi groups, or from Svātmārāma's HYP, which dates from the fifteenth century. Yet not all of the available descriptions of the vajrolī-mudrā implied a sexual context.

In this sense, we could think of the other famous treatise on haṭha yoga, the seventeenth century *Gheraṇḍa-saṃhitā* (GhS), as a more Gorakh-oriented text, as its description of the vajrolī-mudrā is completely deprived of sexual implications. There, the mudrā does not even involve the assistance of a female partner, but the adept is supposed to lift his legs above him with hands on the ground so as to awake the śakti (GhS 3.45). Significantly, the text says this method successfully contributes to the retention of the semen or seed (*bindu-siddhi*). Once the retention has been accomplished, the siddha is able to achieve anything he wants in the world.[21] The vajrolī-mudrā according to the GhS resembles the *viparīta-kāraṇa* as expounded in the *Śiva-saṃhitā* (4.45–47), another renowned text on haṭha yoga. Significantly enough, the *Śiva-saṃhitā* does not even mention the vajrolī, which is in accordance with its rather nontantric oriented ideology and can thus be said to share Gorakh's puritanical spirit. On the other hand, the HYP draws closer from tantric influences, as the connection with Tibetan Buddhism attest, and must necessarily move away from Gorakh's Nāth yoga. At the same time, the conflictive relationship between the texts on haṭha yoga, Matsyendra-based compositions, and the Nāth Panth illustrates the conflictive relationship of the texts on haṭha yoga and Matsyendra-based compositions; the Nāth Panth illustrates very well the mist in which the origins of the order are shrouded.[22] It indeed seems as though the mist extends to cover the panth's development as well, and the various issues dealt with in this pages bear witness to this.

In the tale examined in this paper, we have dealt with more than just a folk tale meant to entertain. We have seen that the legend imaginatively promotes a specific position on a major dispute at the core of the Nāth tradition, a position that proved to be crucial for the shaping of a Nāth identity. This identity has not been stationary but has been subjected to continuous modifications. Through a dialectic borrowed from popular narrating forms, some Nāth factions sought to undermine a former religious and ethical agenda within the roots of the tradition. This—as some schools of *dakṣinacārīs* did, versus the so-called *vāmācārīs* within the tantric foil—would enable some Nāth leaders to purge the Nāth yogi tradition from "impure" practices. It, of course, also evinces a general tendency of Hindu sects to advocate asceticism and sexual abstinence.

In fact, most of the Nāth yogis that I met in India and Nepal in 2004 and 2005 decidedly claimed to be different from, and even opposed to, tantrics. They claimed not to know anything (or pretended not to know) about the tantra-oriented texts attributed to Matsyendra (the *Kaula-jñāna-nirṇaya*, the *Akula-vīra-tantra*, the *Matsyendra-saṃhitā*). Avedyanāth, *mahant* of the Gorakhpur Temple, replied that he had heard of these texts, but that they did not belong to the panth and therefore were not stored or studied by them. The mahant of the Gorakhnāth Temple in Varanasi hadn't even heard of them, but in any case rejected any association of the Nāth Sampradāya with tantra. It is quite significant that the mahant used the terms *dakṣinacārīs* and *vāmācārīs* to distinguish his own lineage of Nāth yogis from some "hard-core" tantric groups as well as from the Aghorīs. That they should label themselves as dakṣinacārīs, as opposed to vāmācārīs, reveals a rejection of many typically tantric practices, such as ritual sex. At the same time, under this logic, the term *vāmācāra* stands for hardcore tantra, whereas for these Nāth leaders *dakṣinācāra* denotes a spiritual path aided by the knowledge of haṭha yoga and the worship of the legendary masters, especially from Gorakh onwards.

Matsyendra's tale is in many senses an exemplary legend on yoga, especially on how yoga is *expected* to be carried on by Nāth *sādhakas* after Gorakh. This is a type of yoga consistent with the ways of an avadhūta and one that denies all contact with women, even on ritual grounds. In this sense, Matsyendra's "golden legend" has an inverted dynamics, so to speak, since he is not an exemplum of abstinence and asceticism, the real hero being Gorakh. Contrary to the European Legenda aurea, Matsyendra's tale depicts him as an example of *how not to behave* if one is a Nāth yogi. Gorakh, on the other hand, is the very example of virtue according to mainstream Nāth ideals in this narrative.

In Nāth poetry, a negation of the Kaula School is not as important as a rebuff of all practices considered to be pernicious to the Nāth Panth. And ritual sex was something that did lie at the core of Kaula practices. There were also other tantric schools close to the yogi's world which made use of ritual sex. On the other hand, contact with tantric schools is not necessarily a requisite for undertaking sexual activity; any yogi, as long as he is still a man, is liable to temptation and arousal. As is well known, sādhus, and yogis in particular, are believed to be highly potential sexual partners on account of their cumulated inner heat. Engaging in sexual relations would eventually lead to producing offspring and therefore becoming a householder. Matsyendra definitely exemplifies this trend.

CHAPTER EIGHT

What Should Mīnanāth Do to Save His Life?

Lubomír Ondračka

The story of yogin Gorakhnāth's rescue of his guru from the Kingdom of Women is one of the most widespread and popular in Indian literature. Full versions of this story or allusions to it are to be found in a vast range of oral narratives and written texts in many Indian languages. Several versions of the story differ rather substantially from each other. The only constant element they share is Gorakhnāth's arduous but finally successful attempt to save his teacher from the clutches of lustful women. One of the noteworthy and, from several points of view, unique adaptations of this tale is available in the Bengali language. Unlike other versions, the Bengali poem contains many verses, or even full songs describing technical details of yogic doctrine and practice. In one such song, Gorakhnāth instructs his guru Mīnanāth in a certain yogic exercise that might be able to save the teacher's life. The instruction is expressed in such a cryptic manner, however, that it remains altogether unclear what Mīnanāth should actually do. In this study, an attempt will be made to interpret this song and answer the question posed in the title.

"THE VICTORY OF GORAKHNĀTH"

The song is part of a lengthy Bengali poem[1] called "The Victory of Gorakhnāth" in most of the preserved manuscripts, or "The Awaking of Mīnanāth" in a few others.[2] The text is available in four different editions ascribed to four different poets.[3] It is discussed in standard histories of Bengali literature (Bandyopādhyāy 1993, 365–90;

Sen 1398, 191–96; Zbavitel 1976, 189–90) and has been briefly summarized in English (Sen 1925, 85–110; Sen 1979, 40–43; Dasgupta 1969, 377–78).[4] The only full translation of the poem is into Russian (Tovstych 1988).[5]

It is not an easy task to determine the date of composition of these texts. Most historians of Bengali literature agree on the conclusion that the present form of the different versions of the poem cannot be dated earlier than the seventeenth century (Bandyopādhyāẏ 1993, 425; Sen 1398, 191–92; Zbavitel 1976, 189).[6] While it is a fact that the grammar of most versions suggest this period, this linguistic argument does not say anything about the age of the story, nor even about when it was composed. Nāth literature in Bengali, like vernacular Nāth literature in other parts of North India, was oral and transmitted by the lower strata of Bengali society. It never reached the status of classical or highly valued poetry and thus was not originally fixed in a written form. Consequently, the language of the versions of the poem has been changing over the course of time, thereby making it impossible to determine the date of their composition on linguistic grounds. We can thus assume that the texts are probably older than the seventeenth century, but it would be unfounded speculation to conjecture how much older.

Although the Bengali version of the Gorakhnāth story differs from adaptations in other languages—it has some episodes and motifs not found elsewhere (e.g., Gorakhnāth's struggle with Śiva's wife Gaurī) and other events are missing in it (e.g., the character Hanumān and Gorakhnāth's combat with him)—the main line of narrative is the same. Siddha Mīnanāth secretly overheard Śiva's lesson to Gaurī on how to achieve immortality. Consequently, Mīnanāth acquired this Great Knowledge (*mahājñān*), but was cursed by Śiva so that he would forget it sometime in the future. Śiva's curse became effective when Mīnanāth reached the Kingdom of Women. He became a king here and embarked upon an unrestrained sensual life with his two queens and another sixteen hundred lustful women inhabiting the kingdom. When Gorakhnāth was informed by Siddha Kānupā about the dangerous circumstances into which his teacher had fallen, he decided to rescue him. After overcoming several obstacles, Gorakhnāth eventually managed to meet his guru and, disguised as a charming woman dancer, he informed him about his perilous situation. Instructed by his pupil, Mīnanāth gradually recovered his yogic knowledge but was reluctant to leave his queens and, feeling weak and tired, he fatalistically accepted his imminent death. In order to break Mīnanāth's hesitancy, Gorakhnāth killed Mīnanāth's son Bindunāth (but later brought him back to life). This shocking event helped Mīnanāth make the irreversible correct decision: together with his son, he followed his pupil and left the Kingdom of Women. In this way, his life was saved.

THE INSTRUCTIVE SONG

The song is a turning point in the narrative. Gorakhnāth had already revealed his true identity and accused Mīnanāth of falling away from the right yogic path, warning him about his disastrous position. Mīnanāth accepted all these words, but argued that his body had become so old and weak that he had no power to return to the yogic way of life. In his own defense, Mīnanāth objected that he was just imitating his own guru Śiva, who is also a householder and took his pleasure with his two wives. In response to Mīnanāth's objections, Gorakhnāth sang the following song.[7] In the first part, he explained the difference between Śiva and Mīnanāth, and in the second part, he instructed his guru on how to overcome the weakness of the body by practicing a certain yogic technique.

Alas, guru Mīnanāth,
you destroyed[8] your body.
Sinning,[9] you have forgotten yoga.
You abandoned your guru's teaching.
Being deluded by amorous passion,
you wanted to taste death. (1)

Guru, think about
and remember:
your guru is Mahādeva.
Hara does not enjoy one thing [only];
he continually enjoys everything,
as if[10] he consumes hashish and datura. (2)

He enjoys amorous sports with women,
[but] he does not forget the doctrine.
He never forgets.
Śiva does not have just one form,
he is the soul of all beings
and consumes all pleasures.[11] (3)

Guru, there are four moons (*cāri candra*)
pervading a body.
If you practice them you will be rescued.
An original moon (*ādicandra*), one's own moon (*nijacandra*)

an excited (*unmattacandra*) and a poisonous moon (*garalcandra*):
these four pervade the body.[12] (4)

He who fixes the original moon,
joins the own moon
with the excited one,
restrains / controls the three moons,
and loads [them] on himself [or: on Khemāi],[13]
he drinks all the poisonous moon. (5)

Having restrained / controlled the four[14] moons,
and having crossed the ocean of existence,
then he is fully protected.
But you did not do this work
and you have forgotten everything.
Tell me guru, what is the way? (6)

You do not have the strength
to run away from here.
There is no hope for life.
I say true words of the teaching.
Think and examine them
if you have a desire to live. (7)

Do a reverse Yoga,
make yourself still
and remember your own mantra.
Keep yourself reversed
and strike at Triveṇī
to fill the channels with water.[15] (8)

The first three verses do not require any special explanation. In the first one, Gorakhnāth blames his guru for forgetting the yogic teaching and for ruining his body by an excessive sexual life, one which ultimately leads to death. This accusation, however, is only partly justified, since the true reason for forgetting the teaching was not Mīnanāth's negligence but Śiva's curse. The aim of the following two verses is to explain how the situation of Śiva, to whom Mīnanāth compares himself, is dissimilar. The answer embodies three arguments, two of them closely connected. Firstly (2d–f), Śiva has a unique capability to enjoy everything simultaneously and constantly, including heady hashish and datura.[16] The second argument (3d–f) is more theological: seen from the point of view of the monistic Śaiva philosophy, Śiva is an Absolute Enjoyer—and in fact, the only enjoyer because all living beings are identical to him. His enjoyment knows no limits.[17] The last argument (3a–c) is the most important for Mīnanāth's situation. Yes, it is true that Śiva also has two wives[18] and takes great delight in erotic activities as does Mīnanāth, yet this does not have any harmful consequences for Śiva. The key difference between them is that Śiva never forgets the doctrine: he is a perpetual holder of the Great Knowledge. We may understand this message as meaning that a siddha can do anything and enjoy any earthly pleasure (such as intoxicants or female contact) providing he has mastered the right yogic proficiency and, especially, possesses the Great Knowledge.

Gorakhnāth's instruction proper is included in the fourth, fifth, and eighth verses. A key term used here is "four moons"(*cāri candra*; 4a, f). The correct understanding of the meaning of these four moons is absolutely essential to answer our question: what should Mīnanāth actually do to save his life? It is obviously not possible to infer the meaning directly from the song. Yet even the whole poem does not help us much since the term is not explained anywhere within the text. For this reason, we will begin our investigation in a different Bengali tradition, one where the term *four moons* plays a cardinal role, in Sahajiyā.[19]

FOUR MOONS IN THE SAHAJIYĀ MILIEU

Although the term "four moons" is not attested in the oldest Sahajiyā texts,[20] it represents a fundamental concept of ritual practice in the contemporary Sahajiyā milieu.[21] The correct meaning of the four moons in Sahajiyā traditions has been known for over a hundred years[22] and has been further researched during the past few decades,[23] especially by the Bengali scholar Saktinath Jha, who in 1995 published an article called "*Cāri-Candra Bhed*: Use of Four Moons" (Jha 1995). This study contains a rich collection of data obtained during fifteen years of the author's field research in different parts of West Bengal. Since his findings are extremely important for our discussion, it is necessary to sum up some essential results.

In the Sahajiyā milieu, the term four moons basically means four bodily products. The more or less standard set consists of sperm, menstrual blood, urine, and feces. These fluids are mixed in various ways and combinations and then consumed orally or applied externally. The ritual is usually called "the piercing of four moons" (*cāri candra bhed*). Technical details of this practice vary quite considerably in different guru lineages. For example, not all *sādhakas* (religious adepts) use all four moons; others take more than four—adding other bodily products, and the manner of usage and frequency of application differ. Naturally, obtaining a full description of these rituals is often very difficult because they are one of the most secret parts of Sahajiyā practice. Nevertheless, despite all the differences, the general principle is clear and indisputable.[24]

What is the purpose of this ritual? Saktinath Jha propounds eighteen various explanations (1995, 94–99) which he finally groups into three main answers (100):

(a) The attainment of, if not an ever-youthful and deathless body, then at least a long and healthy life.
(b) The sustainment of an active body and mind until death, and control of disease.
(c) The retention of semen, control over the sense organs and enjoyment of sensual pleasure.

These findings are confirmed by independent research,[25] and thus we can take them as plausible interpretations of the concept of the four moons within the Sahajiyā milieu.

FOUR MOONS AS BODILY FLUIDS IN GORAKHNĀTH'S SONG?

I am not aware of any specific study devoted to the meaning of four moons in Bengali Nāth texts similar to Saktinath Jha's exploration of four moons in the Sahajiyā milieu. The term has been discussed in the literature only in passing, mostly by the editors of Nāth works. Even from these short remarks, two facts are obvious. First, there is no scholarly consensus on the meaning of this term. Secondly, the four moons are not explained in any Bengali Nāth text, at least not in any edited one. This is not surprising. It would be naive to expect to find an explicit description of the four moons in the texts. The most important things are normally also the most secret in this kind of literature. One author even quotes this song as a perfect example of the *sandhā bhāṣā* (enigmatic language) in Bengali Nāth literature, without trying to interpret it; he merely observes that the song contains "an unknown secret and obscure hints" (Mukhopādhyāẏ 1994, 28). Two or three different explanations have been suggested to date, but none of these offers a convincing argumentation. I will now discuss some arguments for and against these interpretations.

Some authors simply identify the four moons in Nāth texts with the four moons in the Sahajiyā milieu because of the use of the same words *cāri candra*.[26] This would mean that the four moons in the song stand for some set of bodily fluids. What arguments might support this interpretation?

First, we know that yogic techniques and ideas have been widely shared by traditions with different backgrounds (Śaiva, Vaiṣṇava, Tāntric, Śākta, or even Sūfī) and that there has been an exchange of views and particular practices between various groups. It is thus reasonable to assume that the same term could have the same or very close meaning in different traditions, notably when it occurs in a similar context. Unfortunately, there has not yet been sufficient research into the mutual contacts between the Nāth and Sahajiyā traditions in medieval Bengal, and thus we do not have much concrete evidence for such exchanges of views and techniques. Nevertheless, according to Glen Hayes, medieval Sahajiyā borrowed a good number of ideas from the Naths,[27] and this would increase the likelihood that the concept of four moons may also originally belong to the Naths and have been later accepted into the Sahajiyā milieu. There is even textual evidence confirming this possibility.[28] It is, for instance, interesting that there are a few private, secretive Sahajiyā texts that use almost the same names for the individual moons as our song does.[29]

Second, the fact that some fluids are probably involved is suggested by the description of Mīnanāth's serious, in fact fatal, condition. According to the account books held in Yama's realm of death, Mīnanāth will die within the next three days.[30] The main cause of this situation is, as Gorakhnāth repeatedly states, that Mīnanāth's body has become dried up and is now critically "sapless."[31] It is necessary to flood his body right away, as the last line of the song says: "fill the channels with water."[32]

Third, the effects of the practice of the four moons, as summarized by Saktinath Jha and quoted above, would solve all the other problems of Mīnanāth's body. A perfect siddha should be immortal and ever youthful, healthy and full of strength, and he should be able to control his sense organs to preserve his semen. Mīnanāth's state is the exact opposite. He has grown old, and his hair has become grey;[33] his body is weak,[34] and his sensual life has caused an uncontrolled and immense loss of semen.[35] All these defects could be rectified by using the four moons.

Fourth, there is a clear connection between the word *moon* (candra, soma) and two specific bodily fluids. According to a yogic conception (which in fact reflects an ancient Indian idea [Gonda 1985]), the moon is a source of the nectar of immortality (*amṛta*) which is homologized with semen (*śukra, bindu, retas*).[36] And the correlation between menstruation and the cycles of the moon is also apparent.

Fifth, taking into account the importance of this practice for saving Mīnanāth's life, the lack of information about it is striking. This indicates that it might involve something odd and unusual. This is also the case in the contemporary Sahajiyā milieu, where the practice of the four moons is widespread, highly important, yet rarely mentioned in written texts.[37] It is a precious secret, transmitted orally and not to be disclosed to outsiders.[38] The reason is obvious: such a practice is completely unacceptable in Indian society, be it Hindu or Muslim. If the four moons in the song really mean the bodily products, then it is more than understandable why the text does not contain any elaborate description of this technique.

On the other hand, some objections against the interpretation of the four moons as bodily fluids may be raised.

First, the same term does not always bear the same meaning, and there are enough examples where the content of a term has been changed rather substantially when transferred to a different—albeit from certain point of view similar—environment.[39] Thus, we have to be careful when using this argument, especially with the use of such a "code word" that does not have any unified and fixed meaning even in standard haṭha-yoga texts.[40]

Second, it is not easy to answer the question why all the fluids are called moons. We have just seen that this name is quite natural for semen and menstrual blood, but it remains a mystery why any other bodily fluid (be it urine,[41] feces, female sexual secretions, saliva, breast milk, etc.)[42] should be also called moon. We can perhaps assume that this name was transferred from the two more prominent fluids—namely, semen and menstrual blood—to the other two, but this is far from certain.

Third, there is an apparent inconsistency between the negative approach to women in the Nāth texts, on the one hand, and the need for a female partner in the practice of the four moons, on the other. This fact argues strongly against interpreting the four moons in the song as bodily fluids if any of women's fluids (menstruation or sexual secretion) are involved. This objection opens a more general and difficult question about possible modes of relationship between yogis and women, which despite the strong rhetoric of yogic texts, are not without ambivalence. I will not analyze this complex problem in detail here.[43] But perhaps one observation should be made. While it is true that in Bengali Nāth literature women are depicted as thirsty leeches or wild tigresses eager to destroy men's strength, we have seen through the example of Śiva that the danger does not lie in a householder's way of life or in erotic pleasure per se—providing one knows the right way of conduct. In other words, there is not danger if one always has the Great Knowledge, as Śiva does.

OTHER POSSIBLE INTERPRETATIONS OF THE FOUR MOONS

Some authors reject the possibility that the four moons in the Nāth texts could have the same or similar meaning as in the Sahajiyā milieu,[44] but only a few of them offer any alternative explanation. One such attempt was made by Gopinath Kaviraj.[45] Unfortunately, his brief notes on this topic are somewhat ambiguous.[46] According to Kaviraj, the meanings of the particular moons are as follows. The "poisonous moon" (*garalcandra*) stands for the nectar of immortality (*amṛta*); the "excited moon" (*unmattacandra*) means mind (*manas*) or bodily wind/breath (*vāyu*); and "one's own moon" (*nijacandra*) means kuṇḍalinī or some essence/fluid (*rasa*) which is not further specified. The meaning of the "original moon" (*ādicandra*) remains altogether unclear. Kaviraj glosses it merely as a moon (candra) placed in the *sahasrāra-cakra*.[47] Perhaps, he distinguishes between the moon uncontrollably falling down from the *sahasrāra-cakra* in a ordinary man before beginning the proper yoga practice (*ādicandra*) and the same moon turned into the nectar of immortality (*garalcandra*), which in an advanced yogi does not fall down since he is able to drink it and thus become immortal.[48]

The advantage of this interpretation is that it fits into the Nāth's doctrine relatively well: if the mind, breath, and the falling stream of the moon become still, then a yogi can drink the nectar of immortality.[49] On the other hand, precisely this fact could be turned against this theory. We may ask why this essential and well-known part of a doctrine should be concealed under such unclear terms, particularly when it is openly described in other parts of the poem. The next problem is again with the word *moon*. I am not aware of any place in yogic texts where kuṇḍalinī or mind is called candra, and establishing any correlation between them does not appear to be easy. This interpretation also fails to explain how Mīnanāth's dry body could be flooded by an immobilization of mind, breath, and *kuṇḍalinī*, and by stopping the dripping of the nectar.[50] Moreover, according to lines 4b and 4f of the song, the four moons "pervade a body," and it is difficult to understand how the mind can do this.[51]

Another theory has been proposed by Rajmohan Nath in one footnote in his edition of a fragment of "The Victory of Gorakhnāth" (Nāth 1964, 153–54n3). He attempted to overcome the apparent difficulties of the above-mentioned interpretations by assuming that the four moons have two levels of meaning: one material or gross and one immaterial or subtle. According to Nath, on the subtle level the "original moon" (*ādicandra*) refers to the sun in the *mūlādhāra-cakra* (i.e., the lower cakra), the "one's own moon" (*nijacandra*) indicates a drop of soma (*somabindu*) in the *ājñā-cakra*, and the "excited moon" (*unmattacandra*) means a full-blown blossom of datura. On the gross level the original moon denotes menstrual blood and paleness of man's sperm,[52] the one's own moon means whiteness of man's sperm,[53] and the excited moon means a mixture of male and female sexual fluids and ejaculated semen. Finally, the poisonous moon (*garalcandra*) means urine probably on both levels. Unfortunately, Nath does not explain on what grounds he draws such conclusions, which are highly problematic and certainly not convincing.

Three different explanations of the four moons have been offered by another Bengali scholar, Praphulacharan Chakrabartti, in his study on Bengali Nāth literature. The first interpretation is the same as that made by Gopinath Kaviraj and quoted above (Cakrabarttī 1955, 136).[54] The second one appears in a longer note discussing the Sahajiyā concept of the four moons (ibid., 56n14).[55] Here, the author denies the possibility that the meaning could be the same in the Nāth texts. According to Chakrabartti, the four moons stand for semen (*śukra-ras*), the nectar of immortality placed in the moon in the sky, and two bodily breaths: *prāṇa* and *apāna*. The third explanation is rather surprising since it identifies the four moons with the four lower cakras (ibid., 56n18).[56] Like most previous authors, Chakrabartti does not give any reasons for these interpretations and one is obviously reluctant to accept them.

It is apparent that the meaning of the four moons in the Bengali Nāth texts remains obscure for scholars dealing with these works. None of their interpretations is easily acceptable since each of them has serious flaws and fails to offer a coherent explanation of the practice of the four moons. Although, as we have seen, the understanding of the four moons as bodily fluids is certainly not without serious difficulties, it seems to be the only one of the theories proposed so far that deserves further analysis.

WHAT COULD BE THE POSSIBLE SOURCES OF THE PRACTICE OF THE FOUR MOONS?

If we accept the idea of bodily fluids as a working hypothesis for the explanation of the four moons in Gorakhnāth's song, then one of the first and quite natural doubts that would arise is the seeming impropriety of such a practice among the Nāth yogis. However, a cursory search for its possible sources reveals that this practice need not be as unthinkable in yogic circles as might seem at first sight.

The use of different bodily products is now a relatively well-known, yet still not sufficiently researched practice described in several tāntric (including Buddhist)[57] and Kaula texts. David White, for example, has devoted a good part of his book *Kiss of the Yoginī* to the discussion of sexual fluids, but he left aside the problem of urine and feces.[58] The best discussion of the use of bodily products in tāntric ritual, together with a large number of references to various texts, is to be found in the writings of Alexis Sanderson.[59] He shows very clearly that terms like *pañcāmṛta*, *ratnapañcakam*, *pañcadravyam*, etc. occurring in different tāntric (Trika, Krama) and Kaula texts stand for five bodily fluids—namely, semen, menstrual blood, urine, feces, and phlegm or marrow. He notes that the ingestion of a mixture of them was an important part of tāntric and Kaula rituals. We should pay attention to the prominent position of this practice particularly in Kaula texts, since they may be at the origin of the practice in subsequent Nāth works. Although we are still not able to fully reconstruct the exact history of the transmission of Kaula ideas and rituals to later traditions,[60] the association of Matsyendranātha (Mīnanāth?)[61] with a Kaula milieu, and at the same time, his important position in Nāth texts are indisputable.

Nonetheless, the possibility of seeing the source of the four moons in this older ritual is not entirely unproblematic. Without going into too much detail, some of the difficulties should be mentioned here. First, the fluids are probably not called moon (*candra*) anywhere in Sanskrit sources.[62] Second, the number of fluids differs: tāntric and Kaula works apparently always refer to five substances[63] relating them to other pentads of the doctrine, contrary to the usual four in Nāth texts.[64] Third, the aim of the practice is different, since in earlier Śaiva non-dualistic traditions the practice aims primarily to help to overcome any discrimination and to demonstrate the monistic reality in which nothing can be impure per se.[65] Fourth, there does not appear to be any explicit link connecting this practice from the Kaulas to the Naths. To the best of my knowledge, such a ritual is not described, at least not openly, in any haṭha yoga text. Of course, in yogic literature, there are relatively frequent references to *bindu/retas* and *rajas*, which normally stand for semen and menstrual blood (or vaginal excretions), and infrequent references to urine and faeces. These pairs, however, occur separately: bindu/retas and rajas mainly in the context of the vajrolī-mudrā (a method of urethral absorption of fluids), while urine and feces occur in the context of the yogi's power to transmute base metals into gold.[66]

Some yogic texts, however, contain allusions to the ritual use of bodily products. We are informed that the practice of ingestion of these secretions must be prevalent at least in some yogic circles, since a few texts do condemn it.[67] On the other hand, one commentator praises the consumption of urine and faeces and lists its various effects such as health, strength, non-ageing and immortality.[68] Besides ingestion, another way of using the bodily products was possible and probably also more typical. As James Mallinson (2007, 220n328) states: "Practices involving massaging the body with various physical secretions are alluded to fleetingly in many haṭhayogic texts."[69]

Apparently, there is no easy answer to the question of what could be the possible sources of the four moons (if we would understand them as bodily fluids) among the Naths. Despite all the above-mentioned problems, Kaula rituals still seem to be the most natural and probable source. And regarding the missing link, I would suggest, very preliminarily, that the most promising candidate for this might be a group of three haṭha-yoga mudrās (techniques), namely vajrolī, amarolī, and sahajolī, which are variously described in yogic texts and have not been researched well enough to prove this suggestion at present. In any case, these mudrās deal with bodily fluids—namely, with semen, menstrual or other vaginal secretion, and urine, and thus may represent a haṭha-yoga transformation of older Kaula rituals.

WHAT SHOULD MĪNANĀTH THUS DO TO SAVE HIS LIFE?

Until the exact meaning of the four moons is discerned, any answer to this question must remain speculative. We have seen that none of the explanations suggested so far are wholly satisfactory and that neither the song itself nor the full text of the poem offers any clear key to a solution of this problem. The only indisputable point is thus the desirable effect of the practice of the four moons: the fatally sapless body of Mīnanāth should be flooded using this technique. Let us briefly summarize the general possibilities how this objective might be achieved.

(1) All the moons mean only something internal and subtle and the processes with the moons take place within a body, which is flooded by the nectar of immortality.
(2a) Some moon(s) is/are internal and subtle and other(s) is/are external and gross.
(2b) Some moons may have two forms: internal and external.
In these cases (2ab), at least some external bodily fluid is thus involved.
(3a) All the four moons are primarily gross and external, similarly to the Sahajiyā concept. Only the fluids of a yogin are used.
(3b) All the four moons are gross and external, but some female fluid(s) is/are necessary.

Admittedly, the results of my research are rather inconclusive. At the beginning, it was not clear what Mīnanāth should do to save his life and now, at the end, it is still unclear. And, what is worse, the range of possibilities of how to achieve this aim is quite broad, including one (3b) that, at the beginning of our discussion, appeared to be entirely inconceivable for a Nāth yogi but now cannot be so easily excluded. Is it actually possible to make any positive statement in the midst of these uncertainties and is there any promising way of continuing the research?

The identity of at least one of the moons seems to be relatively unproblematic. The poisonous moon (*garalcandra*) stands in all probability for the nectar of immortality, whether taken in its usual subtle form stored in the sahasrāra-cakra, or in an external gross form, i.e., as semen.[70] All occurrences of the term *poison* (garal) within the poem fit this interpretation well.[71]

Further, two lines of the song that refer to a reverse yoga (8a and 8d) clearly allude to the well-known teaching of the Naths.[72] What should be reversed, of course, are various bodily processes, such as ageing and the process of nectar/semen falling down. Or, in more general terms, all natural processes taking place within a body should be reversed or stopped.[73] Consequently, a perfect yogi is a kind of an independent and "closed" system and does not interact materially with his external environment. This means that he does not need to eat and drink,[74] and at the same time, his body does not produce any secretions or waste products.[75] This concept may perhaps also have some connection to the practice of the four moons.[76]

Another relatively clear line is 8e: "strike at Triveṇī." Here, in all probability, Triveṇī stands for the confluence of three main *nāḍīs* (subtle bodily conduits) and the only ambiguity is whether the upper junction in the *ājñā-cakra* or the lower one in the *mūlādhāra-cakra* is meant.[77] Since the following line, 8f, says "to fill the channels with water," the natural choice would be the upper cakra and the filling could then refer to the flooding of the body by the nectar of immortality.

Regarding possible ways of proceeding with the research in order to obtain better results concerning the identity of the four moons, a few facts are quite apparent. The importance of the practice of the four moons for saving Mīnanāth's life seems to be an exclusively Bengali phenomenon. Although other versions of the story also include the event when Gorakhnāth attempts to rescue his guru with the aid of a song, it is only in the Bengali text where the song contains a specific, albeit concealed, yogic instruction on how to achieve the desired goal.[78] Our attention must therefore focus on works in Bengali, primarily on other Nāth texts where the term *four moons* sporadically occurs, and on Bengali works that include the story of these two siddhas. Furthermore, yogic Sūfī literature could turn out to be very important, since many of these works were produced in Bengal, especially the earlier ones, and borrowed a number of ideas and terms from the Naths.[79] Even the term *four moons* is to be found in them. Finally, Nāth texts in other East Indian languages (i.e. Oriya and Assamese) might cast some light on our question, since the Bengali Naths were spread throughout this region and have probably produced works also in these languages. Hopefully, further research along these lines will result in a better understanding of the meaning of the four moons and will answer the question "What should Mīnanāth do to save his life?" more conclusively.

CHAPTER NINE

The Matsyendrasaṃhitā

A Yoginī-centered Thirteenth-century Yoga Text of the South Indian Śāmbhava Cult[1]

Csaba Kiss

INTRODUCTION

In this article, I would like to communicate some basic facts about the *Matsyendrasaṃhitā*[2] (MaSaṃ), a long and significant Sanskrit tantric yoga text—along with some of the results of my three-year-long work on it, which aimed at finding further evidence of the close connection between the tantric cult of Kubjikā and the early haṭha-yogic teachings of the Nāthas.[3] This article is also an update on my preliminary notes on the MaSaṃ (Kiss 2007).

The MaSaṃ that I am dealing with here is available in five nineteenth-century manuscripts. Four of them are to be found in Jodhpur, one in London.[4] No. 1784 of the Jodhpur mss is evidently the best and probably the oldest one of them. The worst one, i.e., the one that gives bad readings against the good readings of the other manuscripts most often, is the London ms.[5]

It was the extremely bad London ms that Debabrata Sensharma, the discoverer of the text, used for his edition of MaSaṃ 1–20 (Matsyendranātha 1994). His edition could be considered the editio princeps. Unfortunately, Sensharma's edition is totally unreliable.[6] My forthcoming critical edition of MaSaṃ 1–13 and 55 (Kiss 2009), based on all five available manuscripts will hopefully clarify that the MaSaṃ is a much more coherent and significant text than it appears to be from the editio princeps. There are some more Sanskrit manuscripts entitled *Matsyendrasaṃhitā*, but they have nothing to do with the MaSaṃ that I am dealing with here.[7] My reasons for choosing *paṭalas* 1–13 and 55 of the MaSaṃ for a critical edition included the following ones: I wanted to present the whole of the frame story (*paṭalas* 1 and 55), which relates an interesting version of Matsyendra's and Gorakṣa's legend; I wanted to include the main yogic sequence of *yogāṅgas* (*paṭalas* 2–7) in the text as well as the rituals of the central mantra and of the seven Yoginīs[8] (Ḍākinī, Rākinī, Lākinī, Kākinī, Sākinī, Hākinī, and Yakṣinī) (*paṭalas* 9–13) that are crucial to the cult of the MaSaṃ; also, by editing *paṭalas* 1–13, my edition will nicely complement James Mallinson's excellent critical edition of the *Khecarīvidyā* (Mallinson 2007), an early haṭha-yogic text that appears in the MaSaṃ as *paṭalas* 14–16 and 28. I am convinced that I have edited and translated in my forthcoming critical edition all those chapters of the MaSaṃ that are crucial for the reconstruction of the unique and significant yogic cult it teaches.

The title of the present article contains four elements that call for further elucidation. In the following sections, I shall describe what I mean by the term *Śāmbhava*, and what traces of the Śāmbhava cult can be found in the MaSaṃ; what the significance of the Yoginī cult of the MaSaṃ is; on what grounds we can date the MaSaṃ to thirteenth-century South India; and finally, how the yogic teaching of the MaSaṃ enriches our understanding of the history of yoga.

TRACES OF THE ŚĀMBHAVA CULT IN THE MASAṂ

The MaSaṃ (The Compendium [attributed, or rather, related to the legendary yogin] Matsyendra[nātha])[9] is a Sanskrit Śaiva text, a Śaiva Tantra,[10] divided into fifty-five *paṭalas*. It contains a total of approximately three thousand stanzas mainly in the *anuṣṭubh* meter, with some verses in other stanza forms. To determine with which tantric tradition the MaSaṃ is most affiliated, a detailed philological study of the text is required. This is so because the text is far from being explicit about its sectarian roots and central deities. An in-depth philological study can reveal passages in other texts that have parallels in the MaSaṃ, and by this, it can shed some light on the MaSaṃ's textual orientation. Moreover, by reconstructing the mantra system of the MaSaṃ and the iconography of its central deities, its sectarian orientation can be confirmed.[11] There are a great number of passages in the MaSaṃ that have parallels in other texts.[12] The MaSaṃ is a Kaula text,[13] as is clear from the frequent occurrence of the word *kula*/*kaula*/*kaulika*.[14] Moreover, there is a whole paṭala (*paṭala* 40) describing *kulācāra* (Kula Conduct).[15] The text clearly refers to the Kulāmnāya (Kula Tradition) in 55.42bc.[16] In 18.66ab, there is a reference to the Goddess of the Kula.[17] Thus it is not surprising that of the four *āmnāyas* of the Kaula tradition (cf. Sanderson 1988, 680 ff.), the Paścimāmnāya (the cult of the goddess Kubjikā), and the Dakṣiṇāmnāya (the cult of Tripurā or Tripurasundarī, in which the goddess is worshipped in/as the Śrīcakra and her mantra, the fifteen-syllable Śrīvidyā), prominently feature in the text.

Kubjikā's cult seems to be the main underlying influence in the MaSaṃ. This cult has been the subject of serious research,[18] and its place of origin and the exact meaning of Kubjikā's name have been debated for a long time.[19] It is also questionable if Kubjikā's cult is still alive.[20] References to Kubjikā and her school in Sanskrit texts outside her cult are rare (Dyczkowski 1989,88), the most important of which is the Kubjikā section of the *Agnipurāṇa* (chapters 143–144).

An important variant of Kubjikā's cult is the so-called Ṣaḍanvayaśāmbhava or Śāmbhavānanda (or simply Śāmbhava) tradition. It is a South Indian manifestation of a masculinized version of the worship of Kubjikā and her partner Navātman—i.e., in this cult the focus shifts from the goddess to Navātman. Texts produced within this tradition include the *Śambhunirṇayatantra*, Śivānandamuni's commentary to the *Śambhunirṇayatantra* (*Śambhunirṇayadīpikā*), Umākānta's *Ṣaḍanvayaśāmbhavakrama*, and Tejānandanātha's *Ānandakalpalatā* (see Sanderson 1988, 687). This tradition coexisted and intermingled with the cult of Tripurasundarī. On the Śāmbhava variant of Kubjikā's cult, Sanderson (2002, 2–3) remarks:

> [the cult of Kubjikā] also flourished in southern India, where it appears as the Ṣaḍanvayaśāmbhava system, also called Śāmbhavānanda, in association with the better known cult of Tripurasundarī. Śivānanda, the South Indian author of the published *Ṛjuvimarśinī* commentary on the *Nityāṣoḍaśikārṇava* and other works in the tradition of the Kaula worship of Tripurasundari [*sic*], also wrote on this system: an incomplete manuscript of his *Sambhunirṇayadīpikā* survives. Maheśvarānanda of Coḷadeśa reports in his auto-commentary (*parimala*) on the *Mahārthamañjarī* [Maṅgala verse 5] that he was initiated into this system. When the Saiddhāntika Jñānaśivācārya, a South Indian settled in Vārāṇasī probably during the twelfth century but not earlier, thinks of the Kaulas it is mostly texts of the cult of Kubjikā that he cites. That it was by no means a marginal phenomenon in the Śaivism of South India is suggested by its assimilation into the tradition of the Smārtas' Śaṅkarācāryas, where it is the basis of the first half of the famous hymn *Saundaryalaharī* attributed to Śaṅkara.

What we see in the probably thirteenth-century MaSaṃ is exactly this mixture of Kubjikā's and Tripurā's cults against a South Indian background. Thus, the many occurrences of the term *śāmbhava* in *paṭala* 1 and throughout the MaSaṃ can also probably be interpreted in the specific sense of the Kubjikā-oriented South Indian Śāmbhava tradition.

Traces of this important tantric tradition, the cult of Kubjikā in general, and its Śāmbhava variant in particular, pervade the teachings of the MaSaṃ in a hidden way: there are very few explicit references to Kubjikā or her partner usually called Navātman.[21] Kubjikā's name is concealed, but the main mantric system of the text and the iconography of the central goddess give away information on the text's affiliation. One of the most important mantras of the MaSaṃ is the Pañcapraṇava (*aiṃ hrīṃ śrīṃ phreṃ hsauṃ*), which is "a set of five syllables . . . serving, as it were, as the signature or hallmark of the Kubjikā cult" (Sanderson 1990, 47).[22] This mantra is used extensively in the MaSaṃ. It usually encloses some other mantra thus: *aiṃ hrīṃ śrīṃ phreṃ hsauṃ*; then some other mantra; and then *hsauṃ phreṃ śrīṃ hrīṃ aiṃ*. The frequent mention of this Pañcapravaṇa mantra reconfirms again and again that the text has close links with the Kubjikā tradition. By enclosing other mantras, the Pañcapravaṇa puts them, so to say, in quotation marks, pervades them, subordinates them, protects them, or makes them appear as if they exist only in relation to Kubjikā's cult. When the Pañcapravaṇa encloses the mantras of the five elements (*bhūta*) in MaSaṃ *paṭala* 2, it transforms a very general set of mantras into something very specifically Kubjikā-oriented. When it encloses the mantras of the five-elements bhūta in MaSaṃ *paṭala* 2, it transforms a very general set of mantras into something very specifically Kubjikā-oriented. When it encloses the Mantrarāja (see below)—i.e., the initials of the six plus one Yoginīs that include the supreme goddess, who is actually Tripurā in disguise—it makes Kubjikā subordinate and rule over the Yoginīs and Tripurā (in MaSaṃ *paṭala* 9). The Pañcapravaṇa the central maṇḍala (see MaSaṃ *paṭala* 10, and also the basic design of the maṇḍala below) at the intermediate points of the compass and at the center to protect it. The Pañcapraṇava is also called the [Five] *tāras* (MaSaṃ 2.21ab, 2.25c, 7.68a, 9.13a, 11.38a). The Pañcapraṇava mantra narrows down the sectarian affiliation of the teaching of the MaSaṃ to a specific cult within the Śaiva religious world, that of the goddess Kubjikā.

There are other important mantras in the MaSaṃ that reveal close connections with the cult of Kubjikā, and specifically with the Śāmbhava cult, such as the Navātman (Nine-fold) mantra. The Navātman mantra consists of nine syllables. One variety of this mantra is *hasakṣamalavayrūṃ* (*hskṣmlvyrūṃ*). It is sometimes called *śāmbhava* and also *hādi*.[23] When coupled with Navātman, Kubjikā's mantra appears as *sahakṣamalavayrīṃ*. This is the *śākta* variant of the Navātman mantra, and is also called *sādi*.[24] Both the Śāmbhava and the Śākta variant of the Navātman mantra appear in highly corrupted forms in the mantras of the seven major Yoginīs of the cult.[25] Although the Navātman mantra is actually a fairly ancient set of mantric syllables, and it is to be found in such early texts as the *Niśvāsatattvasaṅgraha*, the *Brahmayāmala* and the *Svacchandatantra* (mostly as *harakṣamalavayū[ṃ]*; see Hatley 2007, 220), I think that its emphatic appearance in

Reconstruction of the initiation *maṇḍala* of the MaSaṃ
(based on drawings in DEHEJIA 1986:45 & MALLMAN 1963:206)
EAST

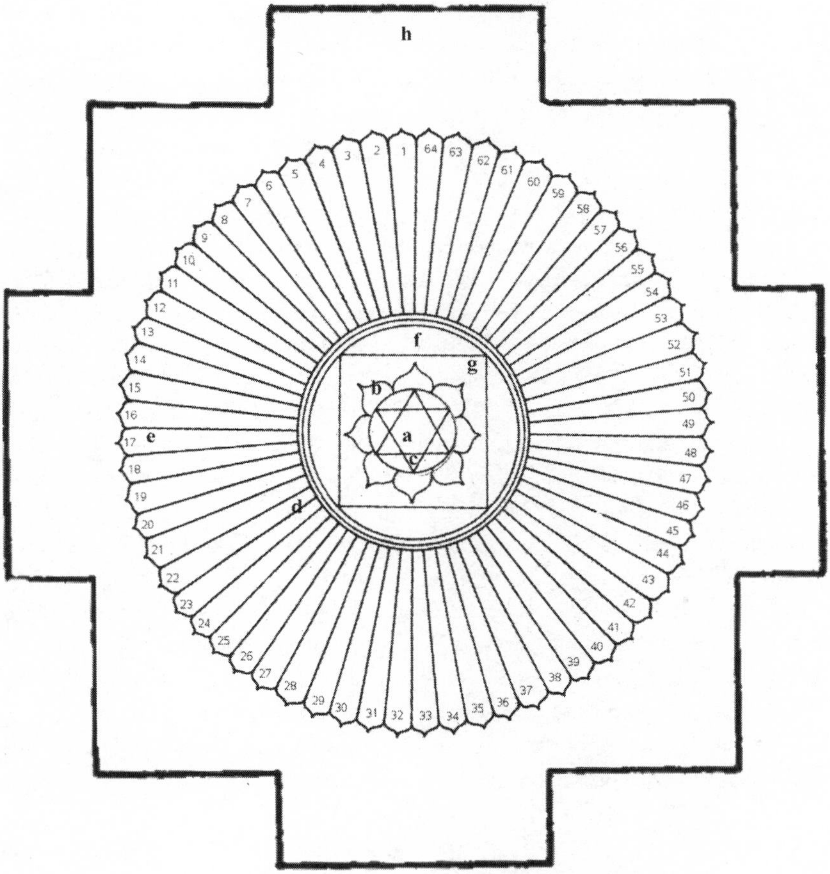

WEST

a = *pātraka* in the centre + fifth *ratna* and fifth *praṇava*
b = at the bases of the eight petals: 8 Bhairavas with 16 Mātṛs
at the points of the eight petals: 8 *nidhi*s and 8 *siddhi*s
c = at the points of the six-pointed star: six lotuses and jars for the six Yoginīs (W, N-W, N-E, E, S-E) with their 50 Kalās
d = 50 Rudras with their Śaktis
e = 64 *yoginīs*
f = four of the five *ratna*s (E, S, W, N)
g = four of the five *praṇava*s (S-E, S-W, N-W, N-E)
h = Baṭuka, Bheruṇḍa, Durgā, Kṣetreśa (E, S, W, N)

significant mantras of the MaSaṃ, a generally Kubjikā-oriented text, in conjunction with its Śākta variant, is a further indication of some influence of the Śāmbhava variant of Kubjikā's cult. In the MaSaṃ, not only is Navātman's mantra incorporated in the mantric system, but his name is given (11.36a and margin of ms Ja f. 21ᵛ) and his visualization in *paṭala* 43 echoes the *Nityāhnikatilaka* (f. 26ʳ lines 2–4). The powerful presence of Navātman's mantra in the MaSaṃ, e.g. in the central mantras of the individual Yoginīs, where it even overshadows Kubjikā's mantra, is thus a strong indication that the text is deeply rooted in the tantric Śāmbhava cult of Kubjikā and Navātman.

As regards the iconography of the deities of the MaSaṃ in its central *dhyāna* section (*paṭala* 7), Caṇḍikā, a six-faced and twelve-armed goddess is evidently a disguised form of Kubjikā (compare MaSaṃ 7.19cdff and *Nityāhnikatilaka* f. 27ʳ line 2ff).[26] Navātman's iconographic description in MaSaṃ paṭala 43 echoes *Nityāhnikatilaka* f. 26ʳ lines 2ff. Also, the embracing position of the divine couple in MaSaṃ 1.83 (i.e., *śaktyāliṅgitadehāya*), otherwise well-known from Buddhist iconography, is rare in the Śaiva realm: it is confined to Navātman and Kubjikā of the Kubjikā/Śāmbhava tradition.[27] Moreover, the central *dhyānaślokas* of the divine couple are rather "de-Śāktaized": Śiva/Bhairava/Navātman seems to be the real focus of the cult, which again points to the Śāmbhava variant of the Kubjikā cult as the root of the MaSaṃ. The presence of the goddess Tripurā in the MaSaṃ, mostly as the leader of the seven major Yoginīs—as well as passages in the MaSaṃ that have parallels in the *Nityāṣoḍaśikārṇava*, the *Svacchandapaddhati*, and other Traipura texts—also suggest that the Śāmbhava variant of Kubjikā's cult, in which Tripurā's and Kubjikā's cults coexisted, is the most probable cultic affiliation of the MaSaṃ. In the MaSaṃ, Tripurā's identity fluctuates between that of a Yoginī (then she is called Yakṣiṇī)[28] and that of the supreme goddess, in which case her difference from Kubjikā is somewhat blurred.

THE YOGINĪ CULT OF THE MASAṂ

Although primarily a text of the Śāmbhava cult, in which the foci of worship are Kubjikā and Tripurā, the MaSaṃ shifts its main focus to a Yoginī cult of the seven Yoginīs: Ḍākinī, Rākinī, Lākinī, Kākinī, Sākinī, Hākinī, and Yakṣiṇī. That the MaSaṃ is an attempt to break free from the sectarian limitations of the Paścimāmnāya and the Dakṣiṇāmnāya to provide a universal yogic cult of Yoginīs for yogins can be inferred primarily from its central mantra, the Mantrarāja. The central mantra of a tantric cult is to be passed on by the guru to the initiated during initiation (*dīkṣā*),[29] and it is one of the indispensable pieces of information for anyone to enter the circle of the initiated of the given cult. It is a PIN code, so to say, which gives access to the cult, and it may also contain much information in a condensed form on the history and basic affiliations of the cult. The Mantrarāja of the MaSaṃ, in my reconstruction, is made up of the initials of six of the seven Yoginīs Ḍākinī, plus the syllable *phreṃ*[30] for Yakṣiṇī, a special Yoginī: *ḍaralakasahaphreṃ* or *ḍrlkshphreṃ*. For a cult to have its central mantra made up of fragments of Yoginī names means that here these Yoginīs dominate and more or less take over the function of the central goddess(es).

While the names of these Yoginīs occur in a great number of Kaula and yogic texts,[31] the sequence *ḍa-ra-la-ka-sa-ha* as a designation for the six (of seven in many cases) Yoginīs seems to be typical of texts within or influenced by the cult of Kubjikā. It can be found three times in the *Kubjikāmatatantra*,[32] once in the *Nityāhnikatilaka*,[33] once in the *Kularatnoddyota*,[34] and once in the Kubjikā section of the *Agnipurāṇa*.[35] Thus, the abbreviation *ḍa-ra-la-ka-sa-ha* seems to designate especially the Yoginīs of the Kubjikā cult, and by its appearance in the MaSaṃ as the most important mantra of the cult, the Yoginīs themselves are raised to central importance. The seven Yoginīs of the MaSaṃ are the presiding deities of the yogic cakras or *ādhāra*s (Mūlādhāra, Svādhiṣṭhāna, etc.), an association which is present perhaps as early as in the *Kubjikāmatatantra*,[36] and is definitely the case in the later *Nityāhnikatilaka*.[37] By focusing on the Yoginīs of the bodily power centers (i.e., ādhāra, cakra) rather than on one single central deity, the cult of the MaSaṃ starts a transition from sectarian Śaiva yoga, more specifically from the yogic teachings of the Kubjikā tradition, to pan-Indian yoga, later to be melted down to haṭha yoga, which gradually gets rid of those sectarian marks that connect a tradition to a specific deity.

It is also of utmost importance to notice how Yoginīs are predominant throughout the initiatory process (MaSaṃ 10–11) over other deities, including Śiva/Navātman and Devī/Kubjikā/Tripurā. It is the mantras of the seven Yoginīs that are to be recited before the actual moment of initiation and then passed on to the initiated secretly. It is their initials, as we have seen, that make up the central mantra that gives access to the cult. It is their Kalās ("digits"; actually goddesses such as Amṛtā, Ākarṣiṇī, etc.) to be repeatedly installed, first on the initiation maṇḍala,[38] then on the initiated's body, and all in all there are 121 deities (7 Yoginīs + 50 Kalās of the seven Yoginīs + 64 minor *yoginīs*) in the maṇḍala that are some kind of yoginīs or are closely connected to the Yoginīs. These facts suggest very emphatically that the cult of the MaSaṃ is primarily a Yoginī cult that overshadows the cult of any individual deity.[39]

Thus, the MaSaṃ is a yogic Yoginī cult that is rooted in the Kubjikā/Śāmbhava tradition but is already in the process of concealing and later totally eliminating all specific references to this tradition and focusing on yogic practices and on the worship of goddesses that were originally intimately connected with the Kubjikā tradition but whose main and important function from now on is to protect the yogin's body and mind. The question when this process exactly began and if it was only one path of many in the history of yoga that contributed to the formation of haṭha yoga is difficult to answer. Nevertheless, I think that to date the MaSaṃ is not as hopeless a task as the case is with many other Śaiva tantras.

THE PROVENANCE OF THE MASAṂ

As regards the date of composition of the MaSaṃ, it is important to note that there does not seem to be any known Sanskrit source that mentions it or refers to it. A certain *Śivamatsyendrasaṃhitā* is mentioned in the margin of f. 5ʳ of the *Bṛhatkhecarīprakāśa*,[40] a commentary to the *Khecarīvidyā*. (The *Khecarīvidyā* is an early haṭha-yogic text that is included in the MaSaṃ as *paṭalas* 14–16 and 28.) This might be the only known reference to the MaSaṃ. The fact that we may have no references to the MaSaṃ at all probably points to the late origin of this collection of texts as we now have it in five nineteenth-century manuscripts.

The pronounced familiarity of the text with the Dakṣiṇāmnāya and the Paścimāmnāya makes it clear that the MaSaṃ, or to be precise, many parts of it, definitely postdate their formation periods.[41] The core of the MaSaṃ seems to postdate Paścimāmnāya texts such as the *Nityāhnikatilaka* (pre-twelfth-century). As far as the Dakṣiṇāmnāya is concerned, the MaSaṃ postdates the *Nityāṣodaśikārṇava* (pre-tenth-century?), while there seems to be no trace of the *Yoginīhṛdaya* in it (of which "there is no evidence . . . before the thirteenth century" [Sanderson 1988, 690]). The *Nityāṣodaśikārṇava* teaches the Kādi-variant of the Śrīvidyā, similarly to the MaSaṃ (1.72 and paṭala 34), while the *Yoginīhṛdaya* belongs to the tradition of the Hādi Śrīvidyā (*Yoginīhṛdaya* 2.21ff). Perhaps the MaSaṃ was composed at a time when or in a region where the *Nityāṣodaśikārṇava* was already a well-known and authoritative text of the Dakṣimāmnāya but the teachings of the *Yoginīhṛdaya* had still not been widely propagated.

There is a list of tantras in MaSaṃ 14.13cd–15, which may theoretically help us date the *Khecarīvidyā*, and by this, the MaSaṃ.[42] This passage mentions five works: *Mahākāla*, *Vivekamārtaṇḍa*,[43] *Śābara*, *Viśuddheśvara* and *Jālaśaṃvara*.[44] Since paṭala 14 is part of the *Khecarīvidyā*, Mallinson has tried to identify these references (2007, 165n6 and 196–97nn201–205). Although any terminus post quem reached thus is valid only for the *Khecarīvidyā* section of the MaSaṃ, it is evidently crucial for dating the rest of the MaSaṃ. Mallinson (2007, 4), after considering all data available to date the *Khecarīvidyā*, concludes that it was composed before 1400 CE. It seems very likely to me that much of the MaSaṃ is earlier than the *Khecarīvidyā* mainly because its basic yoga teaching is closer in contents to the Bhairavatantras[45] and even to the Saiddhāntika yoga-pādas than the slightly more haṭha-yogic *Khecarīvidyā* is. I agree with Mallinson that "the Khecarīvidyā is a later addition to an earlier version of the *Matsyendrasaṃhitā*" (2007, 6). Evidence for this is the sharp contrast in the treatment of cannabis (no mention vs praise) and of the *khecarīmudrā* (pushing the tongue upwards vs a hand-gesture) in the *Khecarīvidyā* and the rest of the MaSaṃ (ibid.). Note also that the word *haṭha* is not to be found in the MaSaṃ at all, making it unlikely that we are dealing with a yoga text composed after haṭha yoga gained popularity.[46] The mention of the "Chola king"(*colo rājā*) in paṭalas 1 and 55 suggests that the frame story was composed during or after the rule of the Chola dynasty in Southern India (ninth to thirteenth centuries). Matsyendra is depicted as a human being in paṭalas 1 and 55. This may perhaps indicate that this version of his legend stems from a relatively early phase of the development of his cult. He is at least very far from being deified as he has been in Nepal and Tibet since perhaps the seventeenth century (see Locke 1980). Also, I have not found any firm evidence that any of the numerous passages in the MaSaṃ that have parallels in other texts (see some of them above) would force us to believe that the MaSaṃ was composed after the thirteenth century. Although I am aware of the fact that my efforts to date the MaSaṃ are much less than conclusive, I am inclined to date the core of the MaSaṃ, i.e., chapters 1–13 and 55, as composed before 1300 CE.

As regards the place of origin of the MaSaṃ, there are several signs that indicate that much of the MaSaṃ originated in Southern India. The text is a mixture of the cults of Kubjikā and Tripurasundarī, is probably from the thirteenth century, and is probably a product of the Śāmbhava tradition. If it is, then a South Indian origin would be natural (see previous section on the Śāmbhava cult).[47]

There are two geographical names suggesting a South Indian origin, both mentioned in the frame story of the MaSaṃ. One is Gomanta (1.109d), which is probably a mountain in Goa.[48] If the Gomanta mentioned in the MaSaṃ is to be located in Goa, the caves of Panhāle-Kājī (ancient name: Praṇālaka; today: Panhale Kazi), a small village in the Sindhudurg district of Maharashtra adjoining Goa from the north, can be of considerable importance. According to Deshpande (1986), two of the caves, nos. 14 and 29, are dedicated entirely to Nātha images. Cave 29 contains images of eighty-four Nāthasiddhas. Several representations of Matsyendra,[49] Gorakṣa, and Tripurasundarī have been found in these caves dated to the thirteenth century. Of course, in the present state of research it is impossible to confirm if there is any direct connection between the redactors/target audience of the MaSaṃ and the caves of Panhāle-Kājī, but at least the stone-images found in caves 14 and 29 provide archeological proof for a close connection between the cult of Tripurasundarī and the Nāthas headed by Matsyendra: a connection that is one of the main underlying themes in the MaSaṃ.[50]

The other geographical name mentioned in the MaSaṃ is the city of Alūra (55.3a). It is very difficult to restrict this name to any definite city or village. The name might refer to Ellora (Maharashtra) of the famous rock temples (which was probably called Elāpura in ancient times; cf. Dey 1927). Other possibilities are Eluru in Andhra Pradesh, or any of the Alūras/Allurs/Alurs, many of which are located around Madras (see e.g., Thornton 1854). At any rate, the ending *-ūra* (modern *-ore*) suggests a Tamil or at least South Indian name. The MaSaṃ also confirms that the location is in the South: *alūrādhipatiṃ bhūpaṃ dākṣiṇātyam* (55.3ab), i.e., the king of Alūra was a southerner.

The fact that the redactor of the text equates Gorakṣanātha, one of the main characters of the frame story, with the Chola king,[51] a surprising feature of the version of Matsyendra's legend in the MaSaṃ, may also point to the Chola region as the place of the origin of the text, or at least of the frame story in *paṭalas* 1 and 55. The Chola king may be a general term, or may refer to a specific king of the Chola dynasty: any of the names Rājarāja Cola I (r. 985–1016CE), Rājendra I (r. 1012–44CE) and Rājendra II (r. 1052–63 CE) or Rājarāja II (r. 1146–73CE) may be meant.

The iconographical item (*mṛga*) mentioned in the *dhyānaślokas* of Śiva (7.31c) is typically South Indian.[52] The occurrence of the name of the exclusively South Indian god Śāstṛ (= Aiyanār) in MaSaṃ 8.31a is a strong evidence of the text's origin in South India, more specifically in the Tamil region.[53] There are interesting parallels between the frame story in the MaSaṃ and the *śaṅkaradigvijayas*, many of which were composed in South India.[54] Moreover, I have not found any passages in other texts that have parallels in the MaSaṃ and are definitely of North Indian origin. In contrast with this fact, many of the texts that contain passages that have parallels in the MaSaṃ probably originated in Southern India (e.g., *Bhāgavatapurāṇa*, *Prapañcasāra*,[55] *Svacchandapaddhati*, *Ṣaḍanvayaśāmbhavakrama*).

All these features of the MaSaṃ point to the same conclusion, namely that at least much of the text of the MaSaṃ was composed in thirteenth-century South India, probably in the Tamil region or, alternatively and less likely, around Goa.

THE YOGA OF THE MASAṂ

To define the position and significance of the MaSaṃ in the history of yoga, it is obvious to turn now to its yogic teaching. In a certain sense, which might correspond very closely to what the redactor(s) of the MaSaṃ intended, the whole MaSaṃ is yogic. It is intended for yogins, which is evident from the very frequent use of the word *yogin* when the text gives instructions. Also, the key topic of the text is Śāmbhava yoga practice (*śāmbhavaṃ yogasādhanam*, 2.2d). In this sense, the yogic teaching of the MaSaṃ is a highly ritualistic one. It includes a great number of outward rites as well as many internalized ones. These rituals, inner and outer, are mixed with haṭha-yogic bodily exercises such as breath control (*prāṇasaṃyamana*, i.e., *prāṇāyāma*) and sitting postures (*āsana*).

In the following short analysis, I will restrict the sense of the term *yoga* to that physical and mental process which leads the yogin to fusion with the deity, and which is described in MaSaṃ 2–7, and I will exclude practices that aim "only" at obtaining worldly siddhis/magical powers (e.g., *japa* and *nyāsa* for obtaining victory over one's enemy). The basic reason for this restriction of the yoga of the MaSaṃ to *paṭala*s 2–7 is that they teach a Pātañjala-like complete sequence of yogāṅga*s*.

The yoga of MaSaṃ *paṭala*s 2–7 can be described, unfortunately, mainly in negative terms. This form of yoga seems to be devoid of the system of five/six/seven power centers (cakra, ādhāra) of the *Kubjikāmata* and haṭha-yogic texts, and of MaSaṃ 8–13.[56] It does not refer to Siddhas. It probably does not teach complex yogic postures (*āsana*) other than intricate sitting postures (note that the text of *paṭala* 3, the *āsana-paṭala*, seems to be highly corrupt). It does not speak of the haṭha-yogic technique of *khecarī* (the blocking of the throat with the tongue pushed upwards), while other parts of the MaSaṃ contain the whole *Khecarīvidyā*. It is not *ṣaḍaṅga* in the tantric sense,[57] since it includes an extra purificatory rite as its seventh *aṅga* and it does not teach *tarka* or japa as an auxiliary, which would be typical of tantric *ṣaḍaṅgayoga*. Most importantly, it does not refer to the seven Yoginīs of MaSaṃ *paṭala*s 1 and 8–13.

In contrast with these, it does refer to yoginīs in general;[58] it mentions sādhakas, a designation that may refer to siddhi-seeking tantric initiates in this context,[59] or simply practitioners. Other, more haṭha-yogic parts of the text often refer to Siddhas instead of sādhakas, and at one point (17.37cd ff.), it distinguishes between the two groups. The system of *aṅga*s in *paṭala*s 2–7 follows Pātañjala yoga almost perfectly. We could treat the purification section (*paṭala* 2) as a kind of *yama-niyama* section that teaches rituals that purify the practitioner and prepare him for yoga. All other aṅgas of the Pātañjala model can be found in the MaSaṃ in the traditional order: āsana (*paṭala* 3), prāṇāyāma (*paṭala* 4), *pratyāhāra* (*paṭala* 5), *dhāraṇā* (*paṭala* 6), dhyāna (*paṭala* 7), and samādhi (not having a separate paṭala in the MaSaṃ, but inserted in *paṭala* 7).

The absence of the yama-niyama rules in a yogic text that is modelled on Pātañjala yoga is significant and can be accounted for by the fact that many of the practices included in the MaSaṃ (e.g., the sexual practices of *paṭala* 40 or practices with human skulls in *paṭala* 33) would be difficult to harmonize with rules such as *brahmacarya* (continence) and *śauca* (purity) (*Yogasūtra* 2.30, 32).

The description of *dehaśuddhi* follows a very general tantric model that can be found in Śaivasiddhānta texts as well as in Bhairavatantras and has nothing to do with Patañjali's tradition or haṭha yoga. What is significant here is, first, the use of the Five-Praṇava-mantra (see above) up to 2.43, which confirms that this section is intended to be associated with Kubjikā; and, second, the appearance of three power centers, the *mūlādhāra*, the heart, and the middle of the eye-brows, after 2.43, which may indicate that this section originates in some other source than Kubjikā's tradition. It may be so because to name three to five centers, some of them by everyday names such as *hṛd* and *bhrūmadhya*, can be typical of Śaivasiddhānta texts,[60] or at least may be indicative of a tradition independent of the well-known teaching of five/six/seven cakras by names such as Svādhiṣṭhāna and Anāhata. Thus, MaSaṃ *paṭala* 2 may be considered as made up of two main sections: one general but "Kubjikized" description of *dehaśuddhi* (called the Aghamarṣaṇa ritual) up to 2.43, and the four-fold sequence of *śoṣaṇa, dāhana, plavana* and deification, which is perhaps ignorant of the cakra-system of the Kubjikā tradition and uses the word *praṇava* in some other sense than the Five Praṇavas (e.g., in the sense of *oṃ*), in sharp contrast with the Kubjikā-oriented first section.

The teaching of āsanas in MaSaṃ *paṭala* 3 is slightly problematic. It teaches fourteen āsanas (i.e. *vīra, kūrma, svastika, kukkuṭa, mayūra, vyāghra, padma, vijaya, dṛḍha, gṛdhra, garuḍa, yakṣa, siddha, vṛṣabha*), some of which are cursory and/or corrupt and difficult to interpret satisfactorily. I have not been able to find any similar sequence of sitting postures in any other texts, and the descriptions in the loci classici (*Haṭhayogapradīpikā, Gheraṇḍasaṃhitā, Śivasaṃhitā*) of āsanas named as they are in the MaSaṃ have little to do with the text of the MaSaṃ.

In contrast with the āsana chapter, the chapter on prāṇāyāma (paṭala 4) contains a great number of passages that have parallels in other Sanskrit sources (*Mṛgendrāgama, Śivapurāṇa, Agnipurāṇa, Sārdhatriśatikālottara, Sarvajñānottara*, and most prominently, the *Prapañcasāra* and the *Mahākālasaṃhitā*). This chapter seems to draw on some common yogic sources, traces of which can be found in a number of pre-thirteenth-century texts. That the āsanas and the prāṇāyāma in MaSaṃ 3–4 originate from some general yogic source is suggested by the fact that there is practically no trace of any sectarian affiliation in them. That the redactor of the MaSaṃ did a slightly less than perfect job when trying to harmonize all aspects of the borrowed sections can be seen for example in the discrepancy in the number of *nāḍī*s in 4.57 ("fifty thousand": the passage parallel with the *Prapañcasāra*) and 4.71 ("seventy-two thousand": the passage parallel with the *Mahākālasaṃhitā*). An interesting aspect of the prāṇāyāma taught in the MaSaṃ is that, unlike in later haṭha-yoga texts, there is only one single method described, namely inhalation through one nostril, holding the breath, then exhaling through the other nostril. The only aim seems to be to slow down one's breathing.

The very short fifth chapter on the next yogāṅga, *pratyāhāra*, displays, similarly to the two previous chapters, no traces of any sectarian affiliation. It is basically a simple teaching to withdraw the senses (the *karmendriya*s and the *buddhīndriya*s of the Sāṅkhya system) into the elements, i.e., bhūta. This is not far from what the *Yogasūtra* suggests.[61]

Up to this point, the similarity of the yoga of the MaSaṃ to Pātañjala yoga is not insignificant. With Chapter six, the teaching on dhāraṇā, the picture slightly changes. The dhāraṇā of the MaSaṃ does not have very much to do with what can be inferred from *Yogasūtra* 3.1 or its commentaries,[62] in which concentration on one's own body (navel, heart, head, nose, tongue) that gets transformed into dhyāna is taught as dhāraṇā. The MaSaṃ echoes tantric concentration techniques similar to those of the *Kiraṇa* (58.18c ff.), the *Raurava* (Vidyāpāda 7.6–10), and the *Mataṅgapārameśvara* (Yogapāda 2.35c–65), which teach *āgneyī/pāvakā, vāruṇī/saumyā, aiśānī* and *amṛtā dhāraṇā*s, as well as those of the *Mālinīvijayottaratantra* (cf. Vasudeva 2004, 319 ff).[63] There are three kinds of dhāraṇā described in the MaSaṃ: *vāyavā, āgneyī,* and *amṛtā*.[64] The three dhāraṇās in the MaSaṃ are little more than a reinterpretation of the *śoṣaṇa-dāhana-plavana* sequence in *paṭala* 2. This seems also to be the case in some other texts, e.g., the *Svacchandatantra* (7.299c–300), the *Parākhya* (14.14c–15b) and the *Jayākhyasaṃhitā* (33.10).[65] Thus, although the teaching of dhāraṇā in the MaSaṃ seems to be a tantric filler for a missing Pātañjala yogāṅga, to supply a ritual derivative of *bhūtaśuddhi* for yogic dhāraṇā is not uncommon in tantric texts. One should also note MaSaṃ 6.1cd (*prāṇāyāmadviṣaṭkaṃ tu dhāraṇāyogam ucyate*), which states that twelve [rounds of] prāṇāyāma result in dhāraṇā and thus it ignores *pratyāhāra*, a Pātañjala aṅga between prāṇāyāma and dhāraṇā.[66] Later, the text tries to make up for this confusion and mentions pratyāhāra in 6.13cd (*sarvendriyavaśīkāraḥ pratyāhāreṇa jāyate*), which echoes *Yogasūtra* 2.55. Most of the remainder of the chapter teaches how to present propitiatory offerings *bali* to ghosts, demons, and deities. Obviously, this chapter is a slightly unsuccessful attempt to go on with the Pātañjala sequence of aṅgas in the MaSaṃ. Lacking any real Pātañjala dhāraṇā text, the redactor supplied a general tantric visualization passage of bhūtaśuddhi, a commonly seen phenomenon in tantric texts, and then quickly switched to the description of bali. By saying that the *dhāraṇā paṭala* is a slightly unsuccessful attempt to force the yogic teaching of the MaSaṃ into the Pātañjala model, I do not want to suggest that Pātañjala yoga is the only reference point to compare a tantric yoga teaching to. Referring to different sequences of yogāṅgas found in tantric texts, Vasudeva (2004, 376) is definitely right when he states:

> . . . these systems are not simply indiscriminately reshuffled versions of an original "correct" order. Many Śaiva scriptures have invested considerable effort in the reformulation of yoga. Upon deeper familiarizating, the internal logic of the respective systems provides their coherence.

The next question is whether the main dhyāna of the MaSaṃ's yoga has any links with Pātañjala yoga. The process of dhyāna in MaSaṃ 7 follows the typical tantric model, i.e., the practitioner visualizes a lotus throne for Śiva and places the mental image of the god and his consort onto it,[67] but it is prefixed by a preliminary exercise of the visualization of the "Great Body"(*mahāvapus*), in which echoes of the *Yogasūtra* quite evidently appear.[68] There are alternative ways of the visualization of the central deities described in the MaSaṃ, the first of which (7.8–18) is briefly the following: the yogin should imagine a lotus in his own heart, with fire as its petals, the sun as its fibers, the moon as its filament,[69] glowing like ten thousand rising suns, together with the nine Śaktis. In the middle of the lotus, one should visualize Parameśāna—who is black like a black cloud, with serpents in his *jaṭā*, the crescent moon on his crest, fearful (*bhīma*), pervading all the directions with the sacred syllable *huṃ*. His attributes (*āyudha*) are: a sword (*khaḍga*), a trident (*śūla*), the gesture of fearlessness (*abhaya*), a serpent-noose (*nāgapāśa*), a skull (*kapāla*), a bell (*ghaṇṭā*), the gesture of generosity (*varada*), and one more (†*viṣārṇa*†). Thus, he is eight-armed. He is wearing a red garment and is ornamented with red garlands and their scent. He has also a necklace of the eight snakes (*nāgas*). He is roaring and has a tiger skin as his upper garment covered with lion skin. His three eyes are the sun, the moon, and fire. He has tusks in his big mouth. His eyes are rolling with intoxication from wine. This description fits a version of Bhairava. Then the yogin should visualize the goddess Caṇḍikā (7.19ff.) as sitting on Bhairava's left. She looks like a black cloud. She is adorned with severed heads (*muṇḍa*), rings of serpents, and red flowers. She has six heads, each having three eyes and twelve arms. She is wearing the same garments as Śiva (tiger skin and lion skin). She is holding a thunderbolt (*vajra*), an elephant-goad (*aṅkuśa*), a disc (*cakra*), a conch (*śaṅkha*), a shield (*kheṭa*), a trident (*triśūla*), a knife (*karttṛkā*), a staff (*daṇḍa*), a pestle (*muśala*), the gesture of fearlessness (*abhaya*), and the gesture of generosity (*varada*). (One āyudha seems to be missing.) She is benevolent (*bhadra*) and young. She has the moon on her crest. She is drunk on wine. She is surrounded by the yoginīs. She swallows/destroys time (*kālagrasanarūpiṇī*).

Although the description of Caṇḍikā is rather detailed and she seems to be at least as powerful as Śiva, this dhyāna section does not give the impression of being Śākta, i.e., the emphasis is still on Śiva/Bhairava. Descriptions of Śiva's other forms are scattered through this paṭala from 7.28 to 7.74. He is to be visualized with the following attributes:

7.31ff.: (six-armed) varada, abhaya, ṭaṅka, mṛgamudrā, akṣasrak, pustaka;
7.37ff.: (four-armed) akṣamālā, varada, †viśiṣṭa†, abhaya;
7.69ff.: (four-armed) varada, pāśa, veda, akṣasūtra;
7.71ff.: (eight-armed) śūla, khaṭvāṅga, ghaṇṭā, kuliśa, varada, kapāla, abhīti} (= abhaya), aravinda.

The very general[70] name of the goddess Caṇḍikā might evoke the figure of Mahiṣāsuramardinī alias Caṇḍikā, who, according to one tradition,[71] is six-faced and twenty-armed (*vajra, aṅkuśa, cakra, śaṅkha, kheṭaka, śūla, gadā, dhvaja, ghaṇṭā, dhanus, abhaya, khaḍga, śakti, ḍamaru, chattra, nāgapāśa, bāṇa, paraśu, darpaṇa, mudgara*), with a golden complexion—handsome, young, wrathful and sitting on a lion. Moreover, the description of the divine couple in the MaSaṃ can also evoke the image of Kubjikā (and Navātman) of the Paścimāmnāya, or its parallel and masculinized tradition, the Śāmbhava.

In fact, Kubjikā and Navātmān's (i.e., Śiva's) description in the *Nityāhnikatilaka*, a text of the Kubjikā tradition, is not only similar to the couple in the MaSaṃ, but there are some passages that have parallels in the MaSaṃ. In the *Nityāhnikatilaka*, Kubjikā is also six-faced and twelve-armed as in the MaSaṃ, with the following attributes: *triśūla, cakra, vajra, aṅkuśa, śara, karttṛkā, nīlotpala, muṇḍa, khaṭvāṅga, ghaṇṭā, pustaka, dhanus*. Only five of these match the description of Caṇḍikā in the MaSaṃ, but it seems very plausible that we are dealing with a variant of the goddess Kubjikā in the MaSaṃ, with her name almost completely concealed. It is also remarkable that Navātman, Kubjikā's partner in the Paścimāmnāya, appears in the MaSaṃ.[72] In MaSaṃ *paṭala* 43, there are some verses that are parallel with Navātman's dhyāna in *Nityāhnikatilaka* f. 26^{r} lines 2–4.

Thus, it seems quite clear that the very central yogic visualization in the MaSaṃ presents Kubjikā in a slightly concealed way with her partner assuming various forms. This visualization seems to be constructed from various sources, some of them with some Kubjikā influence. The image in the MaSaṃ of the goddess sitting on her partner's left while he is in a sitting position, but at the same time, her being twelve-armed, seems rather unusual, since the common iconographic image of the couple of Śiva and Devī is either that of an embracing couple facing each other (in the case of Navātman and Kubjikā) or that of Devī sitting on his left but being two-armed or sitting on his lying body and having more than two arms. The concealment of Kubjikā's and her partner's name in the MaSaṃ and their unusual, or to put it in another way, forced and arbitrary juxtaposition can be seen as a tendency to de-Śāktaize the cult of Kubjikā and to conceal all its sectarian marks. It may indicate again that the yogic core of the text in fact belongs to a Kaula yoga tradition originating from the masculinized Śāmbhava version of Kubjikā's cult, and is in the process of separating itself from any sectarian limitations.

One of the most interesting aspects of the yogic teaching of the MaSaṃ is that it is rather explicit and clear on the nature of samādhi. At the end of *paṭala* 7, samādhi is summarized in seven verses (7.75–81) as a means for the yogin to become Śiva by maintaining an inner vision that has been mastered in the dhyāna phase. There is a flash of light in samādhi and then the yogin can actually see what he wishes to see. This means that he can have total control over his private universe and can create a world of his own mentally in which he can fully immerse. It brings about also total freedom (*mukti*) from the actual world. This point is perhaps the most original one in the yogic teaching of the MaSaṃ and the farthest one from Pātañjala yoga, in which samādhi comes about by the stoppage of all mental activities (*Yogasūtra* 1.2: *yogaś cittavṛttinirodhaḥ*; Vyāsa's *Yogabhāṣya* 1.1: *yogaḥ samādhiḥ*). The most important technique of fully immersing in one's private universe created mentally and of gaining control over this universe is mostly called *bhāva* in the MaSaṃ.

The terminus technicus *bhāva*, and the related verbs (*bhāvayet*, *paribhāvayet*) occur very many times in the MaSaṃ and stand for arguably the most important, if not absolutely original, concept in the MaSaṃ. It is a meditative process during which the yogin visualizes an object, mostly a deity, and usually tries to identify himself with it. This practice is an indispensable part of tantric ritual and yoga in general. It is often denoted in tantric texts by other terms such as bhāvanā, dhyāna, or *smaraṇa*. Sanderson (1995, 42) writes about the same technique and, with respect to the *sādhaka*'s self-identification with Śiva in the Śaiva Siddhānta, says:

> The thinking which the theorists of the Siddhānta had in mind was not the cognition of a fact but a kind of mental work which produces a result through effort. It is seen as imagination with the power to cross from the imaginary (*kālpanikam*) to the real (*satyam*), so transcending the dichotomy between these domains which marks the world on which ritual works. . . . It is certainly the case that the effect, namely Śivaness, is made present in the mind of the ritual agent; but this is not because his ritual has become cognition of a fact (*siddham*)—in this instance, recognition of self—but rather because it is the nature of Tantric ritual to realize in this way what is desired and not yet existent (*sādhyam*).

These observations are not only valid for the MaSaṃ, but describe the very core of the philosophy, or rather the basic underlying theory, of the MaSaṃ.[73] All sections of the MaSaṃ are crowded with instructions on how to create imaginary (*kālpanika*) mental objects and with descriptions of what these mental images, or more precisely the yogin's intense empathic involvement with these images, will result in the real world (*satya*). To put it bluntly: the MaSaṃ, and much of all tantric writing, claim that one can control the real world by intense empathic imagination.

I have attempted to translate most of the occurrences of bhāva in my translation of the critical edition of the MaSaṃ as "empathic imagination." "Empathic mental creation"might be an even closer rendering of *bhāva*, but is too clumsy. The term *mental creation* has been used by Brunner (1994, 442) with reference to dhyāna in Saiddhāntika ritual and yoga. Bhāva is obviously a mental process and the word itself implies the "appearance" or "coming into existence" of something (from √*bhū*; see also the causative form *bhāvayati*: "causes to become" or "creates"). I use the extra qualifier *empathic* to lay stress on the notion that it is not only a "mechanical" mental reproduction of a visual image, but an intense, emotional and empathic "living out" of a dream-like goal by completely losing one's self in the image.[74] I have decided to render *bhāva* by the expression "empathic imagination" and not simply as "visualization" or "meditation" because I suspect that bhāva is preferred in the MaSaṃ to dhyāna (although *dhyāna*, *dhyāyet* etc. also abound) for its extremely wide range of meanings. One of the basic meanings of bhāva is "being, becoming," as already noted above. Another is "emotion, sentiment" or even "passion, love." Bhāva conveys also the meaning "true condition or state, truth." I think that all these rather different senses of the word are condensed in the yogic key term of bhāva. It is a creation of something in the mind by the yogin, toward which he should also create a feeling, an empathic attitude—perhaps, passionate devotion—which will result in the ultimate condition, the desired state of mind: the union with the object, with the deity, with Śiva.

The concept underlying the term *bhāva* is not an invention of the MaSaṃ, but this text is unique in being rather explicit about its technique and aims. After the description of an intricate way of visualization, the MaSaṃ claims:

> bhāvena saha śuddhaś cet sarvaṃ yogam avāpnuyāt ||2.64||
> bhāvahīnasya naivāsti siddhir varṣāyutair api |
> udakumbhasahasreṇa mṛdāḍhakaśatena vā ||2.65||
> api varṣasahasreṇa bhāvaduṣṭo na śudhyati |
> tasmād etāni deveśi bhāvapūtaḥ samācaret |

If bhāva is to be translated as "empathic imagination," as suggested above, a possible translation of the passage reads as follows:

> 2.64cd If he is purified by empathic imagination (*bhāva*), he will obtain complete Yoga.
>
> 2.65ab He who lacks [the capacity for] empathic imagination (*bhāvahīna*) will not have any Power (*siddhi*), not even in tens of thousands of years. Not even by thousands of jars of water, not by hundreds of pounds of mud,
>
> 2.66 not in thousands of years can he whose empathic imagination is defective (*bhāvaduṣta*) be purified. Therefore, O Deveśī, [the yogin should] perform these [practices that follow only when] he has been purified by empathic imagination (*bhāvapūta*).

Of course, it is difficult to be absolutely sure what exactly *bhāvahīna*, *bhāvaduṣṭa* and *bhāvapūta* convey, but if I understand the implications of the passage clearly, the term *bhāva* signifies both the concepts of "emotion, empathy" and "mental creation/imagination": the precise performance of the ritual with all the mantras and visualizations is ineffective without the additional imagination/mental creation (*bhāva* [*nā*]) of "emotion, empathy" (bhāva). Or to put it in a different way, bhāva includes three elements: first, the mental creation, in general, by effort of something which is not normally present in the mind; second, more specifically, the vivid visualization of a predefined object; and third, an empathic, emotional attitude toward the created mental object or a total self-identification with it.

That bhāva basically means "imagination" or "visualization" is evident from the following verses of the paṭala on Inner Worship (*antararcana*), i.e., rites performed mentally:

> pūjayed gandhapuṣpādyair yogī bhāvamayaiḥ śubhaiḥ |
> ṣaḍādhāreṣu vidhivad dvādaśānte viśeṣataḥ ||8.3||
>
> 8.3: the yogin should worship [Śiva] with auspicious (śubha) imaginary (bhāvamaya) scents, flowers and so on in the six Abodes (ādhāra) following the rules [and] especially in the Dvādaśānta.

MaSaṃ 8.30–69 abound in further occurences of bhāva (*avibhedena bhāvena, bhāvapuṣpaiḥ, bhāvasudhayā, naivedyair bhāvasādhitaiḥ, bhāvajvalitapāvake, bhāvacaruṇā, saparyaiṣā bhāvasādhanī, bhāvapuṣpāmṛtādibhiḥ, havibhir bhāvasādhibhiḥ, bhāvasiddhena balinā, bhāvākhyacaruṇā, bhāvagamyam, bhāvamātreṇa, bhāvasādhanaiḥ, bhāvakusumaiḥ*), which befits a chapter devoted to inner—i.e., imaginary,—rituals. Sometimes, bhāva is to be performed on a real visual object such as a maṇḍala to imagine parts of it that are difficult to actually draw (see 10.29–30). On the other hand, there are some occurences of bhāva that cannot be translated as "empathic imagination" (1.26a, 104c; 11.18, 22; 55.33, [38]), which thus perhaps belong to a different layer of the text.

Having said all this, bhāva is sometimes perhaps to be simply taken as a synonym of *dhyāna*. This is what the commentary *Tattvapradīpikā* ad *Siddhāntaśikhāmaṇi* 16.21 (a Vīraśaiva text from Maharashtra) suggests (note its similarity to MaSaṃ 2.64cd–65ab quoted above):

> bhāvaśuddhena manasā pūjayet parameṣṭhinam |
> bhāvahīnā<ṃ> na gṛhṇāti pūjā<ṃ> sumahatīm api ||
> [comm.:] bhāvaśuddhena dhyānaśuddhenety arthaḥ |
>
> He should worship Śiva with his mind purified by bhāva. If [the worship] lacks bhāva, [Śiva will] not accept the worship even if it is grandiose.

[comm.:] "purified by bhāva:" it means "purified by visualization/meditation (dhyāna)."

I am not fully convinced that this simplification of the terminus technicus bhāva is fruitful at all, but it is undeniable that the meanings of bhāva and dhyāna are quite close and sometimes overlap.

The chief aim of the yogic teaching of the MaSaṃ, as I have noted above, is to enable the yogin, through rigorous practice of bhāva/dhyāna, to create mentally the vision of a private reality whenever he pleases, one that is absolutely independent of the pains of everyday life and can give him absolute mental freedom. MaSaṃ 7.81 is a startlingly explicit assertion on this:

samyak samādhau saṃsiddhe yogī yogena cakṣuṣā |
yad yat smarati vai rūpaṃ tat tat paśyati niścitam ||7.81||

7.81 When Samādhi is properly mastered, the yogin will see exactly (niścitam) that vision (rūpa) with his yogic-eyes (yogena cakṣuṣā) which he recalls (smarati).[75]

That is, when the yogin has mastered the technique of visualization (dhyāna), or "empathic imagination" (bhāva), for which a prerequisite is evidently the everyday practice of dehaśuddhi, āsanas, and the other aṅgas (prāṇāyāma, pratyāhāra, dhāraṇā), he can remember (*smarati*) a vision, and it will appear before his mental eyes.

One fundamental, if slightly moralizing, question about this technique of visualizing/creating a different kind of reality is: is it a kind of escapism in the extreme, which tries to ignore everyday reality and requires one to find refuge in an artificially created dream world? Or is it a refined and ingenious mental technique that requires extreme efforts and bestows complete control over one's mental activities? Another basic question would be: is it possible at all? Or is it just an ideal for the yogin to pursue but never to reach? The present article of course cannot answer any of these questions.

CONCLUSIONS

Primarily, the evidence of the MaSaṃ confirms that the Kubjikā tradition had some close links with the early haṭha yoga of the Nāthas, and was probably a major influence on the formation of haṭha-yogic notions.[76]

In general, the main yoga teaching of the MaSaṃ (*paṭalas* 2–7) is more tantric than haṭha yogic, although early haṭha-yogic teachings also appear in it. It is a

Pātañjalised and "de-Śāktaized" form of tantric yoga that has some connection with the Kubjikā/Śāmbhava tradition. This central yogic teaching is probably the earliest layer of yogic passages in the MaSaṃ and is clearly different from the probably later *ṣaḍādhāra* yoga of *paṭala*s 8–13, because *paṭala*s 2–7 do not mention the seven Yoginīs that feature in the frame story and in *paṭala*s 8–13. *Paṭala*s 2–7 are perhaps an originally Saiddhāntika teaching in which the visualization of a goddess resembling Kubjikā was later inserted (7.19–25) to match the strong Kubjikā orientation of other important chapters of the text. MaSaṃ 2–7 are the result of an effort to provide a Pātañjala core yoga teaching for a yogic Yoginī cult originating in the Paścimāmnāya, or more specifically, its Śāmbhava variant.

This Śāmbhava orientation can be mainly observed in the cult of Yoginīs (*paṭala*s 8–13) in which the yogāṅgas of *paṭala*s 2–7 are embedded and which is in the center of the tantric cult of the MaSaṃ. This cult of Yoginīs overshadows the importance of other deities of the tradition, emphasising the general yogic orientation of the text.

It is of course dangerous to draw general conclusions on the evidence of a single text. Nevertheless, I do not think that the MaSaṃ is an exceptional text and is the product of a totally isolated tradition and thus has nothing to say about the history of yoga in a broad sense. Instead, I suppose that the character of the MaSaṃ could be typical of Śaiva tantric yoga texts around the thirteenth century, when the sectarian bonds of Śaiva tantric yoga began to loosen to give way to pan-Indian and more general teachings.

I see the evidence of the cult of the MaSaṃ as an important indication of a phase in the history of yoga when yogic teachings tried to become detached, perhaps not for the first time, from the mainstream religion, in this case tantric Śaivism, by eliminating sectarian boundaries through the concealment of sectarian marks such as easily decodable deity names, mantras, and iconography and to prepare for a formative period of a pan-Indian yoga, which can again become an alternative for the official/conservative religion. This seems to be the process that has eventually produced the well-known cakra-centered haṭha-yogic traditions devoid of any definite claim to belong to any early tantric cult. The MaSaṃ is then both a link between the early Hindu Śaiva tantric traditions (five to tenth centuries) and the full-fledged haṭha-yogic traditions (fifteenth century onwards), as well as an attempt to revitalize the yoga tradition.

Notes

INTRODUCTION

1. A very good example of this was the mahants of Jakhbar, in fifteenth century Punjab. More than once, the Naths received donations by even Muslim rulers, one of which were Akbar, Jahangir, Shah Jahan, and even Aurangzeb. See Goswamy and Grewal 1967, 16, 19, 21 and passim.
2. Daniel Gold has studied this relationship in detail. See Gold 1992 and Gold 1995.

CHAPTER 1. THE NATHS IN HINDI LITERATURE

1. The essay, "Traditions of Non-caste Hinduism: The Kabir Panth," was first published in 1987.
2. See the very first essay in *Yog-pravāh*, "Swami Raghwanand aur Siddhant Panchmatra" (1–22)
3. See *The Communal Problem: Report of the Kanpur Riots Enquiry Committee* 2006, 88.

CHAPTER 2. RELIGIOUS IDENTITY IN GORAKHNATH AND KABIR

1. Lorenzen 2006, 1–36; and Lorenzen 2007. Since 1999, much has been published on this topic by various scholars. See especially Llewellyn 2005;

Pennington 2005; and Oddie 2006.

2. These two terms reappear in *Gorakh-bānī* pad 16.5. Barthwal has an explanatory note, but it is not clear on what his explanation is based.
3. Transcriptions of most Kabir songs from all the early Western collections and manuscripts (but not from the *Kabīr-bījak*) are found in Kabir 2000, edited by Callewaert. Complete editions of the collections by Rajjab (1990) and Gopaldas (1993) have also been published. The *Kabīr-bījak* text is available in Callewaert 1991. For translations of Kabir's texts from the various early collections, see Kabir 1977; Kabir 1983; Kabir 1991; Kabir 1993; and also Hawley 2005, 279–304 (the Fatehpur manuscript songs). For the *Kabīr-granthāvalī* songs, not all of which have been translated, the modern-Hindi commentary by Mataprasad Gupta is useful (Kabir 1969).
4. *Kabīr-bījak, ram.* 39 (Callewaert 1991); *Kabīr-granthāvalī, ram. aṣṭapadī* 3 (Kabir 1969). The readings and interpretation of several key words of this song are somewhat problematic. For the most part, I have followed the text found in the *Kabīr-bījak.* The repeated word *karamata* or *karmata* has been taken as equivalent to *karma te* (modern *karma se*). Some published texts of the *Kabīr-bījak* (and presumably the manuscripts on which they are based) do give the reading *karamate.* Other English translations of this *pad* are found in Kabir 1977 and Kabir 1998.
5. *Kabīr-bījak, pad* 75; *Kabīr-granthāvalī, pad* 57. See Kabir 2000, no. 77.
6. This song is Callewaert's no. 423 (Kabir 2000). The number in the Sabha edition of the *Kabīr-granthāvalī* is 338 (Kabir 1969, 347). See Pashaura Singh's (2003, 31–33) important discussion of Arjan's song and its relation to this song by Kabir. The fact that Kabir's song is only found in the *Kabīr-granthāvalī* and Gopaldas's *Sarvāṅgī* suggests that it could conceivably have been composed by a follower of Kabir sometime *after* Guru Arjan. Against this idea, Arjan does directly quote other texts by Kabir elsewhere in the *Ādi Granth.*
7. Guru Arjan's song is *Ādi Granth, bhairau* 3 (1996, p. 1136). My interpretation of the last verse differs slightly from that offered by Pashaura Singh (2003, 32). The song may also allude indirectly to at least another song by Kabir. This other song appears in most early Kabir collections including the *Ādi Granth* (1996, 1349), the *Kabīr-granthāvalī* (*pad* 259) and the *Kabīr-bījak* (*pad* 97). The song is no. 280 in Callewaert's collection (Kabir 2000).
8. *Kabīr-granthāvalī, ram.* 5.4. Apparently this ramaini has not been previously translated into English, nor is it found in the *Kabīr-bījak* or other collections.
9. *Kabīr-granthāvalī, ram.* 5. 5. A version of this ramaini is also found in the *Kabīr-bījak* (*ram.* 35). The readings of both versions present some conundrums. The *Kabīr-bījak* version is translated in Kabir 1977 and Kabir 1998.

10. Callewaert and Op de Beeck 1991. Callewaert has also produced a word index to the Sikh *Ādi Granth* (1996), but since there is considerable overlap between the Kabir songs in the *Ādi Granth* and the *Kabīr-granthāvalī,* I have not bothered to include the few unique occurrences of these words in the former text.
11. Callewaert and Op de Beeck 1991, vol. 1, 381. See also the fine translation of Hess and Singh (Kabir 1983, 87–88).
12. The phrase that demonstrates the relation is, in the *Kabīr-bījak,* the initial phrase *dar kī bāt kaho daravesā,* and, in the *Gorakh-bānī,* the initial phrase *daraves soi jo dar kī jāṇaiṃ.* These are the only occurrences of the word *daraves* in either text.
13. Callewaert and Op de Beeck 1991. The specific word *Saiva* does not occur in these, but Shiva (also Mahes) is often mentioned. Kabir often uses various names of Vishnu, especially Ram, but in most cases Kabir appears to use these names to refer to the high nirgun God, not to the sagun Vishnu and his avatars.
14. For the Hindi text, see Lorenzen 1991, 129.
15. The version translated here is that of the *Kabīr-granthāvalī* (Kabir 1969, 277). See Kabir 2000: no. 251. The *Adi-granth* song is *asa* 20 481). Its reading is slightly different. There is another translation of the song by Vaudeville (Kabir 1993, 225).
16. See my discussion on the history of tantric religion in Lorenzen 2006, 64–101.
17. Svatmarama 1975: verse 4. 3–4. The translation is taken from this text.
18. *Ādi Granth* (1996, 856). Other versions of this song are found in most other early Western collections including the *Kabīr-granthāvalī.* See Kabir 2000: no. 420. Most of the other versions of the song add criticisms of the "Hindus" and the "Musalmans" to those of the yogis.
19. Kabir 2000, no. 390. The stanza is found with only minor variants in virtually all early Western collections and manuscripts including the *Kabīr-granthāvalī,* the *Ādi Granth,* and Gopaldas's *Sarvāṅgī.*
20. Kabir 2000, no. 420.
21. Lorenzen 1991, 107, 230. For a translation of the full passage, see Lorenzen 2006, 29.
22. On this subject see Vaudeville (1974:, 41–44); Lorenzen (1991, 18–19, 48–54); and Singh (2003, 81–115). On Kamal, see Kamal 1994.
23. *Ādi Granth,* (1996, 524). See Kabir 2000, no. 27. The song is found in most collections of the Western tradition, but only the *Ādi Granth* version includes the first verse.
24. Gorakhanath (1960), *pad* no. 38.
25. Pers. comm. I thank Aditya Behl for all the time and effort he spent on answering my queries about his suggested identification of the Yekamkaris as Sufis.

26. Gorakhanath (1960, 38), sabadi 110.
27. Gorakhanath (1960, 101), *pad* 13, verse 2.
28. *Kabīr-granthāvalī* (1969, 334), *kedarau* 18. See Kabir 2000, no. 360. Versions of this song are found in most early Western collection including the *Ādi Granth* and Gopaldas's *Sarvāṅgī.* For another translation, see Kabir (1993, 233–34). This song, like Gorakh's, contains several linguistic and historical puzzles. For example, the word *dhuṃdha,* here translated as "dark dust," is written as *dhaṃdha* in most other early collections. If *dhaṃdha* is taken as equivalent to modern Hindi *dhaṃdhā*—meaning "trade," "task," or "activity"—this would yield "a fog of tasks," a quite appropriate idea in this context.
29. The respective original phrases are as follows. Gorakh says: *paṃca tatta kī kāyā vinasī rāṣi na sakyā koī / kāla davana jaba gyāṃna prakāsyā.* Kabir says: *je nara joga jugati kari jāṃnaiṃ, khojaiṃ āpa sarīrā / tinakūṃ mukati kā saṃsā nāṃhīṃ.* In the two oldest *Kabīr-granthāvalī* manuscripts the word *joga* does not appear. Callewaert's manuscript "J" of 1681 A. D. reads: *je jana joti jugati sauṃ jāṃnaiṃ / ṣojai āpa sarīrā.* His manuscript S of 1614 has a similar reading. It can be translated: "The devotees who [have] light [as their] means, they know, they search within their own bodies." The *Ādi Granth* version has yet another reading: *rāma nāma binu sabhai bigūte, dekhahu nirakhi sarīrā* ("Without Ram's Name everyone is destroyed. Examine the body and look [within]").
30. Kabir 2000, no. 275. The song is found in the *Kabīr-granthāvalī,* the *Ādi Granth,* Rajjab, and Gopaladas. The *Ādi Granth* version (1996, 476–77) is somewhat different from the others.
31. As cited in Sen 2006, 36.

CHAPTER 3. DRUMS IN GWALIOR

1. David Gordon White (2001, 141–42) gives a concise description of this dual socioreligious role of the Nath.
2. On synthetic characteristics of Maharashtrian religion, see Maxine Berntsen and Eleanor Zelliot 1988, xviii–xix.
3. D. D Kosambi (1975, 46) mentions a March Urs in Navalgund, Dharwar "honouring the Peer Raje Bakshar with an attendance of 100,000." Now in Karnataka state, Navalgund is close to the Maharashtra border.
4. Śrīkānt Gopālnath Purandare, "Maṭh kā Itihās: Ek Vihangāvalokan (the History of the Math: A Bird's-Eye View)." In Krsna Murari Misra et al, eds. 1980. *Smārikā: Param Pūjya Śraddheya Vāsudevnāth Ḍholī Buva Mahārāj Pīṭhārohaṇ Rajat-Mahotsav.* Gwalior, India: Dholi Buwa Math.

Because the article is so short, I haven't tried to reference individual citations.

5. The oldest of Kashi Nath's sons reigned for two-and-half years and the middle one had already died; Gangadhar Nath reigned for thirty years.
6. Pers. comm.
7. Santosh Purandare speaks of this style as being in the sage Narada's performance tradition, which includes the three divisions of music—singing, playing instruments, and dance—and is performed standing up. It contrasts with a parallel tradition attributed to the sage Vyasa, in which storytelling greatly predominates (Pers. comm.).
8. On the Maharashtrian sant tradition, see Charlotte Vaudeville 1974, 102–104; and Catherine Kiehnle 1997, 4–7.
9. Pers. comm.
10. Pers. comm.
11. Pers. comm. (Sandeep Sharma).
12. Pers. comm. (Sandeep Sharma).
13. Many thanks to Aditya Behl for his suggestions about the origin of the name *Raja Bakshar* and some further implications of the Sufi musical traditions associated with the shrine (pers. comm.).
14. For an extended document depicting Sufis as kingmakers, see Digby 2001.
15. Thanks to Richard Wolf of Harvard University for helping me distinguish the music at Raja Bakshar from that normally played in conventional Sufi contexts and other insights into the musical traditions of South Asian Islam.
16. Pers. comm. (Richard Wolf).

CHAPTER 4. INFLUENCE OF THE NATHS ON BHIMA BHOI AND MAHIMA DHARMA

1. *Utkala Deepika*, June 1, 1867, part 2, no. 22.
2. The new faith drew the attention of the colonial government on account of the dramatic effort of a few of its lay followers on March 1, 1881, to enter the temple of Puri and drag out and burn the images of the Jagannath trinity. Following the incident, detailed enquiries were ordered into the beliefs and practices of the faith by the Commissioner of the Orissa Division. The *tehsildars* (revenue collectors) of Angul and Banki, the Manager of Dhenkanal and the Superintendent of Sambalpur all submitted reports to the Commissioner who incorporated them in his report to the Government of Bengal. The accounts of the local officers were filed in the Records of the Board of Revenue, while the

report of the Commissioner was published under the title "On the origin and growth of the sect of Hindu dissenters who profess to be the followers of Alekh" in the *Proceedings of the Asiatic Society of Bengal 1882.*

3. Report of the Commissioner of the Orissa Division, Board of Revenue document no. 445/1, Orissa State Archives, Bhubaneswar.
4. Cf. especially chapters 3 and 5; see also Muñoz's essay in this volume.
5. I thank David Lorenzen for providing me with this very valuable reference.
6. Once again, I thank David Lorenzen for this reference.
7. Reports of the *tehsildars* of Angul and Banki, Board of Revenue Documents nos. 443, 441/1, Orissa State Archives, Bhubaneswar. These reports also mention 1866 as the year of its construction.
8. Pers. comm. (Kasinath Baba).
9. Pers. comm. (Bhagaban Das and others).
10. Pers. comm. (Biswanath Baba).
11. The five mystics were: Balaram Das, Jagannth Das, Achyuta(nanda) Das, Ananta Das, and Yasobanta Das.
12. For a detailed discussion see Banerjee-Dube, "Taming Traditions: Legalities and Histories in Twentieth-Century Oriss,a" in Gautam Bhadra et al 1999: 98–125; see also Banerjee-Dube 2007, chapter 3.
13. For a detailed and critical discussion of Bhima Bhoi's works and ideas see Banerjee-Dube 2007, chapter 3.
14. It is interesting that in his chapter in this volume, White rejects the idea of the body as the microcosm or miniature of the universe, arguing instead that the universe is macranthropic, that is, it has a human form. The body represents the entire universe within it. See "On the Magnitude of the Yogic Body" in this book.
15. Ramesh Samantarai (1976) quotes a phrase current in Western Orissa, which asks a blind man to compose Dalakhai and Rasarakheli for the people to sing, to argue that this blind man is none other than Bhima Bhoi.
16. See Artaballabh Mahanti, foreword to Bhima Bhoi's *Stuti* (Bhoi 1925).
17. *Namati amulya ratana*
Na lage papa dosamana
Sehi namaku kara dhyana
Misai e mana paban
Chada janaku eka mele
Sthapibu e hrudaya kamale. (*Nirveda sadhana,* chapter 2).
18. The theory of creation is elaborated in *Nirveda sadhana,* chapters 5 to 15.
19. It has been argued that Bhima Bhoi's division of the body into cakras was different from the yogic division. The cakras enumerated by the poet were greater

in number than the six—*sada cakra*—used in yoga. The names he gave to them were also different. See Balakrushna Misra. 1981, Brahma nirupana gitare brahmanka sthiti bichara. *Saptarshi* (Sambalpur University Journal) 78: 61–66. On the other hand, Daitari Baba, a *sanyasi* of the Kaupindhari *samaj*, who prepared a schematic pictorial division of the different parts of the body as discussed in Bhima Bhoi, showed that they corresponded with yogic divisions. Daitari Baba gave me a copy of this pictorial division when I met him in 1990.

20. Bhima Bhoi, *Adi Anta Gita*, 13, cited in Bäumer 2008, 163.
21. For a detailed discussion see Johannes Beltz and Kedar Mishra, Ascetic, Layman or Rebellious Guru? Bhima Bhoi and his Female Consorts, in Banerjee-Dube and Beltz 2008, 131–58.

CHAPTER 5. ON THE MAGNITUDE OF THE YOGIC BODY

1. Portions of this paper have appeared in my book *Sinister Yogis* (2009), and are reproduced here with the permission of the University of Chicago Press.
2. Editions of the SSP are listed in Michaël's remarkable French translation (Gorakhnath 2007, 66). The manuscripts of the SSP are catalogued in Gharote and Bedekar 1989, 384–88.
3. Bouy (1994, 19) has established this terminus ante quem on the basis of the fact that the SSP is not cited in any work prior to the seventeenth-century *Gorakṣasiddhāntasaṃgraha* (GSS), which cites it abundantly.
4. Other sources that focus on such identifications include the *Yoga Darśana Upaniṣad* (YDU), translated in Varenne 1976, 200-–222.
5. For different editions, see Gorakhnath 1946 in the bibliography. The *bānīs* are written in a blend of Old Rajasthani (Diṅgal), Old Punjabi, Khaḍī Bolī, and Apabhraṃśa.
6. Edition in Old Bengali, Sanskrit, Tibetan, with an English translation in Kværne, 1986.
7. GB, *pad* 6.1–5, translated in White 1996, 301–302.
8. GB, *pad* 14.1–5.
9. GB, *pad* 26.1–5.
10. GB, *pad* 27.1–6.
11. GB, *pad* 28.1–4.
12. GB, *pad* 29.1–5.
13. GB, *pad* 40.1–4.
14. GB, *pad* 41.1–4.
15. GB, *pad* 42.1–4.

16. GB, *pad* 47.18, discussed in White 1996, 242–43.
17. Editions include Bhambhulnath Yogi, n.d.; and Agravat, n.d.
18. My translation is based on Mallik's 1954 edition.
19. *Kūrma*, the second of Viṣṇu's ten incarnations, who upholds Mount Mandara in the churning of the Ocean of Milk, and the worlds of the cosmic egg.
20. Here, the declension shifts from singular to dual.
21. As an aggregate, the Rudra deities are nearly always eleven in number. However, in the 400–600 CE *Niḥśvāsatattvasaṃhitā* (NTS), an early text of the Śaiva *atimārga*, a group of eight Rudras are identified with eight lower worlds (but not correlated with the Puranic underworlds). This group of eight recurs in other early Śaiva sources; cf. Sanderson 2006, 170–75.
22. *Kālāgnirudra*. For a discussion, see White 1996: 232–33.
23. *Jano loka* in the text.
24. The terminology here is based on plant anatomy: the four worlds are literally identified with the sprout (*aṅkura*), hollow (*kuhara*), stem (*nāla*), and flower (*kamala*).
25. I have emended the reading *śṛṅgāre* to *śṛṅge*.
26. In fact, only nineteen regions have been enumerated, even if one takes the triple world of Indra and the four-fold world of Brahmā to constitute a total of seven separate worlds.
27. Here, a probable reference is to the *kalā*s of moon, sun, and fire, which are discussed in SSP 1.64–66. These do not total sixty-four, however, which leaves open the likelihood that the author was also thinking of the *kalā*s in the sense of the sixty-four practical arts.
28. This list is at variance with the "standard" list of seven island-continents, as found in the *Harivaṃśa* and the Purāṇas, which are, in order, *jambudvīpa*, *plakṣadvīpa*, *śālmalīdvīpa*, *kuśadvīpa*, *krauñcadvīpa*, *śākadvīpa*, and *puṣkaradvīpa*.
29. These are generally referred to as *varṣa*s in the Purāṇas. Apart from Bhārata, the names given here are at variance with those found in the Purāṇas.
30. These are six in number: cold, heat, hunger, thirst, greediness, illusion: Monier-Williams 1984: 222, s.v. *ūrmi*.
31. The text does not specify a particular portion of the body for the location of these pores, and so the entire body appears to be intended. Sites sacred to the tantric goddesses, the *pīṭha*s are scattered across the entire Indian subcontinent, which the Kubjikā Tantras explicitly identify with the entire body of the goddess herself; cf. Dyczkowski 2004, 93—174.
32. Since no *muni*s have been previously evoked in this chapter, the use of the term *other* here is ambiguous.

33. These are śaktis—feminine deities or deified feminine energies—which are lower hypostases of the transcendent Śakti mentioned in verse 5.
34. Varenne 1976, 30–40; Wayman 1982, 172–90; Banerjea 1983, 30, 137; White 1996, 218–62.
35. On-line *Oxford English Dictionary* (http://dictionary.oed.com); cf. *macrocosm* and *microcosmos*.
36. CS 4.4.13 (in Acharya 1992, 318).
37. *Padārthadharmasaṃgraha* (PDhS) 99 (in Jha 1997: 464–650); Cakrapāṇidatta *ad* CS 4.2.35 (in Acharya 1992, 305), with reference to the insertion of the soul into an embryo in a woman's womb.
38. PAS 27. Bhartṛprapañca's work is lost, but is quoted by three commentators, including Śaṅkara. On these sources, see Buoy 2000, 27.
39. *piṇḍaṃ śarīramityuktam* (*Mālinīvijayottara Tantram* 1992).
40. (Abhinavagupta 1987). For a discussion of Abhinavagupta's and the MVUT's analyses of this term, see Vasudeva 2000, 157–62.
41. *Garbholi* is a contraction of *garbhālaya*.
42. Ed. Van Buitenen 1981.
43. Ed. Sukthankar 1933–1960.
44. For example, Vedavyāsa's commentary on YS 1.2 (in Aranya 1981, 6).
45. Monier-Williams 1984, 794 (s.v. "mah").
46. BṛU 1.4.10 (in Limaye and Badekar 1958, 187).
47. MPĀg, *caryāpada* 9.13, translated in Sanderson 2006, 205.
48. This term is also common in such Kashmiri Śākta-Śaiva sources as the 600–1000 CE *Svacchanda Tantra* (SvT 4.297–316, 442, etc.).

CHAPTER 6. AWAKENING GENEROSITY IN NATH TALES FROM RAJASTHAN

1. My recording of Nath tales in 2007 was enabled by generous funding from the William P. Tolley Distinguished Teaching Professorship in the Humanities and the Moynihan Institute of Global Affairs, both at Syracuse University. I am deeply indebted to Shambhu Natisar Nath and his extended family, and (as always) to Bhoju Ram Gujar.
2. I shall use *Nath* and *Jogi* interchangeably in this chapter. While there are nuances to each term that may affect its deployment in particular contexts, in the community where my research is based, both designations are common. Both are used as caste name, surname, and to designate a renouncer. I capitalize both terms when they are names, but employ lower case when they are

generic nouns. From time to time, when my frame of reference goes beyond Rajasthani colloquial contexts, I use the standard term *yogi* as well.

3. According to the *Rajasthani Sabad Kos* (Lalas 1962–1978; hereafter *RSK*, translations mine), *alakh* means "what cannot be equal to any sign; whose attributes cannot be seen; invisible; whose qualities cannot be told; God." The *RSK* also says that *dashnami sanyasis* use this word when begging. *Jagarno* means "to wake up, to bring to consciousness."
4. A fourth allegorical layer in one of the tales—expressed as the image of clay pots that became pure gold—hints at spiritual achievement as well as alchemical transformations; see White 1996 for hints of alchemy in Nath oral traditions.
5. My own work has focused largely on Nath oral traditions including translations and interpretations of the epic tales of King Bharthari and King Gopi Chand as performed by the bard Madhu Natisar Nath in Ghatiyali (A. Gold 1992) and the same bard's rendition of "Lord Shiva's Wedding Song" (A. Gold 2002). Daniel Gold (1996, 1999) has looked at various aspects of Nath identity, practice, and politics in Rajasthan.
6. Naths are distinguished from most other Hindu castes because they bury rather than cremate their dead, another way of marking their identity as linked with that of world renouncers.
7. This is the *bisnami* group of which little is known; but see Khan 1997, 131–35, 155–57.
8. For diverse approaches to Nath practices and oral traditions in other regions of South Asia, see Bouillier 1986; Champion 1994b; Henry 1991.
9. See D. Gold 1999 for more about Banna Nath.
10. Some of the differences apparent in these four performances might provide substance for a fascinating investigation of local variations in a regional oral tradition, of intertextuality within a folklore community, and of the merging and splitting of folkloric motifs. I will not attempt any of this here.
11. Banna Nath, one of the four tellers, actually located the events of the two tales in the former Kingdom of Sawar where he lives. But he nonetheless recited the couplet common to all versions that mentions Alwar and Tijara.
12. Madhu Nath normally sang for ten to fifteen minutes, accompanying himself on the sarangi (a simple stringed instrument played with a bow). Then he paused, rested, cleared his throat, and retold all he had just sung in animated prose. Usually, the narrative would be advanced only in the sung segment; the spoken segment, called "explanation" (*arthav*), retells what was just sung, and elaborates colloquially. I have found it convenient for my purposes to translate *arthav* which is linguistically more accessible and performatively more interest-

ing in that it is more permeable to any given storyteller's innovations and interpretations.

13. *Het* is glossed in the *RSK* with *prem*, *mamta* and other common Hindi terms for "love."
14. Rajasthani religion displays a consistent ambivalence toward the desire for fruits of any ritual or meritorious behaviors; see Gold 1988.
15. See A. Gold 1992, 283–96, 323–26 for the ways that love for sons is explicitly opposed to love for the guru and spiritual awakening in Nath epic traditions.
16. A wildlife sanctuary in Alwar district, part of Project Tiger.
17. This is a conventional number for the nonhuman births through which the soul must wander; the phrase *lakh caurasi yoni* occurs frequently in Nath hymns but is equally common to many non-Nath Hindu religious texts.

CHAPTER 7. MATSYENDRA'S "GOLDEN LEGEND"

1. There is a long list of lately edited tales of yogis, especially in Hindi. The GorakhnāthTemple in Gorakhpur periodically launches his own compilations of these legends under the titles *Gorakh-carit* (GorC 1) and *Gorakhnāth caritra* (GorC 2). Other examples are Harihara's *Bhartṛhari-nirviveda* in Sanskrit (circa fifteenth century), and the more contemporary *Bharthari Piṅgalā* by Dehlavi and *Gopichand* by Balakram Yogishvar (cf. A. Gold 1992, 60–67). Gold's own renderings of Madhunath's telling of yogi tales in Rajasthan have become indispensable now. Her chapter in this book expands her insights in further narrative motifs. Catherine Champion (1989, 1994a, 1994b) and Edward Henry (1991) have also paid attention to folk songs on and by yogis in North India.
2. My calling it a "direct" mood does not imply that this poetry is in the least easier than its Sanskrit counterpart. It is precisely through the topic and the mood of these poems that interesting and unique aesthetic complexities are achieved. On the other hand, Nāth Sanskrit is far from highly stylized.
3. One interesting European parallel is Ramon Llull (1232–1315) who roughly around the same time composed in Spain philosophical and theological works in verse so as to make it easier for disciples to learn them by heart, e.g., *Los cien nombres de Dios* (Hundred Names of God) and *Medicina de pecado* (Medicine of Sin).
4. See Dyczkowski 1989; Dyczkowski 2004; Sanderson 1988; Sanderson 2002; Sanderson 2006, and Csaba Kiss' chapter on this volume for a further discussion on the association of these schools.
5. Religions are communities of persons who follow, or claim to follow, common

systems of beliefs and practices. . . . [T]aken together [these systems] define the group's identity, its membership and its ideology" (Lorenzen 1995, 2).

6. See also *Gogā Mahāpurāṇ* (GogPur), 67–74.
7. See Ondračka's chapter here for a detailed discussion of Bengali versions of this legend. Even though his version presents unique problems (technical terms such as the "four moons"), in broad outline, it deals with the same key issues I discuss. In both cases, Gorakh seems to allude to specific yogic methods to prevent decay and loss of virility.
8. I owe this observation to David White (pers. comm.). I would also like to thank him for his critical remarks concerning this essay.
9. I have mainly derived this version of the tale from the *Gorakh carit*, the *Gorakhnāth caritra*, and the *Gogā Mahāpurāṇ* (see bibliography). The first two in particular can be easily found at the Gorakhpur Mandir and its surroundings, and are thus available to both residents and outsiders of the temple.
10. *kulācārāratāḥ santi guravo bahavo mune / kulācāravihīnastu gurureko hi durlabhaḥ //* (AmY 2.16). This statement seems to mirror the *Kulārṇava-tantra*'s (KulT) advocacy for a Kaula guru, especially at KulT *ullāsa* 13.99 and 13.104–110. See also Padoux 2000, 50.
11. . . . *sacet ho gayā hūṃ* (GorC 2: 45). For another example of polysemic understandings of "waking up," see Ann Gold's chapter in this volume.
12. It is noteworthy that the number and consequently the names of Matsyendra's children vary immensely. In the GorC 2 and the GogPur, the one child is called Mīnānātha (usually a variant of Matsyendra's own name); in Madhunath's rendering (Gold 1992, 284–96), there are two children, called Nīm and Pāras, suggestively connected to Jainism. In another Bengali version (see Ondračka below), the child is called Bindunāth, and his name (*bindu*, "drop, semen") may be symbolical. In all cases, Gorakh takes violently their lives and later resuscitates them to Matsyendra's pleadings.
13. See also GhS 5.79–80, where the intense practice of breathing and retention of breath is said to produce in the adept different sounds such as crickets, a flute, a thunder, and different kinds of drums.
14. See for example KJN 14.57: *aṇimā laghimā devi ūrddhvaretaḥ pravarttanam / ūrddhvaretā bhaved yogī na yogī karata priye //*.
15. I have corrected Barthwal's reading of *torai* as *tīrai*, "on/by the shore" (cf. Barthwal 1994, 137).
16. *tatra vastudvayaṃ vakṣye durlabhaṃ yasya kasyacit / kṣīraṃ caikaṃ dvitīyaṃ nārī ca vaśavartinī //* (HYP 3.84).
17. *mehanena śanaiḥ samyagūrdhvākuñcanamabhyaset / puruṣo 'pyathavā nārī vajrolīsiddhimāpnuyāt //* (HYP 3.85).

18. For the Tibetan Siddha lineage and hagiography, see Dowman 1985. Note that in this Buddhist compilation of legendary accounts, Matsyendra and Mīna (usually synonyms for a single Hindu Yogi) feature independently, as they also do in the HYP and in my sources of the tale. See also Dvivedi 1996, 25–35 and Dasgupta 1995, 202–10.
19. For a more detailed discussion of Haṭhayoga, Rājayoga, and the "six-limbed" yoga in some tantric circles, see Müller-Ortega 2005 and Kiss' chapter in this volume.
20. *brahmacārī mitāhārī tyāgīyogaparāyanaḥ*... (GorŚ 54a).
21. *etad yogaprasādena bindusiddhir bhaved dhruvam / siddhe bindau mahāyatne kiṃ na sidhyati bhūtale //* (GhS 3.47).
22. On the debate of the possible Buddhist or Śaivite origins of the Naths, see Dvivedi 1996, 4–9 and Dasgupta 1995, 191–202.

CHAPTER 8. WHAT SHOULD MĪNANĀTH DO TO SAVE HIS LIFE?

1. The length of the poem varies in different editions, but normally it consists of more than two thousand lines. Most of them are in a popular Bengali medieval meter *paẏār*. In the poem, the songs are in a *tripadī* meter, and their *rāga* is sometimes stated.
2. In Bengali: *Gorakṣabijaẏ* (the spelling varies in the different manuscripts: *Gorakhabijaẏ*, *Gorkhabijaẏ*, etc.) and *Mīncetan*. It is quite probable that the story was known under the title "The Victory of Gorakhnāth" specifically in Eastern India, since one drama by the Maithili poet Vidyāpati is also called *Gorakṣavijaya*. James Mallinson (2007: 186n129) refers to a fourteenth-century Sanskrit work bearing the same title, but unfortunately he does not give more details about it. I am not aware of any Sanskrit text called *Gorakṣavijaya*.
3. Śyāmdās Sen: *Mīn-cetan* (edited by Nalinīkānta Bhaṭṭaśālī in 1915; abbreviated as MC), Sekh Phaẏjullā: *Gorakṣa-bijaẏ* (edited by Munsī Ābdul Karīm in 1917; GBK), Kabicandra Dās: *Gorakṣa-bijaẏ* (edited by Aśvinīkumār Som in 1932; GBS), and Bhīmsen Rāẏ: *Gorkha-bijaẏ* (edited by Pañcānan Maṇḍal in 1949; GBM).
4. The summary made by White (1996, 236–37) is inaccurate and mixed with elements drawn from non-Bengali sources and thus cannot be regarded as faithful to the Bengali versions. White, for example, says that Matsyendra (=Mīnanāth) was cursed by the Goddess for overhearing the teaching, while in fact he was cursed by Śiva (GBM 7, GBK 14, GBS 16, MC 3). Further, he states that the Goddess "curses him [=Matsyendra] to be debauched in the

Kingdom of Women." Precisely, the opposite is true: she gave him a boon (*bar*) fulfilling thus his inner wish (GBM 10, GBK 19, GBS 18, MC 3).

5. Tovstych's translation is based on the edition prepared by Munsī Ābdul Karīm (GBK).
6. Previous attempts to date these texts much earlier (even as early as in the eleventh century) on the grounds of the occurrence of several archaic words were dismissed using the justified argument that these seemingly old words simply belong to the modern colloquial language spoken in peripheral parts of Bengal (Bhaṭṭācāryya 1957, 304–305).
7. The translation is based on the version in GBM 69–72. Slightly different versions of this song are to be found in all other editions: GBS 52–53, GBK 112–115, and MC 21–22. One more variant is available in Nāth 1964, 153–55. The song is composed in a *tripadī* meter (more precisely, in a *nācārī* or *lācārī* meter, also called *dīrgha tripadī*) with prescribed *rāga paṭamañjarī* or *guñjarī*. Most of the different readings do not change the meaning of the verses, although a few exceptions are discussed below.
8. The used verb *karilā* (and similarly other verbs in the song ending with *-lā*) is an irregular form of the second person of the past tense (Chatterji 1970, 980–81 § 711) which is relatively common in medieval Bengali texts. The translator into the Russian takes it as a third person and translates this line as "Mīnanāth destroyed [his] body" (Минонатх погубил [свое] тело, Tovstych 1988, 60). This is definitely wrong, since even the editor of the text on which the Russian translation is based notes that these verb forms in the present work stay in the second person (GBK, appendix, 43, note 31). The Russian translation of the poem as a whole is not accurate and reliable.
9. *Karmmadoṣe* could mean either present bad behavior and actions (sinning), or negative consequences of previous events, in this case the Śiva's curse. An alternative translation would thus be: "because of your bad karma you have forgotten yoga."
10. The translation of *yena* as "as if" is uncertain. Other versions have instead *yena* "poison" (*biṣ*, GBS), "all" and "always" (*sab*, *nitya*, GBK; *niti*, MC).
11. The printed text reads: *sarbbabhoge nā kare āhār*, which does not make good sense and is corrected by the editor (see 278) to *nānārūpe karae āhār*, with a variant in one manuscript *sarbbabhog karen āhār*. I translated this last version, which is also attested in GBS and GBK.
12. Or, according to MC: "these four are the essence of a body" (*ehi cāri śarīrer sār*).
13. The printed text of this line reads: *āpanāke bhār diẏā*. This reading is also attested in some other manuscripts (see GBK 114 and page 21 of the appen-

dix). The editor, however, has corrected the line to: *khemāire bhār diyā* (GBM 278), which is an alternative reading found in some other manuscripts. The word *khemā* may be derived either from the Sanskrit *kṣema* ("safety, security, tranquillity," Dasgupta 1969, 233) or, more probably, from *kṣamā* ("patience, restraint, pardon" Sen 1971, 198, Chatterji 1970, 351, § 172, viii, ab). In Bengali Nāth literature, the word is personified as Khemāi, who is "the best guard to be placed in the different centres of the body so that the wealth within may not be stolen away by Kāla (death, decay, change). Khemāi has sometimes been depicted as a very smart policeman, who arrests all the evil tendencies, pierces the undisciplined and unsteady elephant of mind with the hook." (Dasgupta 1969, 233). The editor of GBM, however, does not seem to take the word *khemāi* in this personified way, since he explained the form *khemāire* as "for stopping, restraining" (*kṣānta karibār janya, kṣamāke, caitanyake*; GBM 247).

14. GBK, however, reads "three moons" and MC "the own moon."

15. (1) *ohe guru mīnanāth / śarīr karilā pāt / karmmadoṣe pāsarilā yog /*
tejilā gurur bol / kāmarase haïyā bhol / maraṇ ichilā tumhi bhog //
(2) *guru bhābi cāẏa man / mane kari saṅgaraṇ / tomā guru mahādeb haẏe /*
ek bhogī nahe har / sarbbabhogī nirantar / bhāṅg dhutūrā yena khāẏe //
(3) *nārī laẏā kare keli / tattvete nā rahe bhuli / bismaraṇ nāhik tāhār /*
ek mūrtti nā haẏe śib / sarbbamūrtti haẏe jīb / sarbbabhog karen āhār //
(4) *guru cāri candra haẏe / śarīr byāpiyā raẏe / tāhāre sādhile paritrāṇ /*
ādi candra nija candra / unmatta garal candra / ei cāri śarīr byāpan //
(5) *ādi candra kari sthita / nijacandra sahita / unmatta kariyā sandhān /*
tin candra sambariyā / āpanāke (khemāire) bhār diyā / garal candra sab kare pān //
(6) *cāri candra sambariyā / bhabasindhu tar giyā / tabe se sakal rakṣā pāye /*
hena karmma nā karilā / sab tumi bismarilā / kaha guru kemata upāẏe //
(7) *sthān hate naṛibār / śakati nāik tomhār / jībaner nā kariya āś /*
āmi kaï tattvabāṇī / cāẏa tumi mane guṇi / yadi thāke jīban habilās //
(8) *ulṭiyā yog dhara / āpanāk sthir kara / nija mantra karaha smaraṇ /*
ulṭi dhara āpanā / tribeṇīte deẏa hānā / khāle jal bharite kāraṇ //

16. The position of hashish (*bhāṅg*) and datura (*dhutūrā*) within this text is rather ambivalent. Śiva's fondness for them is praised in this song, but in other places the status of hashish and datura is not so favorable. In one episode, Śiva is looking for his wife and asks Gorakhnāth whether he knows where she is. Gorakhnāth bursts into laughter and says: "What can I say to you who consume hashish and datura!" (GBM 20). From the context, the meaning of this answer is quite clear: Śiva is so intoxicated that he even does not know where he lost his own wife and Gorakhnāth makes fun of him for this. The position of hashish in non-Bengali Nāth literature is similarly ambivalent. In modern

works, hashish is an integral element of yogic life. As Ann Gold says about the siddhas in Rājasthānī stories: "all the yogis like to smoke hashish and eat sweets" (Gold 1992, 42; in her translation, there is a good number of references to yogis consuming hashish; see 186, 190, 271, 276, 297). The same fondness for hashish is well known among modern sādhus (see, for example, Hausner 2007, 85, 100, 120). On the other hand, in older texts such as *Gorakhbānī*, hashish is clearly rejected (*sabad* 164, 165c, 208, 213, 232a, 241b) and one line of this text also agitates against datura: "Do not drink datura, oh avadhūta!" (*dhotarā na pīvo hai avadhū, sabad* 241a). These different positions may reflect a gradual acceptance of hashish in tantric and yogic circles. According to Alexis Sanderson, the first texts prescribing the use of cannabis in tantric ritual are relatively late East-Indian Śākta *paddhatis*, probably under the influence of Muslim ascetics (Sanderson 2003: 365–66n.43, cf. Mallinson 2007, 169n.23).

17. Although this argument is valid for the Nāth doctrine of monistic Śaivism, it does not correspond well to the first part of the poem describing the origin of the universe, gods, and siddhas. During the cosmogonical process, Śiva appears relatively late and is born from the body of Anādya together with four other siddhas and Gaurī (GBM 3). Śiva is, therefore, on the same ontological level as the siddhas, and nothing suggests his supreme position, except the fact that Śiva is originally the only possessor of the Great Knowledge. On the other hand, his wife Gaurī is sometimes called "the mother of Universe" (*jagater māi*, GBM 3, 5). This cosmogonical section of the text is mostly borrowed from the common medieval Bengali sources (see Dasgupta 1969: 311–21) and, therefore, it is not an entirely coherent—and probably not even an original—part of the poem.
18. Śiva's second wife is Gaṅgā (*gaṅgā gaurī dui nārī*, GBM 9; *tribhubaner karttā śib tān gaṅgā gaurī*, GBM 104).
19. "Sahajiyā" refers to the Vaiṣṇava Sahajiyā. I feel the adjective *vaiṣṇava* in this connection to be pleonastic since there is no other Sahajiyā tradition but Vaiṣṇava. The still relatively frequently used term *Buddhist Sahajiyā/Sahajayāna* is a mere construct of Bengali scholars of the first half of the twentieth century and does not have any real counterpart among Buddhist traditions. Ronald Davidson explains the unsubstantiated coinage of this and other similar terms as "the combination of an immature understanding of the literature, a nascent nationalism in India, and the desire to affirm such subsequent phenomena as Sahajiyā Vaiṣṇavism" (Davidson 2002, 49).
20. Edited by Basu 1932 and Dās 1972, briefly summarized in Bose 1930: 181–193.

21. For the sake of simplicity, I use the term *Sahajiyā milieu* for all different traditions and texts with a Sahajiyā background, be it Sahajiyā texts proper or various traditions such as Bāuls, Kartābhajās, etc., including Muslim fakīrs.
22. One of the first clear explanations is available in Datta 1394 (vol. 1, 232–33), which was originally published in 1870. The first English study known to me is Basu 1889.
23. Among the more important studies on this subject are: Bhaṭṭācārya 1408, 424–37 and Jhā 1999, 267–311 in Bengali, and Jha 1995; Openshaw 2002. 225–39 and Fakir 2005, 201–219 in English.
24. There are, however, isolated attempts to reject the identification of four moons with bodily products. H. C. Paul (1973), for example, argues that the four moons mean four states of mind. His view is, surprisingly, accepted by Banerji 1992, 232.
25. Rudrani Fakir, for example, offers similar explanations: health, longevity, stopping ageing, immortality (2005, 183, 203, 207, 221); or to put it succintly, it is "a means to renew the body" (Salomon 1991, 274). Jeanne Openshaw formulates analogous interpretations (2002, 228–33). A less usual explanation was formulated by one Bāul: "When the 'moons' are absorbed by ingestion, the body is thought to be purified and the *sādhaka* is requested to sublimate his subsequent sexual intercourse so as to perceive the 'essence' of the universe itself." (Ferrari 2007, 253).
26. The degree of such identification is, however, different. The editor of GBM, for example, quotes in the introduction a number of Bāul songs to demonstrate the common technical vocabulary, including the term *cāri candra*. Asitkumār Bandyopādhyāẏ (1993, 380n38) is more explicit, but still careful to make a definite identification. Clear and explicit identification is made by Kalyāṇī Mallik (1950, 140). This is important, since her voluminous book on the history, philosophy and practice of the Naths, though partly outdated, still remains the most comprehensive and valuable survey of this subject.
27. In several places in his dissertation, Glen Hayes discusses parallel concepts in Nāth and Sahajiyā texts, and in most cases, he believes that the Sahajiyas adopted them from the Naths (Hayes 1985, 84, 93, 180, 186, 191, 198, 200–201, 203, 263, 309–10).
28. Saktinath Jha (1995, 85) quotes four lines, occurring in the context of debate on the four moons, from a Sahajiyā work called *Caitanyakārikā* and translates them: "*Candra-sādhan* is chief among *sādhanās*; he who knows nothing of it is like a mere beast. The original *siddhas* like Mīnanāth and Gorakṣanāth developed the power to utter infallible words through *candra-sādhanā*." One partner in this debate is Rūp Kabirāj, who "lived in the middle part of the 17th

century" (ibid., 106n75). Despite uncertainty about the date and author of the *Caitanyakārikā* (cf. ibid., 105n49), its message is very important: the Sahajiyas themselves seemed to be aware of their indebtedness to the Nāth predecessor and gurus regarding the practice of the four moons. This view is even shared by the orthodox Vaiṣṇavas who "speak of the four moons as a non-Vedic *sādhanā* of the Aghor-panthīs or Nāth-panthīs" (ibid., 85).

29. All authors agree that the names of particular moons vary in different guru lineages, but the most commonly used terms are *rūp* (for menstruation), *mati* (for feces), *ras* (for urine or semen) and *rati* (for semen or female sexual fluids). Jeanne Openshaw (2002, 225n2), however, quotes one manuscript with these two sets of names: 1) *ādya*, *āpta*, *unmat*, *garal*; 2) *sādhya*, *nij*, *unmād*, *garal*, which are very close to the terms used in the song: *ādi*, *nij*, *unmatta* and *garal*. According to Openshaw, "[t]hese probably refer to fluids produced in sexual intercourse, urine, faeces and menstrual fluids respectively."

30. "Three days remain, life is finished" (*tin din bākī āche, āyu haïla śeṣ*, GBM 26), "there are three days of live" (*tin diner āẏu āche*, 54). Cf. "there are four days of live" (*din cāri āche āẏu*, 109).

31. "All fluid that was present is lost" (*yatek āchila ras sab nila hari*, GBM 30); "the body became dry" (*kāẏā śukhāila*, 62; *śarīr śukhāila*, 66); "a sand bed has been dried up, there is no water in Gaṅgā" (*śukhāila bālucar, gāṅge nāi pāni*, 74); "there is no water in a pond" (*pukurete jal nāi*, p. 86); "a pond has been dried up" (*sarobar śukhāila*, 91); "Gaṅgā has been dried up" (*śukhāila gaṅgā*, 99).

32. One episode of the text, however, questions the idea that a body of a siddha should be flooded by some fluid(s). When Gorakhnāth is forced by Śiva to marry a princess, he became a small child to avoid consuming the marriage. Then, he explains to his wailing bride that she was cheated by Śiva because Gorakhnāth is neither man, nor woman; he has no man's sexual power; his body is like dry wood and is sapless (*strīpuruṣ nahi āmhi, nāi bīryya bal, śukhnā kāṣṭher mata śarīr sakal; śarīrete ras nāi kāṣṭha samatul*; GBM 23). This image indicates that a perfect siddha should be a totally asexual being without any typical man's characteristics, even without sperm.

33. "Having grown old, you are passing away" (*buṛā haïẏā ghucā haïcha*, GBM 61); "your hair became gray" (*pākiche māthār keś*, 61; *pākila māthār keś*, 82; *pākiche māthār cūl*, 88, 91); "there is a white umbrella above your head" (*tomār upare dhare dhabal chattar*, 105; cf. *māthāe dharae mor dhabal chattar*, 68).

34. "Mīnanāth is without strength and power" (*mīnanāthar bal śakti nāi*, GBM 25); "there is no strength within [my] body" (*gāẏe nāi bal*, 82); "there is no strength in [my] body to practice yoga" (*sādhite yog gāẏe bal nāi*, 72).

35. "Giving away your treasure [= sperm] you have emptied out the room [= body], you have thrown out all the treasure that was there" (*āpanār dhan diẏā*

ghar kailā khāli, āchila yatek dhan sab dilā ḍāli, GBM 67; cf. 98: *yatek āchila dhan sab nilā hari*).

36. The *Gorakṣaśataka*, for example, says clearly: "semen is connected with the moon" (76a: *śukrañ candreṇa saṃyuktaṃ*) or "the *bindu* is the moon" (74b: *bindur indū*).
37. We should not, therefore, be surprised that the oldest Sahajiyā texts do not contain any description or clear allusion to this practice. From this absence, we cannot conclude that this technique was unknown to them. While discussing these old texts, Glen Hayes (1985, 116) admits that "such a mixture of sexual fluids may have been consumed in obscure V[aiṣṇava] S[ahajiyā] rituals (the texts refer to "sweet confections"; *bhiyāna*, which are to be consumed)."
38. For how this esoteric teaching is imparted, see Openshaw 2002, 233–39.
39. David Cashin, working with medieval yogic Islamic texts in Bengali, correctly notes that "the similarity of hidden language forms or even of ritual acts does not necessarily indicate a direct line of transfer or influence. Esoteric code-words have been maintained over centuries intact while, in fact, changing their meaning completely" (Cashin 1995, 39).
40. For example, one of the dictionaries of yogic terms (Digambarji 1991, 113–14) lists seven different meanings of the word *candra* throughout the yogic literature. Most commonly, *candra* refers either to the source of the nectar of immortality in the head of a yogin, or to the *nāḍī* in the left side of the body (*iḍā*). For this second meaning, our text seems to use another synonym for the word moon, namely, *śaśī* (GBM 92, 117, 119). It is paired with the term *rabi* (meaning sun) and this couple stands here for the pair *sūrya-candra/soma* in Sanskrit haṭha-yogic texts.
41. Interestingly, Buddhist Kālacakra tradition connects urine with the moon (Wallace 2001, 84, table 5.9).
42. While the figure four seems to be the most common regarding the number of moons in the contemporary Sahajiyā milieu, there are some traditions using a wider range of bodily fluids. According to Jha (1995, 70), "[s]ome maintain that the use of all substances emerging from the nine (or ten) doors is essential, and call this 'the *sādhanā* of *navarasiks*', or the '*sādhanā* of *ras*'." (cf. Openshaw 2002, 236n26). Narasingha Sil quotes an encounter of the Bengali saint Ramakrishna with the Navarasika women (2003, 48–49; 2009, 292, that he glosses as belonging to a Kartābhajā sect, which is an uncertain identification (but Urban 2001, 246n101 makes the same identification). Describing the same event, Jeffrey Kripal, calls the Navarasikas a 'Tantric sect' (1998, 123).
43. A few notes will be sufficient to show this ambivalence. Yogic texts are in general misogynistic and portray an ideal yogin as an ascetic avoiding the company of women. On the other hand, the same texts contain verses (most often in the

context of the vajrolī-mudrā) in which woman figures as a ritual partner of the yogin. Such passages, of course, belong to the older strata of tāntric and Kaula ideas and practices which were later incorporated into some haṭhayogic texts. Thus, while the "Gorakhnāthīs are under a vow of celibacy," at the same time, "[i]t is possible that the rule of celibacy does not require absolute continence for, to cite one exception, Yogīs acknowledge the practice of śākta rites" (Briggs 2001, 46). David Cashin (1995, 50) holds a similar opinion: "[w]omen were, nevertheless, essential to the Nāth sādhanā." Briggs himself observed that "[w]omen who have been initiated into the sect are numerous" (ibid, 48, cf. also 34). Even nowadays it is still possible to meet women yoginīs, usually called Nāthnī, (see, for example, Fakir 2005, 236–38). A good modern discussion, albeit sometimes rather speculative, on the complicated relationship between Śaiva ascetics and women is the chapter "Shakti bhakti" in William Pinch's study on warrior ascetics (2006, 194–230).

44. Tovstych (1988, 100–101n122), for example, says that the lines 5a–6c are "the most obscure verses of the poem," and although she is aware of the Bāul meaning of the four moons as bodily fluids, she rejects this possibility and states that the four moons "mean obviously something else among the Naths," but what exactly remains unclear.

45. There are at least two places within the large work of Gopinath Kaviraj where he briefly discusses this topic: Kavirāj 1995, 172–73 in Bengali and Kavirāj 1994, 277–78 in Hindi (which is actually a translation of an unpublished manuscript written in Bengali). While these two passages are almost identical, the Hindi one is more important for us, since it explains the meaning of the moons in more detail. Therefore, I quote from it. However, I have some doubt as to the reliability of the Hindi translation, for at one important point in this passage, it says exactly the opposite of what is written in the Bengali version. Moreover, Kaviraj unfortunately does not provide any reference to the textual sources and so we do not know whether his explanation is to be applied to our song. It probably is since he uses exactly the same terms for the individual moons. On the other hand, we have to bear in mind that pandit Kaviraj had a vast knowledge based on a considerable number of various manuscripts, so the textual source of his analysis might be different from our text.

46. It is possible, however, that he has explained this problem in another essay. Klaus Klostermaier (1986, 88) refers to an article called "Kāyasiddhike prakāra," published in a special issue of the journal *Kalyāṇa* 43 [February 1969]: 144–51; ibid., 85 and 104n5), in which Gopinath Kaviraj apparently analyzes the four moons more profoundly. Unfortunately, I did not have access to this essay when writing this paper.

47. "The original moon is the initial moon placed in the root of the lotus with a thousand [petals]." (*ādicandra—yah sahasrār kamal kī jaṛ mẽ sthit yoniniṣṭha candra hai*); Kavirāj 1994, 277.
48. This understanding is supported by two statements by Gopinath Kaviraj (ibid.). First, the lotus with a thousand petals is originally directed down, causing a steady fall of a stream of the "original moon." A yogin should turn the direction of the lotus to stop this outflow and to keep the nectar within it (*adhomukh sahasradal kamal ko ūrdhvamukh kar*). Second, a bodily fluid (*deharas*, the fallen original moon) is to be transformed into the nectar of immortality and then carried up by an upward breath up to the *sahasrāra-cakra* where it is collected (*deharas amṛt ke ākār mẽ pariṇat hokar ūrdhvagāmī vāyu se ūpar pahũcāyā jātā hai aur sahasrār mẽ saṃcit hotā hai*). It is thus possible that in Gopinath Kaviraj's understanding of the four moons, three of them are in fact only different forms of the same: the initial form stored in the lotus with a thousand petals and flowing from it is called the "original moon" (*ādicandra*), the fallen form of it is a bodily fluid (*deharas*) and called the "own moon" (*nija-candra*), and finally, when it is transformed into the nectar of immortality and carried up, it is called the "poisonous moon" (*garalcandra*).
49. The problem, however, remains with the kuṇḍalinī. This energy should be first awakened and then carried up, not stilled. Of course, after reaching the final stage we can see it as nonactive from a certain point of view, but this is not yet the case of Mīnanāth.
50. This problem reflects a basic question about the actual effect of the khecarīmudrā. James Mallinson has summarized his findings clearly (2007, 29): "there are two contradictory aims of *khecarīmudrā* in the texts of *haṭhayoga*. In one, *amṛtaplāvana*, the store of *amṛta* is to be accessed and used to flood the body; in the other, *bindudhāraṇa*, *amṛta* (or *bindu*) is to be kept where it is. Many texts describe both aims." Gopinath Kaviraj's understanding of the practice of the four moons seems to follow the second possibility (*bindudhāraṇa*). It is thus difficult to reconcile it with the Gorakhnāth's advice to flood the body.
51. However, I must confess that the precise conception of the mind (*manas*) in Nāth texts remains unclear to me. I cannot exclude the possibility that at least some texts accept the Nyāya theory of atomic mind moving within a body (see, for example, Potter 1995, 93–95, cf. Chakrabarti 1999, 283n1). In this case, the idea of the mind pervading a body is conceivable.
52. I do not understand what exactly the phrase *puruṣer bīryer pāṇḍurabarṇāṃśa* might mean.
53. The author seems to somehow distinguish between two words that are usually taken as synonymous, both meaning sperm: *vīrya* and *śukra*. One can merely

speculate whether one term stands for the sperm proper and the second for a pre-ejaculatory fluid.

54. Cf. also 56n19 of the edited text. This cannot be a coincidence. Either both authors were working from the same text unknown to me, or Gopinath Kaviraj simply quotes from this book without mentioning the source, which is more probable in my opinion. The manuscript of his book, written in Bengali, was completed in 1961 (this is stated in a foreword to the first edition) and the Hindi translation was published in 1963. And what is also interesting is that in his later Bengali work (published in 1975), he borrowed the full passage on the four moons from this Hindi book intact, except this explicit interpretation of particular moons. Does this mean that Gopinath Kaviraj changed his mind about this question and was later dissatisfied with this previous explanation but unable to offer a better one?
55. However, there is an exact identification of particular moons among the Sahajiyas in note 19 on the same page. According to the author, ādicandra is menstrual blood, nijacandra is sperm, unmattacandra is feces, and garalcandra urine. This classification differs from the opinion of Jeanne Openshaw (see n29 in this chapter).
56. The passage reads: "If one is able to pierce the four moons—*mūlādhār*, *svādhiṣṭhān*, *maṇipur* and *anāhat*, then the piercing of the *viśuddha* and *ājñā* is not difficult." It is necessary to add, however, that this note comments on the phrase "piercing of the four moons" (*cāri candra bhed*) occurring in other Bengali Nāth text and not in Gorakhnāth's song. Moreover, taking into account the context of this phrase, I have strong doubts about the correctness of this interpretation.
57. Some references to a few Buddhist texts describing the usage of bodily products were collected by Saktinath Jha (1995, 84–85). For a discussion of this practice in other Buddhist traditions, see, for example, Wallace 2001, 121–22, 225n65; Garson 2004, 57, 120–121, 357, 363; and Gray 2007, 103–124.
58. Although he does mention this pair a few times (White, 2003, 71, 211, 254–5), he does not discuss them further at all.
59. There are three passages known to me in Sanderson's work discussing this topic: 1995, 82–83 (here he quotes mostly from the twenty-ninth chapter of the *Tantrāloka*); Sanderson 2005, 110–114n63 (this is actually a footnote that is over three full large pages in length and contains a number of references, relevant Sanskrit verses and important analysis of the collected material); and Sanderson 2007, 287n178, adding further references to this practice. See also Mallinson 2007b, 221n333.
60. Regarding this question, Csaba Kiss's research on the text *Matsyendrasaṃhitā*

seems to be very promising. He says about this work: "It provides some clues for, among other things, the understanding of the transition from the early Indian yoga traditions (Pātañjala and Śaiva) to the late and fully developed *haṭha*-yogic teachings as well as of the transition from the early Kula traditions to the later Kaula teachings associated with the figure of Matsyendranātha. It can also throw some light on the connection between the Kaula traditions of the Paścimāmnāya and Dakṣiṇāmnāya, and the Nātha tradition of *haṭha*-yogins." (Kiss 2007, 155; see also notes 26 and 28 for references to other works dealing with the connection between the Kaula and Nāth environments.)

61. I leave aside here the question of whether these two names are to be taken as synonymous or not. Most authors take it for granted that Matsyendranātha and Mīnanāth is one person while others deny it (e.g., White 1996, 85).
62. The terms used for them are, for example, *ratna*, *dravya*, *tattva* and *caru*.
63. I am grateful to Alexis Sanderson (pers. comm.) and Mark Dyczkowski (pers. comm.) for answering in the negative my questions: whether the Śaiva sources use the word *candra* for bodily fluids anywhere, and whether the number four is mentioned anywhere in connection with them.
64. Although the number four is standard also in the Sahajiyā milieu, Saktinath Jha notes that "the number of moons used varies" (1995, 69) and quotes one Bāul song where the number five occurs (ibid., 103n14).
65. For the justification of these practices, see Sanderson 1995, 83–87. The same reasoning for a contact with substances (including consumption) which are regarded as impure by Hindus is to be found among contemporary Aghorīs, whom we can see as modern successors of older Kula ideas and practices (see, for example, Barrett 2008, 152–54 and passim for practicing nondiscrimination as part of their sādhanā). Although this purpose is certainly not the principal one in the Sahajiyā milieu, "one of the reasons given for performing the *candra bhed sādhanā* is to overcome aversion, shame and fear, and thus to attain a stage of 'non-duality' and non-discrimination." (Jha 1995, 94)
66. See Mallinson 2007, 222n336 where he quotes *Śivasaṃhitā* 3.61 (*viṇmūtralepane svarṇam adṛśyakaraṇaṃ tathā*) and *Dattātreyayogaśāstra* 197 (*malamūtrapralepena lohādīnāṃ suvarṇatā*) and White 1996, 456n107 referring to *Yogatattvopaniṣad* 74 (*malamūtralepena lohadehaḥ svarṇatā bhavet*). To these we can add *Yogakarṇikā* 6.29 (*malamūtrapralepena lauhānāṃ svarṇatāṃ tathā*). Similar verses are also to be found in alchemical texts (White 1996, 456n107; Mallinson 2007, 220n328).
67. "Some drink urine, own excretion . . . [but] they do not get a perfection of the body" (*kecinmūtraṃ pibanti svamalam . . . naiteṣām dehasiddhir*, *Amanaskayoga* 2.33 and *Amaraughaprabodha* 8; cf. Mallinson 2007, 220n328). The Hindi

translation of this line (in the *Amanaskayoga*) glosses the word *some* by "Aghorīs" (*aghorpanthī*). An alchemical work *Rasārṇava* sneers at the futility of this practice (1.11c–12b): "If liberation [comes] from using semen, urine and faeces, then why are dogs and pigs not liberated, o great goddess?" (Mallinson's translation, 220n328; cf. White 1996, 172).

68. According to Ballāla, the commentator of the *Khecarīvidyā*, the consumption of feces (called *amarī kriyā*) gives freedom from illness and strength (*tatphalam nirāmayatvaṃ balavattvaṃ ceti*) and drinking of urine (*ajarī kriyā*) removes wrinkles (*tatphalam valītyāgādīty āhuḥ*). The names of these techniques are not accidental: *amarī* causes immortality and *ajarī* non-ageing (*amarī hy amarakāriṇī, ajarī ajarākāriṇī*). The full passage of the commentary is quoted in Mallinson 2007, 222n336.

69. The *Khecarīvidyā* contains a full passage on this subject (2.72–79). See Mallinson's notes 328–39 on 220–23 for an analysis of these verses and further references to other yogic texts. The effects of this practice are similar to the results of the ingestion: "Rubbing the body with that, the yogin truly becomes free from disease in this life, mighty [and] free of wrinkles and grey hair," "rubbing the body [with them], both pallor and itching truly disappear" (ibid, 127, verses 77c–78b and 86cd of the *Khecarīvidyā*). See also Cashin 1995, 196–97.

70. "The poisonous moon meaning semen" (*garalcandra arthe śukra*), Mallik 1950, 140.

71. "Release the nectar and drink the poison" (*amṛt chāṛiyā kara garal bhakṣaṇ*, GBM: 84); "drink the poison" (*garal bhakṣaṇ kari. . .* , 92 and 110). Connection between nectar and poison is expressed also in one Bāul song: "Where is poison, there is nectar" (*yathā garal tathā sudhā*, Bhaṭṭācāryya 1408, 856, song no. 445; cf. also 401–402 for *garal-ras*). Saktinath Jha, however, quotes an alternative and unusual view of some group of sādhakas (1995, 81), who interpret the "poisonous moon" as "the moon of poisonous desire which kills the male."

72. A useful account of the "reverse practice" in the Nāth yoga is Dasgupta 1969, 229–35. See also Mallik 1950, 533.

73. Verse 8b of the song says clearly: "make yourself still" (*āpanāke sthir kara*, GBM), or in another version: "make your body still" (*kāẏā tomhār sthir kara*, GBK). What should be primarily made still are breath and mind: "imprison [your] breath" (*bāẏu kara bandī*, GBM 91); "make still [your] mind and breath" (*man-paban sthir kara*, p. 96), etc. Within this category of things which are to be made still, we can also include nectar/semen. Interestingly, one of the effects of the Matsyendranātha's position (*matsyendrāsana*) referred to in *Haṭhapradīpikā* 1.27 is the "stillness of the moon" (*candrasthiratvam*).

74. There are many verses in yogic texts that say this. Some of the Sanskrit sources are quoted by Mallinson 2007, 175n70 (cf. also note 377 on 228). Further references are, for example, in the Hindi work *Gorakhbānī*, where it is stated that a yogin should "eat [only] his breath" (*sāsa usāsa bāi kau bhaṣibā, sabad* 52a) and give up or reduce food (*avadhū ahāra toṛau*, 33a; *avadhū ahāra kūṃ toṛibā*, 215a; see also 32a, 36a, and 84). The additional reason for reducing or finally giving up food is fear that eating causes spilling of semen (145a, and probably also 35b: "in eating is a house of a thief," *ahāra kai ghari coraṃ*).
75. Some haṭha-yogic mudrās are said to reduce excretion (e.g., *mūlabandha* in *Haṭhapradīpikā* 3.64).
76. If we understand the four moons as bodily fluids, then the mechanism would be clear: Mīnanāth's sapless body would be saved by ingestion of these improperly discharged fluids. This concept of a yogin as a "closed system" is also one of the explanations offered by Saktinath Jha (1995, 98–99) for the practice of the four moons in Sahajiyā milieu: "Decay of the body is a natural law, and the sādhakas think that this occurs through the process of excretion. Thus one should stop the excretion of those substances where this is possible, for example in the case of semen. . . . But the outflow of some substances, for example, urine and faeces, cannot be arrested. By taking these back within the body, the rejected portion is again absorbed, and the proportion of retention over excretion is increased." A similar idea is to be found in the *Gorakhbānī*: "[a yogin should] take inside what goes outside" (*bāhari jātā bhītari āṇai, sabad* 44b). And according to David Cashin (1995, 194), the same logic is behind one passage in Śekh Mansur's *Śrī nāmā*: "Mansur is Nāthist in orientation. . . . The implication seems to be that the substances poured out are in some way consumed again."
77. These two Triveṇīs are sometimes referred to in the literature (e.g., Woodroffe 1997, 111–12) as *yuktatriveṇī* (in the *mūlādhāra-cakra*) and *muktatriveṇī* (in the *ājñā-cakra*). Textual sources of this terminology are unknown to me.
78. Taking into account the character of these works, this fact is not surprising. In Hindi, for example, there is either a contemporary folk version (A. Gold 1992; for the song; see 283–84), or a number of relatively modern and highly brahmanised texts (see, for example, *Gorakhnāth caritra*, the "song"—in fact, it is the sound of a drum—is on 53–54; and a few similar texts published by the Gorakhnāth temple in Gorakhpur). In none of these works can we expect any technical yogic instructions. In fact, I am not aware of any old version of the story in Hindi comparable to the Bengali poem.
79. "The Muslim esoteric tradition in Bengal seems to be largely the product of three influences, the Naths, Vaiṣṇava Sahajiyas, and Sufism. Practically speak-

ing it is the former two sources which are most important. Further, it is the view of this author that most Sufi texts of the Middle Bengali period can be shown to be either exclusively Nāthist or exclusively Vaiṣṇava Sahajiyā." (Cashin 1995, 40) According to David Cashin, the Nāth elements were earlier and the Sahajiyā ones came later (ibid., 55). It is not, however, always easy to tell whether the particular text is "Nāthist or Sahajiyā oriented" (ibid., 197) and this fact complicates any interpretation of passages dealing with bodily substances and their usefulness for solving our problem. A distinction suggested by the author (ibid.): "Where *rasa* is primarily a physical substance to be utilized in gaining immortality and super-human powers, the Nāthist viewpoint is ascendant. Where *rasa* is regarded as a sentiment utilized in the realization of man as God, the Sahajiyā viewpoint is primary" is not satisfactory, since in medieval Sahajiyā texts the term *rasa* stands primarily for bodily substances (according to Hayes, especially for semen: Hayes 1985, 57n63, 85n97, 100–114).

CHAPTER 9. THE MATSYENDRASAṂHITĀ

1. I would like to thank Professor David Lorenzen for inviting me to contribute to this volume, as well as the following people and institutions for the invaluable help they have given me in my research: Professor Alexis Sanderson (Oxford), Dr. James Mallinson (Oxford), Professor Dr Harunaga Isaacson (Hamburg), Dr Adrián Muñoz, Dr. Somadeva Vasudeva (Oxford), Dr. Dominic Goodall (Pondicherry), Dr. Csaba Dezső (Budapest), Dr. Judit Törzsök (Lille), Gergely Hidas (Oxford), Ralf Kramer (Oxford), Dr. Diwakar Acharya (Kathmandu), Dr. Ferenc Ruzsa (Budapest), Dr. Peter Bisschop (Edinbourgh), Dr. Alex Watson (Oxford), Mr. Kr. Mahendra Singh Tanwar (Jodhpur), Dr. Shaman Hatley (Montreal), Dr. Nikolaj Serikoff (Wellcome Library, London), Nina Mirnig (Oxford), Péter Szántó (Oxford), Dr. Imre Bangha (Oxford), Mrinal Kaul (Oxford), Ms. Zita Gábor (Budapest), my family, the Clarendon Fund (Oxford), the Boden Fund (Oxford), and the Max Müller Memorial Fund (Oxford).
2. The title *Matsyendrasaṃhitā* is actually slightly doubtful. It is confirmed in all the colophons of the MaSaṃ manuscript (*iti śrīmatsyendrasaṃhitāyāṃ prathamaḥ* [etc.] *paṭalaḥ* except in those of the best and probably oldest one (Ja; see note 4 below). The colophons of Ja show signs of rather indelicate corrections in a different hand. There are several patterns of these corrections, the most interesting being that of *paṭala* 1 and 55. It displays extensive corrections

with a long gap and may have read originally (illegible akṣaras marked by stars): *iti śrīmatsyendranāthaviracitāyāṃ* * * * * * * * *. The marginal colophons in Ja up to the beginning of *paṭala* 7 and in *paṭala* 26 and those in Jb up to only 1.47 give *ma nā saṃ*, evidently referring to an original *Matsyendranāthasaṃhitā*. The marginal colophons of ms W give *ma saṃ tā*, which is to be read as *ma° saṃ nā*, i.e., *ma nā saṃ*. Thus, the "original" title was probably *Matsyendranāthasaṃhitā*. Colophons in Ja in *paṭalas* 9–10 read *iti śrīmatsyendra* ** [*nātha*?] *saṃhitāyāṃ*. . . . One wonders why any evident association with the Nātha tradition was something to be concealed in the colophons by any scribe.

3. See two remarks by Heilijgers (1994, 9) that touch on the problem of the origins of the Nātha tradition: 1) "there was indeed a certain connection between the Kubjikāmata and the early Nātha tradition as represented by the Yoginīkaulamata . . . this connection is attested by some later Kubjikā texts, which incorporated the doctrine of the Nāthas and the Siddhas"; 2) "To what extent both traditions [Kubjikā and Nātha] influenced each other . . . is a subject for further research." See also Bharati 1965, 66; Schoterman 1977, 934; *Ṣaṭsāhasrasaṃhitā* 1982: 6n2; Goudriaan and Gupta 1981, 56, and Heilijgers 1994, 1, 7.
4. The four Jodhpur MSS are: MSS nos. 1784 (hereinafter Ja), 1783 (Jb), 1782 (Jc), 1785 (Jd) in the Maharaja Man Singh Library, Jodhpur; the London MS (W) is: MS Sanskrit β 1115 in the Wellcome Library for the History and Understanding of Medicine, London. I am grateful to Dr James Mallinson for lending me his copy of MS W. See the detailed description of these MSS in Kiss 2009].
5. A simplified version of the *stemma codicorum* would look like this (the sigla of hypothetical MSS in square brackets):

```
                  [Σ]
               ____|____
              /         \
             /        [Jcdw]
            /         /    \
        [Jab]      [Jcd]    \
          /         /        \
        Ja  Jb    Jc  Jd      W
```

6. On obtaining the manuscript, Sensharma worked from and on starting to compare it to his edition, I found that the edition bristles with editorial blunders, misreadings, and type errors to a surprisingly great extent. Two typical examples will suffice here. In 1.5a, all five manuscripts I worked from read *śivaśaivāgamāṃbhodhau*, and this is given by Sensharma as *śivaśaivāgamāṃ*

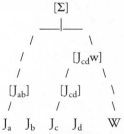

bhoyau and emended to *śivaśaivāgamābhyāṃ yo*; all five manuscripts I worked from read *athāsanakramaṃ* in 3.1a, at the very beginning of a chapter that is devoted exclusively to āsanas. Sensharma gives *yathāsatakramaṃ* and proposes *yathāgatakrama* as an emendation. There are hundreds of problems of this kind in Sensharma's edition. It seems probable to me that the editor had never seen the manuscript itself, but relied on a transcript prepared by people who did not have a firm knowledge of the Sanskrit language and sometimes had problems deciphering nineteenth-century Devanāgarī script. The "critically edited"text gives the impression of being in significantly worse condition than the original manuscript, which is the worst one of those now available to us.

7. There are two *Matsyendrasaṃhitā* MSS in the National Archives, Kathmandu: 1) Access No.: 2/102, Reel No.: B 39/11. This manuscript actually contains two texts in the same hand in the Maithilī script: a *Matsyendraśataka*, which is an unpublished haṭha-yogic text, and a *Matsyendrasaṃhitā*, which is also a haṭha-yogic text and is totally different from the text that I am dealing with in this article; 2) Access No.: 5/2717, Reel No.: B 39/23. This manuscript is a Devanāgarī transcription of the MaSaṃ MS mentioned above in 1). These manuscripts may have confused David Gordon White (1996, 421), who says somewhat misleadingly that: "A very late haṭhayogic source, entitled the *Matsyendra Saṃhitā* is found in manuscript form in the MSL [= Maharaja Man Singh Library] and the NNA [= National Archives, Kathmandu]. Cf. Pandeya 1976, introduction to *Gorakṣa Saṃhitā*, vol. 1, p. gha." Janārdana Pandeya actually writes in the passage referred to by White: *Matsyendranāthaviraciteṣu grantheṣv ete prasiddhāḥ—1. Matsyendrasaṃhitā* [etc.] *Itaḥ param api bahavo granthā etatpraṇītā Nepāladaravāragranthasaṃgrahe Jodhapurarājasaṃgrahe ca santīti śrūyate. Anyā ca ekā Matsyendrasaṃhitā bṛhadākārā Muktāpuramaṅgalūrataḥ prakāśitā vartate. Sā ca yady api Matsyendrapraṇītasaṃhitāto bhinnā tathāpi Matsyendrasambandhinī pracurā sāmagrī tatra dṛśyate.* In translation: "The most well-known texts composed by Matsyendranātha are the following ones—1. *Matsyendrasaṃhitā* [etc.] Moreover, there are said to be (*śrūyate*) a great number of texts composed by him in the Darbar Library, Nepal and in the [Maha]raja [Man Singh] Library, Jodhpur. A certain other long *Matsyendrasaṃhitā* is published by/in Muktāpura[?], Mangalore. This [text], though different from the *Saṃhitā* composed by Matsyendra, contains a lot of material relating to Matsyendra." Thus, Pandeya does not state at all that the manuscripts in Nepal and in Jodhpur are identical. Thus, White wrongly equates the MaSaṃ MSS to be found in Jodhpur and those in Kathmandu, while he does not mention the better-known MaSaṃ MS in the Wellcome Library (W), which was published by Sensharma in 1994. It is, perhaps, needless to say that

his opinion that the MaSaṃ is a "very late haṭhayogic source" is highly debatable since most of the text of the MaSaṃ is tantric in nature.

8. Note that I always spell *Yoginī* with a capital initial *Y* when referring to the set of six/seven Yoginīs of the ādhāras/cakras and with a small *y* when any other type of yoginī is meant. See MaSaṃ 1.63a, where the text indicates that the Yoginīs of the ādhāras are great (*ḍākinyādimahāsaptayoginī*).
9. Hereinafter, the text I refer to and quote as MaSaṃ is that of my critical edition of MaSaṃ 1–13 and 55 (Kiss 2009) [Cf. previous comment.] and of my draft edition of the remaining paṭalas. This means that some quotations from the text may involve significant emendations and conjectures, some made by others, mostly Prof. Alexis Sanderson and Dr. James Mallinson, all reported in my critical edition, but here I will report any alterations to the readings of the manuscripts only at crucial textual problems.
10. It is Śaiva because most of the text (*paṭala*s 2–54) is presented in the traditional form of a dialogue between Śiva (Bhairava, Īśvara) and Pārvatī (Devī); because the first and last (fifty-fifth) *paṭala*s constitute a narrative framework relating a unique version of the legend of the great yogin Matsyendra and his disciple Gorakṣa (mostly mentioned as the Chola king), whose connection with the Śaiva Kaula tradition is very well-established (cf. e.g. Sanderson 1988, 156 and Sanderson 1985, 214n110; Goudriaan and Gupta 1981, 50: and Heilijgers 1994, 9.); and because the main topic of the text is Śāmbhava/Śaiva yoga practice (*śāmbhavaṃ yogasādhanam*) (2.2d and 44.88b); see information suggests that the term *Śāmbhava* is even more specific than just being a synonym of Śaiva. The MaSaṃ is a tantra primarily because there are instances when it refers to itself as "tantra" or "great tantra"(14.16c, 43.34b, 55.39a) and secondarily because it touches on all the topics that make up a Tantra: mantras, construction of maṇḍalas, nyāsa, dhyāna, *pūjā*, *dīkṣā*, yoga, fearsome and erotic practices, results (*phala*) of rites, supernatural powers (siddhi), rules of conduct (e.g., *kulācāra*), praise of deities, the legendary history of the school. (It is rather the presence of these tantric elements in a text than that of some generally shared tantric "philosophical" content that determines that a text is "tantric." Cf. Goudriaan and Gupta 1981, 1, 10.)
11. "[T]he *mantras* are inevitably the most basic constituents of any Tantric system" (Sanderson 1990, 37).
12. The most significant parallel passages in the MaSaṃ include: MaSaṃ 7.43cd–44ab ≈ *Kubjikāmatatantra* (KMT) 6.23; MaSaṃ 44.74–79 ≈ KMT 21.2–3; MaSaṃ 54.10: ≈ KMT 7.111; MaSaṃ 43.27–33 ≈ *Nityāhnikatilaka* f. 27^r lines 2ff ≈ *Ṣaḍanvayaśāmbhavakrama* f. 9^v lines 3ff.; MaSaṃ 1.74cd = line 13 on p. 86 of the *Śambhunirṇayatantra* MS (=*Ṣaḍanvayaśāmbhavakrama* f. 12^v

line 11); MaSaṃ 1.75 ≈ *Nityāṣoḍaśikārṇava* (NṢA) 1.2cd; MaSaṃ 11.2cd–3ab = NṢA 3.16cd–17ab; MaSaṃ 11.4ab ≈ NṢA 3.9ab; MaSaṃ 12.5ab ≈ NṢA 5.7; MaSaṃ 12.5cd = NṢA 5.6cd; MaSaṃ 22.9cd = NṢA 4.7ab; MaSaṃ 22.10ab ≈ NṢA 4.6cd; MaSaṃ 22.23cd ≈ NṢA 4.13; MaSaṃ 22.24 ≈ NṢA 4.14; MaSaṃ 22.25 ≈ NṢA 4.15ab; MaSaṃ 4.3 ≈ *Mṛgendrāgama* Caryāpāda 30; MaSaṃ 4.62–75 ≈ *Mahākālasaṃhitā* (Kāmakalā, 71–73); the *Agnipurāṇa*'s yogic section (chapters 372–73) has some passages that have significant parallels in the MaSaṃ (MaSaṃ 3.17, 4.9–11, 7.41–45ab, 8.81); the *Bhāgavatapurāṇa* has some passages that are parallel with MaSaṃ 12.16cd–17, 20–21ab; MaSaṃ 4.44–47ab ≈ *Prapañcasāra* 1.48–86; MaSaṃ 4.57–60ab ≈ *Prapañcasāra* 1.90–93.

13. In the sense on which Sanderson 1985, 214n110 remarks: "The distinction between Kula and Kaula traditions . . . is best taken to refer to the clan-structured tradition of cremation-grounds seen in the BY-PM [*Brahmayāmala-Picumata*], JY [*Jayadrathayāmala*], TS [*Tantrasadbhāva*], SYMT [*Siddhayogeśvarīmatatantra*], etc. (with its Kāpālika *kaulikā vidhayaḥ*) on the one hand and on the other its reformation and domestication through the banning of mortuary and all sect-identifying signs (*vyaktaliṅgatā*), generally associated with Macchanda / Matsyendra."
14. E.g., MaSaṃ 14.22cd: *granthiṃ nodgranthayed asya vinā kaulikatarpaṇāt*; 14.25cd: *tatra sarvārthadāyinyo vasanti kuladevatāḥ*; 17.27a: *kulāmṛtaiś ca māṃsaiś ca*; 18.10c: *kulāmṛtaṃ divyaṃ*; 20.14cd: *śītalāmṛtakallolad-hārāvṛṣṭikulāmṛtam*; 40.1ab: *atha devi pravakṣyāmi kulācāravidhikramam*; 54.15cd: *tasmāt parīkṣya dātavyā vidyeṣā kulaśāsane*; 55.42cd: *kulāmnāyam aśeṣaṃ tu tasmād uddhṛtya sārayet*.
15. In spite of all these, the words *kula*/*kaula* are not to be found in their technical senses in *paṭala*s 2–7, the main yogic section, nor can they be found in *paṭala*s 8–13, the main dīkṣā and Yoginī chapters.
16. *śatakoṭipravistaraṃ kulāmnāyam*.
17. *akṣayaṃ candradvīpaṃ tu yatra devī kulāmbikā*.
18. See Schoterman 1977, 1980, 1990, 1992; *Ṣaṭsāhasrasaṃhitā* 1982; Goudriaan 1983, 1986; *Kubjikāmatatantra* 1988; *Kubjikopaniṣad* 1994; Goudriaan 1983, 1986; Goudriaan and Schoterman 1988; Goudriaan and Schoterman 1994; Sanderson 1988: 686–88; Sanderson 2002; Dyczkowski 1989; Dyczkowski 2001; Heilijgers 1990; Heilijgers 1994; and Padoux 1994.
19. Bagchi (1931, 2) quotes the *Kubjikātantra* (which is different from the *Kubjikāmatatantra* that Goudriaan and Schoterman edited in 1988) to hint at the cult's foreign origin. Dyczkowski (1989, 92) tends to place it in the Western Himalayas, but later says (2001, 27) that "there seems to be little reason to

doubt that, at some stage in the early development of the tradition, Kubjikā was a South Indian goddess." Schoterman (1982, 5) mentions Nepal as a possibility, but prefers (Northern) India, and especially Koṅkana, and says that the cult's "historical origins [are] still a mystery" (ibid., 6). Goudriaan and Gupta 1981, 52 suggest the Himalayan region, "Kashmir, Nepal, or somewhere between." As regards Kubjikā's name, it basically means "humped-back" or "crooked." On the one hand, it refers to her deformed or bent-over body, for which reasons are given in texts by quoting different myths (Dyczkowski 1989, 88 and see Sanderson's remarks in Padoux 1986, 166), on the other hand it indicates her connection with the coiled Kuṇḍalinī Śakti (Schoterman 1982, 11; Dyczkowski 1989: 88–89; Dyczkowski, 2001,42n89). Note that the *Kubjikāmatatantra*, the root text of the tradition is probably the oldest source of the system of power centers (cakra) closely associated with Kuṇḍalinī-yoga. See Sanderson 1988, 687.

20. Schoterman doubts if Kubjikā's cult is still alive, and says that it "seems that Kubjikā ceased to be worshipped sometime around the 15*th* or 16*th* century AD in Nepal" (1982, 6). Dyczkowski (1989, 88) says that "Kubjikā is still worshipped on certain occasions in the Kathmandu valley although her cult is now hardly known to anybody." According to Dyczkowski (2001, 22), Kubjikā is "the goddess of most, if not all of the higher caste priests of the Hindu Newars." He gives further examples of contemporary nyāsa rituals with Kubjikā's mantras in Nepal (2001, 23n.38). Also, Kubjikā is "virtually unknown outside the circles of her Newar initiates in the Kathmandu valley," but it "does not mean that Kubjikā is a Nepalese Goddess" (Dyczkowski 2001, 25).
21. For a reference to Kubjeśvara, see MaSaṃ 18.67–68ab. For a mention of the 'Navāntarātman' mantra, see MaSaṃ 11.36a.
22. That the Pañcapraṇava mantra is given in Sanderson 1990, 47 slightly differently, with a final *hsauḥ*, although *Kubjikāmatatantra* 5.39d says *au-paścimavibhūṣitam* (i.e., "on the western side, or left of the letter *au* [in the grid of the Mālinī Gahvara code]"), which is ṃ (see Schoterman 1982, 185–86).
23. Not to be confused with the *hādi* variety of the Śrīvidyā mantra. The name *hādi* appears in a corrupted form in MaSaṃ 1.71a and 11.14c.
24. *Nityāhnikatilaka* f. 5r marginalia. It is given as *sahakṣamalavarayīṃ* in *Kubjikopaniṣad* 1.2; see Goudriaan and Schoterman 1994, 73n4. According to Schoterman (1982, 311), the final *l-v-r-y* of these mantras represent the four elements earth, water, fire, and air. *hlvryūṃ* appears in *Kubjikopaniṣad* 5.1 as Kubjikā's mantra (see Goudriaan and Schoterman 1994, 85n2).
25. The mantras of the Yoginīs can be reconstructed as: *ḍāṃ **ḍākinyai** namaḥ ḍa ma la va ra yūṃ ḍāṃ ḍīṃ ḍūṃ ḍeṃ ḍaiṃ ḍoṃ ḍauṃ ḍaḥ; ḍāṃ ḍīṃ ḍūṃ ḍaiṃ*

ḍauṃ ḍaḥ ḍa ma la va ra yūṃ ***ḍākini*** *māṃ rakṣa rakṣa mat tvacaṃ rakṣa rakṣa sarvaśatruvaśaṃkari devi namaś cāmuṇḍe varada vicce ha sa kṣa ma laṃ vyūṃ ha sa kṣa ma la va yaṃ aiṃ klīṃ kṣauḥ śrīṃ haṃsānanda nāthaśrīpādukāṃ pūjayāmi kṣauḥ klīṃ aiṃ ḍāṃ* ***ḍākinyai*** *namaḥ; rāṃ* ***rākinyai*** *namaḥ. . . .*

26. I owe sincere thanks to Prof. Sanderson for drawing my attention to the *Nityāhnikatilaka*, lending me his manuscript of it and sending me his transcription of some of its passages.
27. See an image of the two embracing deities in Rawson 1988, 19.
28. Yakṣiṇī's attributes are those of Tripurā: a noose (*pāśa*), an elephant goad (*aṅkuśa*), a bow (*dhanus*), and five arrows (*bāṇa*).
29. Cf. MaSaṃ 11.51: *pravaded dakṣiṇe karṇe mantrarājaṃ guruḥ svayam.*
30. *phre[ṃ]* is encoded as *vahnipīṭhaśikhī yonir* in MaSaṃ 9.12c.
31. E.g.: *Kubjikāmatatantra*, *Ṣaḍanvayaśāmbhavakrama*, *Svacchandapaddhati*, *Jñānārṇavatantra*, Amṛtānanda's commentary to the *Yoginīhṛdaya*, *Rudrayāmala*, the *Kularatnoddyota*, *Kulārṇavatantra*, *Śāradātilaka*, *Kramasadbhāva*, *Lalitāsahasranāmastotra*, *Nityāhnikatilaka*, *Vāmakeśvaratantra*, *Toḍalatantra*, *Bhūtaśuddhitantra*, *Gandharvatantra*, *Ṣaṭcakranirūpaṇa*, *Śivasaṃhitā*.
32. *Kubjikāmatatantra* (KMT) 1.81d: *yuktā hṛtpaṅkajena ḍaralakasahajā pātu māṃ rudraśaktiḥ*; KMT 14.4ab: *ḍaralakasahajotthāḥ saṃsthitāḥ kulagocare*; KMT 23.92–93ab (coded in the Mālinī Gahvara: see Heilijgers 1994, 123n11 and Schoterman 1982, 181ff): *ū-ḍha-madhyagataṃ [ḍa] gṛhya ṇa-ṭa-madhyagataṃ [ra] tathā | va-kha-pūrvadvayoddhṛtya [laka] dha-ha-madhyagataṃ punaḥ [śa] || ya-sa-madhyagataṃ [ha] gṛhya etat ṣaṭkaṃ samuddhṛtam.* I.e. *ḍaralakaśaha*: note the *śa* instead of *sa*. It appears as *ḍādihāntābhidhānakam* in *Ṣaṭsāhasrasaṃhitā* 2.30d.
33. *Nityāhnikatilaka* f. 50v line 2: *athavā ḍaralakasahavarṇāḥ dīrghasvaravibhūṣitāḥ*.
34. *Kularatnoddyota* 3.57ab: *ḍaralakasahayasaṃjñā dhātujā dhātulipsavaḥ* (hypermetrical).
35. *Agnipurāṇa* 143.7: *yajed ravalakasahān śivendrāgniyame 'gnipe*, which should possibly be emended to *yajed ḍaralakasahān. . . .* (The same emendation is proposed in Heilijgers 1994, 123n13).
36. According to Heilijgers (1994, 226n2), *Kubjikāmatatantra* (KMT) 14.1d (*ṣaḍyoginyo vada prabho*; *ṣaḍyoginyo* being in the nominative instead of the accusative; Cf. Goudriaan 1989, 88) is clearly a reference to Ḍākinī, Rākinī, Lākinī, Kākinī, Sākinī, and Hākinī and "they are the deities of the fourth *cakra* [the Yoginīcakra] and also the presiding deities of the six *cakras* from ādhāra to ājñā" [described in the preceding chapters 11–13]. The KMT is not very explicit on the correspondences between Yoginīs and the six-cakra system. If

Heilijgers is right, the six Yoginīs were regarded as the presiding deities of the six power centers as early as the composition of the KMT. Otherwise, basing her opinion perhaps exclusively on KMT 14.2–5, she might be projecting later conceptions back onto the KMT. Actually, in KMT 11–13, in the description of the six power centers, there is no mention of the six Yoginīs.

37. *Nityāhnikatilaka* f. 50^{v} lines 2ff.
38. See the basic design of the maṇḍala below. Note that it is a variant of Kubjikā's maṇḍala in the *Agnipurāṇa* and has no traces of Tripurā's Śrīcakra (see Mallman 1963, 206).
39. Except that the supreme Yoginī is perhaps the manifestation of Kuṇḍaliṇī.
40. Mentioned by Mallinson 2007, 169n22. The marginal note reads: *śivamatsyeṃdrasaṃhitādau*. Mallinson dates the MS of the *Bṛhatkhecarīprakāśa* (witness 'S' in Mallinson 2007) to 1750–1800CE (Mallinson 2007, 40).
41. But note that the teachings of Yoginīs in Amṛtānandanātha''s commentary on the *Yoginīhṛdaya*, or at least teachings quoted in it from the *Svacchandasaṃgraha* are akin to those of the MaSaṃ.
42. *tantrāś ca bahavo devi mayā proktāḥ surārcite* || *na teṣu khecarī siddhir ākhyātā mṛtyunāśinī* | *mahākālaṃ ca mārtaṇḍaṃ vivekādyaṃ ca śābaram* (*em.* Mallinson; *śābharaṃ/śāṃvaraṃ* Codd) || *viśuddheśvarasaṃjñaṃ ca tathā vai jālaśaṃvaram* | *eteṣu tantravaryeṣu tadabhyāsaṃ prakāśitam*.
43. The *Vivekamārtaṇḍa* is probably the haṭha-yogic text well-known by the title *Gorakṣaśataka* (cf. Bouy 1994, 18 and Mallinson 2007, 166–67n9).
44. Compare this list of tantras with that of *Nityāṣodaśikārṇava* 1.13ff, which includes a *Śambara-*, a *Jālaśaṃvara-*, a *Tattvaśambaraka-*, a *Kālasāra-*, and a *Viśuddheśvaratantra*.
45. On the category of Bhairavatantra, see Sanderson 1988, 669.
46. In contrast with this, the *Bṛhatkhecarīprakāśa* uses the word *haṭha*, e.g., in f. 1^{v}: *namaskurmo haṭhasyāsya rājayogasya cāptaye* | *ādināthaṃ ca matsyeṃdraṃ gorakṣaṃ cānya* [sic] *yoginaḥ* ||.
47. On the intermingling of Kubjikā's and Tripurā's cults in South India, see also Khanna (1986, 65): "For the presence of the Kubjikā cult among the Southern Traipuras cf. *Ṣaḍanvayaśāmbhavakrama* of Umākānta. . . ; *Ānandakalpalatā* of Tejānandanātha. . . ."
48. It is an "isolated mountain in the Western Ghats, where Kṛishṇa and Balarâma defeated Jarâsindhu (Harivaṁśa, ch 42). There is a Tîrtha called Gorakṣa on top of Gomanta-giri. The mountain is situated in the country about Goa *i.e.*, the Konkan, called the country of Gomanta (*Padma P.* Âdi Kh., ch. 6)" (Dey 1927, 70). In addition, the "Harivaṃsa [*sic*] locates a mountain Gomanta-giri in North Kanara" (ibid.). And the "'Raivata hill in Gujarat was also called

Gomanta (*Mbh.* Sabhâ, ch. 14[:38; in a list of *janapadas*])" (ibid.). This latter interpretation is the one accepted by White (1996, 331).

49. See also a fine stone-image of Matsyendra sitting on a fish from Kadri exhibited in the State Government Museum, Mangalore in Deshpande 1986, 164.
50. As regards Maharashtra, the *Siddhāntaśikhāmaṇi*, a Maharashtra *vīraśaiva* text, also shows some resemblance to some of the passages of the MaSaṃ.
51. Matsyendra gives the Chola king the name Gorakṣeśa in MaSaṃ 55.17cd–18ab: *tataḥ svaśiṣyaṃ colendraṃ dīkṣayitvāgamoditaiḥ || dadau vidyākaro nāma gorakṣeśeti yogirāṭ*.
52. See images of Chola bronzes e.g. in Dehejia et al. 2006 or *Rauravāgama*, vol. 2.
53. See e.g. Huntington and Huntington 1985, 308: "Aiyanār-Śāstā, a hunter god . . . is known only in south India'." I owe thanks to Professor Sanderson for drawing my attention to the fact that Śāstṛ is an exclusively South Indian god and for providing the following references to South-Indian sources: *Rauravāgama* vol. 3, *paṭala* 49 (it outlines the procedure for a festival of the village deities [*grāmadevatāḥ*]: Gaṇeśa, Subrahmaṇya, Viṣṇu, Durgā, and Śāstṛ; *Ajitāgama*, vol 3. paṭala 83 (*śāstṛpratiṣṭhotsavavidhiḥ*), ibid.; the editor cites other *āgamic* sources (evidently from the same region) that deal with Śāstṛ: the *Suprabheda*, the *Bhīmasaṃhitā*, the *Padmasaṃhitā*, and the *Kulālaśāstra*. See also *Īśānaśivagurudevapaddhati* Kriyāpāda *paṭala* 58 on the pratiṣṭhā, etc. of Śāstṛ and his visualization, ibid. 32.9–15. See also Adiceam 1967.
54. For details, see Kiss 2009, 57.
55. More specifically, the *Prapañcasāra* probably originates in pre-thirteenth-century Orissa. See Sanderson 2007, 230–33.
56. A minor exception is 4.90b.
57. On *ṣaḍaṅgayoga* cf. Vasudeva 2004, 282 ff. Śaiva *ṣaḍaṅgayoga* very frequently includes tarka, which is absent from the MaSaṃ. Vasudeva (2004, 290) treats the MaSaṃ (with reference to MS W) first as if it had only four aṅgas (prāṇāyāma, dhāraṇā, pratyāhāra, dhyāna), then, on the same page, as *aṣṭāṅga* (*yama, niyama,* āsana, prāṇāyāma, dhāraṇā, pratyāhāra, dhyāna, samādhi). In fact, the MaSaṃ teaches neither yamas nor niyamas in the Pātañjala sense of the word, but it does have all the ancillaries of the *Yogasūtra* except yama and niyama for which it has a dehaśuddhi section (note also niyama mentioned in 6.31, 52.35, and 55.46).
58. 2.9b: *yoginīmelanaṃ*, 6.27c: *yoginīḥ* [*tarpayet*], 7.25a: *yoginīgaṇasammukhāṃ*.
59. 3.1b: *sādhakānāṃ hitāya vai*. On the sādhakas as the "target audience" of Śaiva (Saiddhāntika) yoga, see Brunner 1994, 431–35.
60. Cf. Brunner (1994, 437), who deals with yoga in Śaivasiddhānta texts. She says that though Śaivasiddhānta texts "sometimes use the terms *mūlādhāra* and

brahmarandhra, [they] ignore the names *svādhiṣṭhāna*, *maṇipūra*, *anāhata* and *viśuddha*."

61. *Yogasūtra* 2.54–55: *svaviṣayāsamprayoge cittasya svarūpānukāra ivendriyāṇāṃ pratyāhāraḥ*: "When they are separated from their objects, the senses' imitation, so to say, of the mind's true nature is Withdrawal."
62. *deśabandhaś cittasya dhāraṇā*: "'Fixation is the mind's binding to a spot'." In the MaSaṃ, it is not clear if the fixations are attached to single points of the body or involve the whole body. Since fixation in the MaSaṃ is a paraphrase of bhūtaśuddhi in paṭala 2, and the *śoṣaṇa*, etc. sequence in the bhūtaśuddhi ritual is attached to the Mūlādhāra, the heart, the middle of the eyebrows, and the whole body, one can say that the Pātañjala teaching of dhāraṇā is not so distant from the teaching of the MaSaṃ.
63. Vasudeva (2004, 319n113) says: "A derivative of the four fixations is also taught in the *Matsyendrasaṃhitā*. . . ." I agree, but clearly there are only three kinds of dhāraṇās in the text. Cf. MaSaṃ 6.2a: *dhāraṇā trividhā devi*.
64. There seems to be also a reference to *vāruṇī dhāraṇā* in 6.4b in MS W, but all other MSS read *dhāraṇā°* for W's *vāruṇā*.
65. These are noted in Vasudeva 2004, 411.
66. Note that *Gorakṣaśataka* (ed. by Nowotny), 114–15 is more careful and does not miss out *pratyāhāra* when teaching almost the same. See the Apparatus ad MaSaṃ 6.1cd.
67. On this process of "mental creation," see Brunner 1994, 442.
68. Compare MaSaṃ 7.7 (*iti pradhyāya tat samyak yoginaś cittavṛttayaḥ || śanair niścalatāṃ yānti divyajñānavicintanāt* and *Yogasūtra* 1.2 (*yogaś cittavṛttinirodhaḥ*).
69. The difference between the last two (fibers and filament, i.e. *kesara* and *kiñjalka*) is not clear to me.
70. See e.g. Hatley 2007, 69–70, who mentions that Caṇḍikā's "identity may subsume any number of fierce Śaiva goddesses, especially Durgā and Cāmuṇḍā."
71. See Rao 1914 vol. 1, part 2, 346.
72. In the margin of MS Ja f .21v bottom: '*navāntarātmā*'; also the Navātman mantra is incorporated in the main mantric system of the MaSaṃ.
73. Since there is very little theology in the MaSaṃ, it is difficult to say with absolute certainty whether the text is dualistic or non-dualistic. Rather, the MaSaṃ, being very practice-oriented, concentrates on mental techniques that can be related to both.
74. See Brunner 1994, 457 on how Saiddhāntika texts insist that the mere "imagination" of the rites can have no fruit "without the real transformation of the worshipper."

75. Note the somewhat similar verse in the *Siddhāntaśikhāmaṇi*, a Vīraśaiva text from Maharashtra quoted above (17.21): *yad yat paśyan dṛśā yogī manasā cintayaty api || tat tat sarvaṃ śivākāraṃ saṃvidrūpaṃ prakāśyate.* (Whatever the yogin sees with his eyes or even thinks of with his mind, all that shines in the form of Śiva [and his] consciousness.)

76. See note 3.

Bibliography

This bibliography includes works cited in this volume, as well as some available Nāth texts and/or on yoga and relevant manuscripts. In most cases, original sources are referred to according to the "traditional" author, e.g. Gorakhnath or Kabir. Since there are many editions of the original sources—and different collaborators have employed different editions—all editions cited in the text are included in this bibliography.

Abhinavagupta. 1987. *The Tantrāloka of Abhinavagupta with commentary by Rājānaka Jayaratha*, ed. Mukund Ram Shastri et al., 12 vols. Allahabad: Indian Press, 1918–1938. [Reprinted with introduction and notes by R. C. Dwivedi and Navjivan Rastogi, 8 vols. Delhi: Motilal Banarsidass.]

Acharya, Jadavji Trikamji. 1992. *Caraka saṃhitā with the commentary of Cakrapāṇidatta*. Benares: Chaukhamba Surabharati Prakashan. [First published in 1941.]

Adi Granth [as *Sri Guru Granth Sahib: With Complete Index*]. 1996. Prepared by Winand M. Callewaert. 2 parts. Delhi: Motilal Banarsidass.

Adiceam, Marguerite E. 1967. *Contribution á l'étude d'Aiyanār-Sāstā*. Pondicherry: Institut français d'Indologie.

Agnipurāṇam. 2001. Ed. K. L. Joshi. Sanskrit text and English Translation by M. N. Dutt. Delhi: Parimal Publications. Parimal Sanskrit Series No. 53.

Agrawal, Purushottam. 2004. Seeking an Alternative to Religion Itself. In *Theatology: Literary Studies in India*, ed. Sibaji Bandyopadhyay, 208–29. Kolkata: Jadavpur University.

Ajitāgama. 1964–1991. 3 vols. Édition critique par N. R. Bhatt. Publications de l'Institut français d'indologie no. 24. Pondichéry: Institut français d'indologie.

Appiah, Kwame Anthony. 2005. *The Ethics of Identity*. Princeton, NJ: Princeton University Press.

Aranya, Swami Hariharananda, ed. and trans. 1981. *Yoga Philosophy of Patañjali Containing his aphorisms with the commentary of Vyāsa in the original Sanskrit, and annotations thereon with copious hints on the practice of Yoga.* Calcutta: University of Calcutta.

Bagchi, P. C. 1931. On Foreign Element in the Tantra. *Indian Historical Quarterly* 7, no. 1 (March): 1–16.

Bandyopādhyāẏ, Asitkumār. 1993. *Bāṃlā sāhityer itibṛtta: tṛtīẏa khaṇḍa, pratham parba: saptadaś śatābdī.* 3ẏa saṃ. Kalikātā: Maḍārṇ buk ejensī. [First published in 1966.]

Banerjea, Akshaya Kumar. 1988. *Philosophy of Gorakhnath with Goraksha-Vacana-Sangraha.* Delhi/Varanasi: Motilal Banarsidass. [First published in 1962. The 1983 edition was published by the Gorakhnath Mandir, Gorakhpur.]

Banerji, S. C. 1992. *Tantra in Bengal: A Study in its Origin, Development and Influence,* 2nd . New Delhi, India: Manohar. [First published in 1978.]

Banerjee-Dube, Ishita. 2007. *Religion, Law, and Power: Tales of Time in Eastern India, 1860–2000.* London: Anthem Press.

Banerjee-Dube, Ishita and Johannes Beltz. eds. 2008. *Popular Religion and Ascetic Practices: New Studies on Mahima Dharma.* New Delhi: Manohar.

Banerjee-Dube, Ishita and Saurabh Dube, eds. 2009. *Ancient to Modern: Religion, Power, and Community in India.* New Delhi: Oxford University Press.

Barrett, Ron. 2008. *Aghor Medicine: Pollution, Death, and Healing in Northern India.* Berkeley, CA: University of California Press.

Barry, Brian. 2002. *Culture and Equality: An Egalitarian Critique of Multiculturalism.* Cambridge, MA: Harvard University Press.

Barth, Fredrik, ed. 1998. *Ethnic Groups and Boundaries: The Social Organization of Culture Difference.* Long Grove, IL: Waveland Press, Inc. [First published in 1969.]

Barthwal, Pitambar Datt. 1946. *Hindī kavitā meṃ yog-pravāh* In *Yoga-pravāh. Cune hue lekhoṅ kā saṃgraha,* 54–8. Varanasi: Śrī Kāśī-vidyāpīṭha. [This essay was first published in 1930.]

———. 1955. *Rāmānand kī hindī rachnāem.* Kashi: Nagari Pracharini Sabha.

———. 1978. *Traditions of Indian Mysticism based upon Nirguna School of Hindi Poetry.* New Delhi: Heritage Publishers. [[First published in 1936 as *Nirguna School of Hindi Poetry.*]

———. 2004. "The Times and their Need." In *Religious Movements in South Asia 600–1800,* ed. D. Lorenzen, 253–68. Oxford/NY/Delhi: Oxford University Press.

Bartz, Richard K. and Monika Thiel-Horstmann, eds. 1989. *Living Texts from India.* Wiesbaden: Otto Harrassowitz:

Basu, Kedarnath. 1889. "On the Minor Vaishnava Sects of Bengal." *Journal of the Anthropological Society of Bombay* 1, no. 8: 477–504.

Basu, Maṇīndramohan. 1932. *Sahajiẏā sāhitya*. Kalikātā, India: Kalikātā biśvabidyālaẏ.

Bäumer, Bettina. 2008. Tantric elements in Bhima Bhoi's *ouvre*. In *Popular Religion and Ascetic Practices: New Studies on Mahima Dharma*, ed. Ishita Banerjee-Dube and Johannes Beltz, 159–72. New Delhi: Manohar.

Bersten, Maxine, and Eleanor Zelliot. 1988. *The Experience of Hinduism: Essays on Religion in Maharashtra*. Albany, NY: State University of New York Press.

Bhadra, Gautam et al., eds. 1999. *Subaltern Studies X: Writings on South Asian History and Society.* New Delhi: Oxford University Press.

Bhāgavatapurāṇa. 1996. The Bhāgavata. [*Śrīmad Bhāgavata Mahāpurāṇa*]. 6 vols. Critically edited by H. G. Shastri. Ahmedabad. B. J. Institute of Learning and Research. [Previous editions referred to in this critical edition: K. (Kumbhakonam), G. (Gorakhpur), N. (Nadiad).]

Bharati, Agehananda. 1965. *The Tantric Tradition*. London: Rider.

Bharati, Dharmavir. 1968. *Siddha-sāhitya*. Ilāhābād: Kitāb Sahal.

Bhaṭṭācārya, Upendranāth. 1408. *Bāṃlār bāul o bāul gān*. 3ẏa saṃ. Kalikātā, India: Oriẏenṭ buk kompāni. [First published in 1364.]

Bhaṭṭācāryya, Āśutoṣ. 1957. *Bāṃlār lok-sāhitya*. Paribarddhita 2ẏa saṃ. Kalikātā, India: Kyālkāṭā buk hāus. [First published in 1954.]

Bhattacharya, Ahbhushan et al, ed. and trans. 1972. *The Kūrma Purāṇa (with English translation)*. Varanasi: All-India Kashiraj Trust.

Bhattacharya, France. 1996. La secte des Naths et le *Manasā Maṅgal*. In *Traditions orales dans le monde indien. Études reunies par C. Champion (Puruṣārtha 18)*, ed. Catherine Champion, 315–25. Paris: École des Hautes Etudes en Sciences Sociales.

Bhoi, Bhima. 1925. *Stuti Chintamoni*. In *Bhima Bhoi Granthabali*. Comp. A. Mahanti. Cuttack: Prachi Samiti.

———. 1971. *Bhaktakabi Bhima Bhoinka Granthabali*. Cuttack: Dharma Grantha Store.

Biardeau, Madeleine and Charles Malamoud. 1976. *Le sacrifice dans l'Inde ancienne*. Paris: Presses Universitaires de France.

Bisschop, Peter. 2005. Pañcārthabhāṣyam on Pāśupatasūtra 1.37–39. Recovered from a Newly Discovered Manuscript. *Journal of Indian Philosophy* 33: 259–51.

Bose, Manindra Mohan. 1930. *The Post-Caitanya Sahajiā Cult of Bengal*. Calcutta, India: The University of Calcutta.

Bouillier, Veronique. 1986. La caste sectaire des Kanphata Jogi dans le royaume du Népal: l'exemple de Gorkha. *Bulletin de l'Ecole française d'Extrême-Orient* 75: 125–167.

———. 1991. Growth and decay of a Khanphata Yogi monastery in south-west Nepal. *The Indian Economic and Social History Review* 28, no. 2: 151–70.

———. 2008. *Itinérance et vie monastique. Les ascètes Nāth Yogī en Inde contemporaine*. Paris: Éditions de la Maison des sciences d l'homme.

Bouy, Christian. 1994. *Les Nātha-yogin et les Upaniṣads. Étude d'histoire de la littérature hindoue*. Paris: Editions de Boccard.

Brahmayāmala. NAK 3–370, Nepalese-German Manuscript Preservation Project, reel no. A42/6.

Bṛhatkhecarīprakāśa. Scindia Oriental Research Institute Library MS 14575. Ujjain, Madhya Pradesh.

Briggs, George Weston. 1920. *The Chamars*. Delhi: Low Price Publications.

———. 2001. *Gorakhnāth and the Kānphaṭa Yogīs*. Delhi/Varanasi/Patna: Motilal Banarsidass. [First published by YMCA in 1938.]

Brooks, Douglas Renfrew. 1992. *Auspicious Wisdom: The Texts and Traditions of Śrīvidyā Śākta Tantrism in South India*. Albany, NY : State University of New York Press.

Brunner, Hélène. 1994. The Place of Yoga in the Śaivāgamas. In *Paṇḍit N. R. Bhatt Felicitation Volume,* ed. P-S. Filliozat, S. P. Narang, and C. P. Bhatta, 425–61. Delhi, India: Motilal Banarsidass.

Cakrabarttī, Praphullacaraṇ. 1955. *Nāthdharma o sāhitya*. Ālipurduẏār, India: Praphulla Caraṇ Cakrabarttī.

Callewaert, Winand, and Bart Op de Beeck. 1991. *Nirguṇ Bhakti Sagar. Devotional Hindi Literature. A critical edition of the* Pañc-Vānī *or Five Works of Dādū, Kabīr, Nāmdev, Rāidās, Hardās with the Hindi Songs of Gorakhnāth and Sundardās, and a complete word-index*. 2 vols. Delhi: Manohar. [Kabir's *Bijak* is included from the edition of Shukdeo Singh. The *Kabir-granthavali* used is the abridged version of P. N. Tiwari. The *Adi Granth* (*Guru Granth Sahib*) songs and verses are not included.]

Cashin, David. 1995. *The Ocean of Love: Middle Bengali Sufi Literature and the Fakirs of Bengal*. Stockholm, Sweden: Association of Oriental Studies, Stockholm University.

Chakrabarti, Kisor Kumar. 1999. *Classical Indian Philosophy of Mind: The Nyāya Dualist Tradition*. Albany, NY: SUNY Press.

Chakravarti, Chintaharan. 1963. *Tantras. Studies on Their Religion and Literature*. Calcutta: Punthi Pustak.

Champion, Catherine. 1989. A contre courant (*ulṭā sādhanā*). Tradition orale du Nord-est de l'Inde: l'exemple des récits chantés bhojpuri. In *Living Texts from India*, ed. Richard K. Bartz and Monika Thiel-Horstmann, 63–85. Wiesbaden: Otto Harrassowitz:

———. 1994a. Entre la Caste et la Secte: Un *kissa* du répertoire des Bhartrhari Jogi Musulmans de la Région de Gorakhpur (Uttar Pradesh). *Puruṣārtha* 17: 25–41.

———. 1994b. The Nayanā-Yogin Songs in the Devotional Literature of Mithila. In *Studies in South Asian Devotional Literature*, ed. Alan W. Entwistle and Francoise Mallison, 65–81. New Delhi/Paris: Manohar/École Française d'Extrême-Orient.

———, ed. 1996. *Traditions orales dans le monde indien. Études reunies par C. Champion (Puruṣārtha 18)*. Paris: École des Hautes Etudes en Sciences Sociales.

The Communal Problem: Report of the Kanpur Riots Enquiry Committee. 2006. With an Introduction by Bipan Chandra. New Delhi: National Book Trust.

Chatterji, Suniti Kumar. 1970. *The Origin and Development of the Bengali Language*. London: George Allen & Unwin. [First published in 1926.]

Das, Paritosh. 1972. *Caitanyottar pratham cāriṭi sahajiẏā pūthi*. Kalikātā, India: Bhāratī buk sṭal.

———. 1988. *Sahajiya Cult of Bengal and Pancha Sakha Cult of Orissa*. Calcutta: Firma KLM.

Dasgupta, Shashibhushan. 1995. *Obscure Religious Cults*. Calcutta: KLM Private Ltd. [First published in 1946, 3rd edition.]

Datta, Akṣaẏkumār. 1394. *Bhāratbarṣīya upāsak-sampradāẏ*. Pratham bhāg. Kalkātā, India: Karuṇā prakāśānī. [First published in 1318.]

Davidson, Ronald M. 2002. "Reframing *Sahaja*: Genre, Representation, Ritual and Lineage." *Journal of Indian Philosophy* 30, no.1: 45–83.

Dehejia, Vidya. 1986. *Yoginī Cult and Temples. A Tantric Tradition*. Delhi: National Museum.

Dehejia, Vidya et al. 2006. *Chola. Sacred Bronzes of Southern India*. London: Royal Academy of Arts.

Deshpande, M. N. 1986. *The Caves of Panhāle-Kājī (Ancient Pranālaka). An art historical study of transition from Hinayana, Tantric Vajrayana to Nath* Sampradāya. Memoirs of the Archaeological Survey of India. New Delhi: Archaeological Survey of India.

Dey, Nundo Lal. 1927. *The Geographical Dictionary of Ancient and Mediaeval India*. London: Luzac & Co.

Dezső, Csaba. ed. 2007. *Indian languages and texts through the ages. Essays of Hungarian indologists in honour of Prof. Csaba Tottossy*. New Delhi: Manohar.

Digambarji, Swami et al. 1991. *Yoga Kośa: Yoga Terms: Explained with Reference to Context*. 2nd. ed. Lonavla, India: Kaivalyadhama S.M.Y.M. Samiti. [First published in 1972.]

Digby, Simon. 2000. *Wonder-Tales of South Asia*. New Delhi: Manohar.

———. 2001. *Sufis and Soldiers in Awrangzeb's Deccan: Malfúzát-i-Naqshbandiyya*. New Delhi/ New York: Oxford University Press.

Djurdjevic, Gordan. 2005. Masters of magical powers: the Nāth Siddhas in the light of esoteric notions. PhD diss., University of British Columbia.

Doniger, Wendy O'Flaherty. 1973. *Ascetism and Eroticism in the Mythology of Śiva*. London/NY/Toronto: Oxford University Press.

Dowman, Keith. 1985. *Masters of Mahamudra: Songs and Histories of the Eighty-Four Buddhist Siddhas*. Albany, NY: State University of New York Press.

Dvivedi, Hazariprasad, ed. 1980. *Nāth siddhoṃ kī bāniyāṃ*. Kāśī: Nāgarīpracāraṇī Sabhā. [First published in 1957.]

———. 1981. *Collected Works.* vol. 5. Delhi: Rajakamal Prakasan.

———. 1996. *Nāth-Sampradāy.* Ilāhābād: Lok Bhāratī Prakāśan. [First published in about 1950.]

———. 2000. *Kabir.* Delhi: Rajakamal Prakasan. [First published in 1942.]

———. 2004. Kabir's Place in Indian Religious Practice. In *Religious Movements in South Asia 600–1800,* ed. David N. Lorenzon, 269–87. Oxford/NY/Delhi: Oxford University Press. [Translated from the Hindi by D. Lorenzen and taken from *Kabir.* Delhi, 1971.]

———. 2006. *Hindi Sahitya ki Bhumika*—An Introduction to Hindi Literature. New Delhi: Rajkamal Prakashan.

Dyczkowski, Mark S. G. 1988. *The Canon of the Śaivāgama and the Kubjikā Tantras of the Western Kaula Tradition.* Delhi/Varanasi: Motilal Banarsidass.

———. 2001. *The Cult of the Goddess Kubjikā. A Preliminary Comparative Textual and Anthropological Survey of a Secret Newar Goddess.* Stuttgart: Franz Steiner Verlag.

———. 2004. *A Journey in the World of the Tantras.* Benares: Indica Books.

Eliade, Mircea. 1969. *Yoga, Immortality and Freedom.* Princeton, NJ: Princeton University Press.

Entwistle, Alan W. and Francoise Mallison, eds. 1994. *Studies in South Asian Devotional Literature.* New Delhi/Paris: Manohar/École Française d'Extrême-Orient.

Eschmann, Anncharlot. 2008. Mahima Dharma and Tradition. In *Popular Religion and Ascetic Practices: New Studies on Mahima Dharma,* ed. Ishita Banerjee-Dube and Johannes Beltz, 31–42. New Delhi: Manohar.

Fakir, Rudrani. 2005. *The Goddess and the Slave: The Fakir, the Mother and Maldevelopment.* Varanasi, India: Indica Books.

Ferrari, Fabrizio. 2007. "The Jewel of the Secret Path or the Neglected *guru*? Some Remarks on the *guruvāda* among the Bāuls of Bengal." In *Guru, the Spiritual Master in Eastern and Western Traditions: Authority and Charisma,* edited by Antonio Rigopoulos. New Delhi, India: D. K. Printworld; pp. 247–83. [First published in 2004 by the Venetian Academy of Indian Studies.]

Friedlander, Peter G. 1994. The Core of the *Vāṇī* of Raidās. In *Studies in South Asian Devotional Literature,* ed. Alan W. Entwistle and Francoise Mallison, 455–79. New Delhi/Paris: Manohar/École Française d'Extrême-Orient.

Gaeffke, Peter. 1992. How a Muslim looks at Hindu bhakti. In *Devotional Literature in South Asia. Current Research, 1985–1988,* ed. R. S. McGregor, 80–88. Cambridge: Cambridge University Press.

Gandhi, Rajmohan. 2006. *Mohandas: A True Story of a Man, his People and an Empire.* New Delhi: Penguin Books.

Garson, Nathaniel DeWitt. 2004. "Penetrating the Secret Essence Tantra: Context and Philosophy in the Mahāyoga System of rNying-ma Tantra" PhD diss., University of Virginia.

Garzilli, Enrica. 1988. [Review of] Matsyendra Saṃhitā Ascribed to Matsyendranātha, Part I. Edited by Debabrata Sensharma. *Journal of the American Oriental Society* 118, no. 4: 543–45.

Gauḍapāda. 2000. *L'Āgamaśāstra Un traité vedāntique en quatre chapitres.*texte, traduction et notes de Christian Bouy. Publications de L'Institut de Civilisation Indienne, No. 69. Paris: De Boccard.

Gharote, M. L., and V. A. Bedekar. 1989. *Descriptive Catalogue of Yoga Manuscripts.* Lonavla: Kaivalyadhama.

The Gheranda Samhita. 1976. A Treatise on Hatha Yoga. Trans. Sris Chandra Vasu. Madras: The Adyar Library. [First published in 1895; the 1979 edition is by Satguru Publications.]

Gogā Mahāpurāṇ. n.d. Delhi: Lakṣmī Prakāśan.

Gold, Ann Grodzins. 1988. *Fruitful Journeys: The Ways of Rajasthani Pilgrims.* Berkeley, CA: University of California Press.

———. 1989. The Once and Future Yogi: Sentiments and Signs in the Tale of a Renouncer-King. *The Journal of Asian Studies* 48, no. 4 (Nov. 1989): 770–86.

———. 1991. Gender and Illusion in a Rajasthani Yogi Tradition. In *Gender, Genre, and Power in South Asian Expressive Traditions,* ed. Arjun Appadurai, Frank J. Korom, and Margaret A. Mills, 102–35. Philadelphia, PA: University of Pennsylvania.

———. 1992. *A Carnival of Parting: The Tales of King Bharthari and King Gopi Chand as Sung and Told by Madhu Natisar Nath of Ghatiyali, Rajasthan, India.* Berkeley, CA: University of California Press.

———. 2002 The Tender Trap: Lord Shiva's Wedding in Vernacular Mythology, in *Multiple Histories: Culture and Society in the Study of Rajasthan,* ed. L. A. Babb, Varsha Joshi, and Michael W. Meister, 84–116. Jaipur: Rawat Publications.

Gold, Daniel. 1987a. Clan and Lineage among the Sants: seed, substance, service. In *The Sants. Studies in a Devotional Tradition of India,* ed. Karine Schomer and W. H. McLeod, 305–27. Delhi/Varanasi/Patna: Motilal Banarsidass.

———. 1987b. *The Lord as Guru. Hindi Sants in North Indian Tradition.* NY/Oxford: Oxford University Press.

———. 1992. Ascenso y caída del poder de los yoguis: Jodhpur 1803–1842. *Estudios de Asia y Africa, El Colegio de México* 27, no. 1: 9–27.

———. 1995. The Instability of the King: Magical Insanity and the Yogi's Power in the Politics of Jodhpur, 1803–1843. In *Bhakti Religion in North India. Community Identity and Political Action,* ed. David N. Lorenzen, 120–32. Delhi: Manohar.

———. 1996. Experiences of Ear-Cutting: The Significances of a Ritual of Bodily Alteration for Householder Yogis. *Journal of Ritual Studies* 10, no. 1: 91–112.

———. 1999. Nath Yogis as Established Alternatives: Householders and Ascetics Today. *JAAS* 34, no. 1: 68–88.

———. 2005. The Sufi Shrines of Gwalior City: Communal Sensibilities and the Accessible Exotic Under Hindu Rule. *Journal of Asian Studies* 64, no. 1: 127–50.

Gold, Daniel and Ann Grodzins Gold. 1984. The Fate of the Householder Nath. *History of Religions* 24, no. 2 (November 1984): 113–32.

Gonda, Jan. 1985. "Soma, Amṛta and the Moon". In J. Gonda, *Change and Continuity in Indian Religion.* 1st Indian ed. Delhi, India: Munshiram Manoharlal, pp. 38–70. [First published in 1965.]

Goodall, Dominic. 1998, ed. and trans. *Bhaṭṭa Rāmakaṇṭa's Commentary on the Kiraṇatantra.* vol. 1: chapters 1–6. Collection Indologie—98. Paris: Institut français de Pondichéry—École française d'Extrême-Orient.

Gopaladas. 1993. *The Sarvangi of Gopaldas: A 17th Century Anthology of Bhakti Literature.* Ed. by Winand M. Callewaert. New Delhi: Manohar.

Gorakh Bodh arthāt Gorakṣanāth Matsyendranāth Samvād. n.d. Ed. Yogi Bhambhulnath. Hardwar: Sampatnath Yogi.

Gorakh bodh vāṇī saṃgrah. Bhajanamālā n.d. Ed. Maharaj Ramprakash Agravat. Ajmer: Ṣrī Sarasvatī Prakāśan.

Gorakhnath. 1918. *Amaraugha-śāsana. The Amaraugha-shāsan of Goraksha-nātha.* Ed. Mahāmahopādhyāya Paṇḍit Mukund Rām Shāstrī. Bombay: Research Department, Jammu and Kashmir/Nirnaya Sagar Press.

———. 1946/1955/1960/1994. *Gorakh bānī*, 3rd ed. Ed. Pitāmbaradatta Baḍathval (P. D. Barthwal). Allahabad: Hindi Sahitya-sammelan. [First published in 1942.] Another version was edited by Ramlal Srivastav and published by the Gorakhnāth Mandir as *"Gorakh bānī," Viśeṣaṅk* in *Yog Vānī*, special issue no. 1, Gorakhpur, 1979). This edition contains extra material and interpretations not avaliable in Barthwal's edition.

———. 1954. *Amaraughaprabodha.* In *Siddha-siddhanta-paddhati & Other Works of the Nath Yogis*, ed. Kalyani Mallik. Poona: Poona Oriental Book House.

———. 1954. *Siddha-siddhānta-paddhati* In *Siddha-siddhanta-paddhati & Other Works of the Nath Yogis*, ed. Kalyani Mallik. Poona: Poona Oriental Book House.

———. 1976. *Das Gorakṣaśataka.* Ed. Fausta Nowotny. Köln: K. A. Nowotny.

———. 1980/2002. *Amanaskayoga.* Ed. Rāmlāl Śrīvāstav. Gorakhpur: Gorakhnāth Mandir.

———. 2007. *La centurie de Gorakṣa, suivi du Guide des Principes des Siddhas.* Trans. Tara Michaël. Paris: Éditions Almora.

———. 1981. *Gorakṣaśataka.* Ed. Rāmlāl Śrīvāstav. Gorakhpur: Gorakhnāth Mandir.

Gorakh carit. N.d. Ed. Rāmlāl Śrīvāstav. Gorakhpur: Gorakhnāth Mandir.

Gorakhnāth caritra. 1981. Ed. Camanlāl Gautam. Mathurā: Saṃskṛti Saṃsthān.

Gorakṣanātha (see Gorakhnath).

Gorakṣasaṃhitā. 1976. part 1. Ed. Janārdana Pāṇḍeya. Varanasi: Sampūrṇānanda Saṃskṛta Viśvavidyālaya.

Gorakṣa-siddhānta-saṃgraha. 1925. Ed. Gopinath Kaviraj. Princess of Wales Saraswati Bhavana Texts N°18. Varanasi: Vidya Vila Press.

———. 1973. Ed. Janārdana Śāstrī Pāṇḍeya. Varanasi: Varanaseya Sanskrit Vishvavidyalaya.

———. 1979. Ed. Rāmlāl Śrīvāstav. Gorakhpur. Gorakhnāth Mandir.

Goudriaan, Teun. 1983. Some beliefs and rituals concerning time and death in the Kubjikāmata. In *Selected Studies On Ritual In The Indian Religions. Essays to D.J Hoens*, ed. Ria Kloppenborg, 92–117. Leiden: E. J. Brill.

———. 1986. Kubjikā's Samayamantra and its Manipulation in the Kubjikāmata. In *Mantras et diagrammes rituels dans l'hindouisme*, ed. André Padoux, 141–68. Paris: Éditions du Centre National de la recherche scientifique.

———, ed.1992. *Ritual and Speculation in Early Tantrism. Studies in Honor of Andre Padoux*. Albany, NY: SUNY Press.

Goudriaan, Teun and Sanjukta Gupta. 1981. *Hindu Tantric and Śākta Literature*. Wiesbaden: Harrasowitz.

Goswamy, B. N. and J. S. Grewal. 1967. *The Mughals and the Jogis of Jakhbar. Some Madad-i-Ma'sh and Other Documents*. Simla: Indian Institute of Advanced Study.

Gray, David B. 2007. *The Cakrasamvara Tantra: The Discourse of Śrī Heruka*. New York: The American Institute of Buddhist Studies.

Gupta, Maithilisharan. 2006. *Bhārat Bhāratī*. Jhansi: Saket Prakashan.

Hamer, Dean. 2004. *The God Gene: How Faith is Hardwired into Our Genes*. New York: Doubleday.

Hatley, Shaman. 2007. The *Brahmayāmalatantra* and Early Śaiva Cult of Yoginīs. PhD, diss., University of Pennsylvania.

Hausner, Sondra L. 2007. *Wandering with Sadhus: Ascetics in the Hindu Himalayas*. Bloomington, IN: Indiana University Press.

Hawley, John Stratton. 1995. The *Nirguṇ/Sagun* Distinction in Early Manuscript Anthologies of Hindu Devotion. In *Bhakti Religion in North India. Community Identity and Political Action*, ed. David N. Lorenzon, 160–80. Delhi: Manohar.

———. 2005. *Three Bhakti Voices: Mirabai, Surdas, and Kabir in Their Time and Ours*. New Delhi: Oxford University Press.

Hawley, John Stratton and Mark Juergensmeyer. 1988. *Songs of the Saints of India*. NY/London: Oxford University Press.

Hayes, Glen. 1985. "Shapes for the Soul: A Study of Body Symbolism in the Vaiṣṇava-Sahajiyā Tradition of Medieval Bengal" PhD diss., University of Chicago.

Hazra, R. C. 1975. *Studies in the Purāṇic Records on Hindu Rites and Customs*. Delhi: Motilal Banarsidass.

Heilijgers-Seelen, Dory. 1990. The Doctrine of the Ṣaṭcakra according to the Kubjikāmata. In *The Sanskrit Tradition and Tantrism*, ed. T. Goudriaan, 56–65. Leiden: Brill. [Originally presented at the Seventh World Sanskrit Conference, Kern Institute, Leiden, (August 3–29, 1987)].

———. 1994. *The System of Five Cakras in Kubjikāmata-tantra 14–16*. Groningen Oriental Studies, vol. 9. The Netherlands, Groningen: Egbert Forsten.

Henry, Edward O. 1991. Jogis and Nirgun Bhajans in Bhojpuri-Speaking India. *Ethnomusicology* 35, no. 2: 221–42.

Hess, Linda. 1987. Kabir's Rough Rhetoric. In *The Sants. Studies in a Devotional Tradition of India*, ed. Karine Schomer and W. H. McLeod, 143–65. Delhi/Varanasi/Patna: Motilal Banarsidass.

Huntington, Samuel P. 1997. *The Clash of Civilizations and the Remaking of World Order.* New York: Touchstone.

Huntington, Susan L. and John C. Huntington 1985. *The Art of Ancient India: Buddhist, Hindu and Jain*. Tokyo: John Weatherhill.

Īśānaśivagurudevapaddhati. 1990. Ed. Gaṇapati Śāstrī. 2 vols. Delhi: Bharatiya Vidya Prakashan. [First published in 1920.]

Jacobsen, Knut A., ed. 2005. *Theory and Practice of Yoga. Essays in honour of Gerald James Larson*. Leiden: Brill.

Jha, Durgadhara, ed. 1997. *Padārthadharmasaṅgraha* of Praśastapāda. *Praśastapādabhāṣyam (Padārthadharmasaṅgraha) of Praśastapādācārya with the Commentary Nyāyakandalī by Śrīdhara Bhaṭṭa along with Hindi Translation*. Ganganathajaha-Granthamala, vol. 1. Varanasi: Sampurnanand Sanskrit University.

Jha, Sakti Nath. 1995. "Cāri-Candra Bhed: Use of the Four Moons." In *Mind Body and Society: Life and Mentality in Colonial Bengal,* edited by Rajat Kanta Ray. Calcutta, India: Oxford University Press, 65–108.

———. 1999. *Bastubādī bāul: udbhab, samāj, saṃskṛti o darśan*. Kalkātā, India: Loksaṃskṛti o ādibāsī saṃskṛti kendra, Tathya o saṃskṛti bibhāg, Paścimbaṅga sarkār.

Junejā, Ved Prakāś. 1984. *Nāth-sampradāy aur sāhitya*. Gorakhpur: Gorakhpur mandir.

Kabir. 1969. *Kabir-gramthavali*. Ed. by Mataprasad Gupta with a modern-Hindi commentary. Allahabad: Lokabharati Prakasan.

———. 1977. *The Bijak of Kabir.* Trans. by Ahmad Shah. New Delhi: Asian Publication Services. [First published in 1917.]

———. 1983. *The Bijak of Kabir.* Trans. by Linda Hess and Shukdev Singh. San Francisco, CA: North Point Press. [Essays and notes by Linda Hess. These are the best translations but are not complete.]

———. 1991. *Songs of Kabir from the Adi Granth*. Trans. and introduction by Nirmal Dass. Albany, NY: State University of New York Press.

———. 1993. *A Weaver Named Kabir: Selected Verses with a Detailed Biographical and Historical Introduction.* Trans. and introduction by Charlotte Vaudeville. Delhi: Oxford University Press.

———. 1998. *The Bijak of Guru Kabir.* Vol. 1, *Ramainis.* Trans. Jagessar Das. Surrey, Canada: The Kabir Association of Canada.

———. 2000. *The Millennium Kabir Vani: A Collection of Pad-s.* Edited by Winand M. Callewaert with Swapna Sharma and Dieter Taillieu. New Delhi: Manohar.

Kamal. 1994. Las canciones de Kamal. Ed. and trans. by David N. Lorenzen and Uma Thukral. *Estudios de Asia y África* 29, no. 2: 259–71.

Kapani, Lakshmi. 1992, 1993. *La notion du saṃskāra dans l'Inde brahmanique et bouddique*, 2 vols. Publications de l'Institut de Civilisation Indienne, no. 59. Paris: De Boccard.

Kaviraj, Gopinath. 1995. *Tāntrik sādhanā o siddhānta.* Dvitīẏa khaṇḍa. Bardhamān, India: Bardhamān biśvabidyālaẏ. [First published in 1975.]

———. 1994. *Tāntrik vāṅmaya mẽ śākta dṛṣṭi.* Tṛtīyāvṛtti. Paṭnā, India: Bihār rāṣṭrabhāṣā pariṣad. [First published in 1963.]

Khan, Dominique-Sila. 1997. *Conversions and Shifting Identities: Ramdev Pir and the Ismailis in Rajasthan.* New Delhi: Manohar.

Khanna, Madhu. 1986. The Concept and Liturgy of the Śrīcakra based on Śivānanda's Trilogy. Ph.D diss., Oxford University.

Kiehnle, Catharina. 1997. *The Conservative Vaiṣṇava: Anonymous Songs of the Jñāndev Gāthā.* Stuttgart: F. Steiner Verlag.

Kiss, Csaba. 2007. Notes on the *Matsyendrasaṃhitā.*' In *Indian languages and texts through the ages. Essays of Hungarian indologists in honour of Prof. Csaba Tottoss*, ed. Csaba Dezső. New Delhi: Manohar.

———. 2009. "Matsyendra's Compendium. Matsyendrasaṃhita. A critical edition and annotated translation of Matsyendrasaṃhita 1–13 and 55 with analysis." D. Phil. thesis. Balliol College, Oxford University.

Klostermaier, Klaus K. 1986. "Contemporary Conceptions of Karma and Rebirth Among North Indian Vaiṣṇavas." In *Karma and Rebirth: Post Classical Developments*, edited by Ronald W. Neufeldt, 83–108. Albany, NY: SUNY Press.

Knipe, David M. 1977. Sapiṇḍikaraṇa: The Hindu Rite of Entry into Heaven. In *Religious Encounters with Death*, ed. Frank Reynolds and Earle Waught, 111–24. University Park, PA: Pennsylvania State University Press.

Kosambi, K. K. 1975. *An Introduction to the Study of Indian History.* Bombay: Popular Prakashan.

Kripal, Jeffrey J. 1998. *Kālī's Child: The Mystical and the Erotic in the Life and Teachings of Ramakrishna.* Chicago: University of Chicago Press. [First published in 1995.]

Kubjikāmatatantra 1988. *The Kulālikāmnāya version.* Critical edition by T. Goudriaan and J. Schoterman. Leiden: E. J. Brill.

Kubjikopaniṣad. 1994. Ed. by Teun Goudriaan and Jan A. Schoterman. Groningen: Egbert Forsten.

Kukareti, Visnudatta. 1986. *Nāthpanth: Garhvāl ke paripreksya meṃ.* Gorakhnāth Mandir: Gorakhpur.

Kularatnoddyota, E-text prepared by Mark S. G. Dyczkowski based on several MSS

(Bodlian Library, Oxford: CSS MS no. C 348; NAK MS no: 1–1653 NGMPP reel no: B119/3, NAK MS no: 1–16, NGMPP reel no: A 206/10 etc.), http://muktalib5.org/DL_CATALOG/TEXTS/ETEXTS/kularatnoddyotaDEV.pdf.

Kulārṇava Tantra. 2002. Introduction by Arthur Avalon (Sir John Woodroffe), Readings by M. P. Pandit. Sanskrit Text by Tārānātha Vidyāratna. Delhi: Motilal Banarsidass. [First published in 1965.]

Kūrma Purāṇa. 1972. Ed. and trans. A. Bhattacharyya, A.S. Gupta, and S. Mukherji. Varanasi, India: All India Trust.

Kværne, Per. 1986. *An Anthology of Buddhist Tantric Songs: A Study of the Caryāgītī.* Bangkok: White Orchid.

Lalas, Sitaram. 1962–1978. Rajasthani *Sabad Kos*, 9 vols. Jodhpur: Rajasthani Shodh Sansthan.

Limaye, V. P and R. D. Vadekar, eds. 1958. *Eighteen Principal Upaniṣads (Upaniṣadic Text with Parallels from extant Vedic Literature, Exegetical and Grammatical Notes).* Poona: Vaidika Samsodhana Mandala.

Llewellyn, J. E., ed. 2005. *Defining Hinduism: A Reader.* London: Equinox.

Locke, John. 1980. *Karunamaya. The Cult of Avalokitesvara—Matsyendranath in the Valley of Nepal.* Kathmandu: Sahayogi Prakashan For Research Centre for Nepal and Asian Studies/Tribhuvan University.

Lorenzen, David N. 1972. *The Kāpālikas and Kālāmukhas: Two Lost Śaivite Sects.* Berkeley, CA: University of California Press.

———. 1987. Gorakhnāth. In *The Encyclopedia of Religion*, vol. 6, ed. Mircea Eliade,77–78. London and New York: MacMillan Publishing Co.

———. 1991. *Kabir Legends and Ananta-das's Kabir Parachai.* With a translation of the Kabir Parachai, prepared in collaboration with Jagdish Kumar and Uma Thukral, and with an edition of the Niranjani Panthi recenssion of this work. Albany, NY: State University of New York Press.

———, ed. 1995. *Bhakti Religion in North India. Community Identity and Political Action.* Delhi: Manohar.

———. 1996. *Praises to a Formless God: Nirguni Texts from North India.* Albany: State University of New York Press.

———, ed. 2004. *Religious Movements in South Asia 600–1800.* Oxford/NY/Delhi: Oxford University Press.

———. 2006. *Who Invented Hinduism? Essays on Religion in History.* New Delhi: Yoda Press.

———. 2007. Gentile Religion in South India, China, and Tibet: Studies by Three Jesuit Missionaries. *Comparative Studies of South Asia, Africa, and the Middle East* [Toronto] 27, no. 1: 205–15.

Lorenzen, David N. and Uma Thukral. 2005. Los diálogos religiosos entre Kabir y Gorakh. *Estudios de Asia y África* 40, no. 1: 161–77.

Mādhava-vidyāraṇya. 1967. *ŚrīŚaṅkara-dig-vijaya.* Śrī śrāvaṇa jñān-mandir: Hardvār.

Mahākālasaṃhitā. 1976. Guhyakālīkhaṇḍaḥ, parts 1–3, ed. Dr. Kiśoranāth Jhā. Illāhābād: Gaṅgānātha Jhā Kendrīya Saṃskṛta Vidyāpīṭha.

———. 1976. Kāmakalākhaṇḍaḥ. Ed. Dr. Kiśoranāth Jhā. Illāhābād Vidyāpīṭha: Gaṅganātha Jhā Kendrīya Saṃskṛta.

Mālinivijayottara Tantram. 1922. Ed. Madhusudan Kaul. Kashmir Series of Texts and Studies, no. 37. Bombay: Tattva-vivechaka Press.

Mallik, Kalyani. 1950. *Nāthsampradāẏer itihās, darśan o sādhanpraṇālī*. Kalikātā, India: Kalikātā biśvabidyālaẏ.

———. 1954. *Siddha-siddhānta-paddhati and Other Works of the Nātha Yogīs* . Poona: Poona Oriental Book House.

Mallinson, James. 2007. *The Khecarīvidyā of Ādinātha. A critical edition and annotated translation of an early text of haṭhayoga*. London: Routledge.

Mallison, Françoise, ed. 1991. *Littératures médiévales de l'Inde du nord. Contributions de Charlotte Vaudeville et de ses élèves*. Paris: École Française D'Extrême Orient.

Mallman, Maria-Thérèse de. 1963. *Les enseignements iconographiques de l'Agni-purana*. Paris: Presses Universitaires de France.

Manjhan Shattari Rajgiri, Mir Sayyid. 2000. *Madhumālatī: An Indian Sufi Romance*. Trans. with and introduction and notes by Aditya Behl and Simon Weightman. Oxford: Oxford University Press.

Mataṅgapārameśvara. 1982. (*Kriyāpāda, Yogapāda, Caryāpāda*) Ed. N. R. Bhatt. Pondichérry: Institut Français D'Indologie.

Matsyendranātha. *Akula-vīra-tantra*. 1996–2006. E-text in Mike Magee. *Shiva Shakti Mandalam. The inner wisdom of the hindu tantrik tradition*, www.shivashakti.com.

———. *Kaula-jñāna-nirṇaya*. 1986. In *Kaula-jñāna-nirṇaya of The School of Matsyendranatha*. Text edited with an Exhaustive Introduction by P.C. Bagchi, Translated into English by Michael Magee. Varanasi: Prachya Prakashan. [The original edition of 1934, besides the KJN, included other texts attributed to Matsyendra such as the *Akulavīra-tantra*, the *Kulānanda-tantra*, and the *Jñānakārikā*.]

———. 1994. *Matsyendrasaṃhita*, part 1. Ascribed to Matsyendranatha. Ed. Debabrata Sensharma. Calcutta: The Asiatic Society." [It corresponds to author Matsyendranatha.]

McGregor, R. S., ed. 1992. *Devotional Literature in South Asia. Current Research, 1985–1988*. Cambridge: Cambridge University Press.

McLeod, W. H. 1980a. *Early Sikh Tradition: A Study of the Janam-sakhis*. Oxford: Clarendon Press.

———. 1980b. (Trans. and introduction). *The B40 Janam-Sakhi*. Amritsar: Guru Nanak Dev University.

———. 1989. *The Sikhs. History, Religion, and Society*. New York: Columbia University Press.

Mishra, Bandhu. 1956 . *Miśra Bandu Vinod*. Lucknow: Ganga Granthagar.

Misra, Balakrushna.1981. Brahma nirupana gitare brahmanka sthiti bichara. In *Saptarshi* (Sambalpur University Journal) 78: 61–66.

Misra, Krsna Murari, et al, eds. 1980. *Smārikā: Param Pūjya Śraddheya Vāsudevnāth Ḍholī Buva Mahārāj Pīṭhārohaṇ Rajat-Mahotsav*. Gwalior, India: Dholi Buwa Math.

Monier-Williams, Monier [Sir]. 1984. *A Sanskrit-English Dictionary etymologically and philologically arranged with special reference to cognate Indo-European languages*. London: Oxford University Press. Reprint, Delhi: Motilal Banarsidass. [Originally published in 1899.]

———. 1982. *A Dictionary, English and Sanskrit*, reprint of 4th ed. London: Allen. Reprint, Delhi: Motilal Banarsidass. [Originally published in 1851.]

Mṛgendrāgama. 1985. Section des rites et section du comportement avec la vṛtti de Bhaṭṭanārāyaṇakaṇṭha. Traduction, Introduction et Notes par Hélène Brunner-Lachaux. Pondichéry, India: Institut de civilization indienne.

Mukhopādhyāẏ, Sukhmaẏ. 1994. *Bāṃlār nāth-sāhitya*. Kalkātā, India: Subarṇarekhā.

Muller-Ortega, Paul Eduardo. 2005. "*tarko yogāṅgam uttamam*": On subtle knowledge and the refinement of thought in Abhinavagupta's liberative Tantric method. In *Theory and Practice of Yoga. Essays in honour of Gerald James Larson*, ed. Knut A. Jacobsen, 181–212. Leiden: Brill.

Muñoz, Adrián. 2010. *La piel de tigre y la serpiente*: *La identidad de los Nāth Yoguis a través de sus leyendas*. Mexico City: El Colegio de México.

Nayak, P. M. 1984. A Study of the Contribution of the Sonepur Durbar to Literature (1837–1937), Ph.D diss., Sambalpur University.

Nāth, Rājmohan. 1964. *Baṅgīya nāth-panther prācīn-pũthi*. Kalikātā, India: Āsāmbaṅga yogi-sammilanī.

Nāth-siddha Carit Viśeṣāṅk. 1984. Ed. Rāmlāl Śrīvāstav. Gorakhpur: Gorakhnath Mandir.

Nityāhnikatilaka. Nepalese-German Manuscript Preservation Project. Access No.: 3/384, Reel No.: A 41/11. University of Hamburg.

Niśvāsatattvasaṅgraha. E-texts transcripts of Nepalese MSS No. 1–127 NGMPP A 41/14 and No. 5–2406 NGMPP A 159/18.

Oddie, Geofrrey A. 2006. *Imagined Hinduism: British Protestant Missionary Constructions of Hinduism, 1793–1900*. New Delhi: Sage Publications.

Openshaw, Jeanne. 2002. *Seeking Bāuls of Bengal*. Cambridge, UK: Cambridge University Press.

Padma Saṃhitā. 1974–1982. Critically edited by Smt. Seetha Padmanabhan and R. N. Sampath. Madras: Pancaratra Parisodhana Parisad.

Padoux, André, ed. 1986. *Mantras et diagrammes rituels dans l'hindouisme*. Paris: Éditions du Centre National de la recherche scientifique.

———. 1994. *Le coeur de la yoginī. Yoginīhṛdaya. Texte sanskrit traduit et annoté par André Padoux*. Paris: Collège de France, Publications de l'Institut de civilisation indienne Série in-8° Fascicule 63.

———. 2000. The Tantric Guru. In Tantra in Practice, ed. David Gordon White, 41–51. Princeton, NJ and Oxford: Princeton University Press.

Parākhyatantra, The. 2004. A Scripture of the Śaivasiddhānta. A critical edition and annotated translation by Dominic Goodall. Collection Indologie—98. Pondichéry, India: Institut français de Pondichéry—École française d'Extrême-Orient.

Patañjali. 1989. *Yoga sūtra.* The Kashi Sanskrit Series 110. Varanasi, India: Chaukhambha Sanskrit Sansthan.

———. 1996. *Yoga. Discipline of Freedom. The* Yoga Sutra *Attributed to Patanjali.* Trans. Barbara Stoler Miller. Berkeley, CA: University of California Press.

Paul, H. C. 1973. "*Bāul*-Poets on *Chāri-Chandra* (Or Four States of the Mind)." *Journal of the Asiatic Society of Bangladesh* 18, no. 1: 1–53.

Pennington, Brian K. 2005. *Was Hinduism Invented? Britons, Indians, and the Colonial Construction of Religion.* New York: Oxford University Press.

Pinch, William R. 2006. *Warrior Ascetics and Indian Empires.* Cambridge, UK: Cambridge University Press.

Plukker, D. F. 1981. The *Miragavati* of Kutubana: Avadhi Text with Critical Notes. Ph. D diss., University of Amsterdam.

Potter, Karl H., ed. 1995. *Encyclopedia of Indian Philosophies.* Vol. 2, *Indian Metaphysics and Epistemology: The Tradition of Nyāya-Vaiśeṣika up to Gaṅgeśa.* Delhi, India: Motilal Banarsidass. [First published in 1977.]

Pradhan, N. 1986. *Prachin Oriya Sahityare Nirguna Dhara.* Cuttack: Basati Kumari Pradhan.

Prapañcasāra. 1935. 2 Vols. Arthur Avalon's Tantrik Texts 18 and 19. Calcutta: The Sanskrit Press Depository.

Pratap Singh, Anuj. 1989. *Gorakhnāth aur nāth siddh.* Gorakhpur: Gorakhnāth mandir.

Raghav, Rangey. 2004 *Gorakhnāth aur unkā yug.* Delhi/Lucknow: Ātmārām and Sons. [First published in 1963.]

Rajjab. 1990. *Sarvangi* [as *Sarabamgi*]. Ed. Dharmapal Simhal. Jalandhar: Dipak Publishing.

Rao, Gopinath. 1914. *Elements of Hindu Iconography.* 2 Vols (4 parts). Madras: Law Printing House, 1914–1916.

Rauravāgama. 1985–1988. 3 vols. A critical edition by N. R. Bhatt. Pondichéry: Institute Francaise d'Indologie.

Rawls, John. 1993. *Political Liberalism.* New York: Columbia University Press.

Rawson, Philip. 1988 *The Art of Tantra.* London: Thames and Hudson. [First published in 1973.]

Rigopoulos, Antonio. 1993. *The Life and Teachings of Sai Baba of Shirdi.* Albany, NY: State University of New York Press.

Ṣaḍanvayaśāmbhavakrama (alias *Ṣaḍanvayamahāratnacitradhātuka*) of Umākānta. MS β 353, London: Wellcome Library for the History and Understanding of Medicine.

Salomon, Carol. 1991. "The Cosmogonic Riddles of Lalan Fakir." In *Gender, Genre, and Power in South Asian Expressive Traditions*, edited by Arjun Appadurai, Frank J. Korom, and Margaret A. Mills, 267–304. Philadelphia, PA: University of Pennsylvania Press.

Samantarai, Romesh. 1976. *Oriya Sahityare Bhima Bhoi*. Cuttack: Dharmagrantha Store.

Śambhunirṇayadīpikā of Śivānandamuni. R. No. 3203d, Madras Govt. Lib.

Śambhunirṇayatantra. R. No. 3203c, Madras Govt. Lib.

Sandel, Michael J. 1998. *Liberalism and the Limits of Justice*, 2nd ed. Cambridge: Cambridge University Press.

Sanderson, Alexis. 1985. Purity and power among the Brahmans of Kashmir.' In *The Category of the Person*, ed. Michael Cassithers et al, 190–216. Cambridge: Cambridge University Press.

———. 1988. Śaivism and the Tantric Traditions. In *The World's Religions/Religions of Asia*, ed. Friedhelm Hardy, 660–704. London: Routledge. [Reprint: 1990]

———. 1990. The visualization of the deities of the Trika. In *L'image divine. Cult et méditation dans l'Hindouisme*, ed. A. Padoux, 31–88. Paris: Éditions du Centre National de la Recherche Scientifique.

———. 1995. Meaning in Tantric Ritual. In *Essais sur le rituel III: Colloque du Centenaire de la Section des Sciences religieuses de l'École Pratique des Hautes Études*, Ed. A.-M. Blondeau and K. Schipper, 15–95. Bibliothèque de l'Ecole des Hautes Études, Sciences Religieuses, Volume 102. Louvain-Paris: Peeters.

———. 2002. Remarks on the Text of the Kubjikāmatatantra. *Indo-Iranian Journal* 45: 1–24.

———. 2003. "The Śaiva Religion among the Khmers, Part I." *Bulletin de l'École française d'Extrême-Orient* 90–91 (2003–2004): 349–462.

———. 2005. "A Commentary on the Opening Verses of the Tantrasāra of Abhinavagupta." In *Sāmarasya: Studies in Indian Arts, Philosophy, and Interreligious Dialogue in Honour of Bettina Bäumer*, edited by Sadananda Das and Ernst Fürlinger, 89–148. New Delhi, India: D. K. Printworld.

———. 2006. The Lākulas: New Evidence of a System Intermediate Between Pāñcārthika Pāśupatism and *Āgamic* Śaivism. *Indian Philosophical Annual* 24: 143–217.

———. 2007a. Atharvavedins in Tantric Territory: The *Āṅgirasakalpa*. Texts of the Oriya Paippalādins and their Connection with the Trika and the Kālīkula, with critical editions of the *Parājapavidhi*, the *Parāmantravidhi*, and the *Bhadrakālīmantravidhiprakaraṇa*. In *The Atharvaveda and its Paippalāda Śākhā: Historical and Philological Papers on a Vedic Tradition*, edited by Arlo Griffiths and Annette Schmiedchen, 195–311. Āchen: Shaker Verlag, 2007. [Geisteskultur Indiens: Texte und Studien, 11, Indologica Halensis.]

———. 2007b. "The Śaiva Exegesis of Kashmir". In *Mélanges Tantriques à la mémoire d'Hélène Brunner*, edited by Dominic Goodall and André Padoux,

231–442. Paris: École française d'Extrême-Orient; Pondichéry, India: Institut Française de Pondichéry.

Sārdhatriśatikālottarāgama. 1979. Avec le commentaire de Bhaṭṭa Rāmakaṇṭha. Édition critique par N. R. Bhatt. Publications de l'Institut français d'indologie no. 61. Pondichéry: Institut français d'indologie.

Sarkar, Jagdish Narayan. 1985. A Study of Sufism—Its Background and Its Syncretic Significance in Medieval India. *Indo-Iranica* 38, nos. 1 and 2 (March–June 1985): 1–24.

Śāstri, H. P. 1905. *A Catalogue of Palm-leaf & Selected Paper MSS belonging to the Durbar Library, Nepal*, vol 1. Calcutta

Ṣaṭsāhasrasaṃhitā. 1982. Ed. and trans. Jan A. Schoterman. Leiden: E .J. Brill.

Schomer, Karine. 1987. The *Dohā* as a Vehicle of Sant Teachings. In *The Sants. Studies in a Devotional Tradition of India*, ed. Karine Schomer and W. H. McLeod, 61–90. Delhi/Varanasi/Patna: Motilal Banarsidass.

Schomer, Karine and W. H. McLeod, eds. 1987. *The Sants. Studies in a Devotional Tradition of India*. Delhi/Varanasi/Patna: Motilal Banarsidass.

Schoterman, J. A. 1977. Some Remarks on the *Kubjikāmatatantra*. In *Zeitschrift der Deutschen Morgenländischen Gesellschaft* (ZDMG), supplement III-2, 932–40.

———. 1980. A link between Purāṇa and Tantra: Agnipurāṇa. In *Zeitschrift der Deutschen Morgenl\"andischen Gesellschaft*, supplement 4.

———. 1990. Kubjikāmata Tantra: the Laghvikāmnāya version. In *The Sanskrit Tradition and Tantrism*, ed. Teun Goudriaan, 76–84. Leiden, The Netherlands: E. J. Brill.

———. 1992. "The Kubjikā Upaniṣad and its Atharvavedic Character." In Goudriaan, *Ritual and Speculation in Early Tantrism. Studies in Honor of Andre Padoux*. Albany, NY: SUNY Press, 312–26.

Sen, Amartya. 2006. *Identity and Violence: The Illusion of Destiny*. New York: W. W. Norton.

Sen, Dinesh Chandra. 1925. *Glimpses of Bengal Life*. Calcutta, India: Calcutta University Press.

Sen, Sukumār. 1398. *Bāṅgālā sāhityer itihās: dvitīya khaṇḍa: saptadaś–aṣṭādaś śatābdī*. Kalkātā, India: Ānanda pābliśārs. [First published in 1940.]

———. 1971. *An Etymological Dictionary of Bengali: c. 1000–1800 A. D.* Calcutta, India: Eastern Publishers.

———. 1979. *History of Bengali Literature*. 3rd ed. New Delhi, India: Sahitya Akademi. [First published in 1960.]

Shapiro, Michael C. 1995. The Theology of the Locative Case in Sacred Sikh Scripture (Gurabāṇī). In *Bhakti Religion in North India. Community Identity and Political Action*, ed. David N. Lorenzen, 145–59. Delhi: Manohar.

Sharma, Krishna. 2004. Towards a New Perspective. In *Religious Movements in South Asia 600–1800*, ed. David N. Lorenzen, 292–332. Oxford/NY/Delhi: Oxford University Press.

Sharma, Ramvilas. 1977. *Mahavirprasad Dwivedi aur Hindi Navjagaran*. New Delhi: Rajkamal Prakashan.

Shukla, Ramchandra. 1973. *Surdas*. Varanasi: Nagari Pracharini Sabha.

———. 1978. *Hindi Sahitya ka Itihaas*. Varanasi: Nagari Pracharini Sabha.

Sil, Narasingha P. 2003. *Divine Dowager: The Life and Teachings of Saradamani: The Holy Mother*. Selinsgrove, PA: Susquehanna University Press.

———. 2009. "Kali's Child and Krishna's Lover: An Anatomy of Ramakrishna's *Caritas Divina*." *Religion* 39, no. 2: 289–98.

Singh, Pashaura. 2003. *The Bhagats of the Guru Granth Sahib: Sikh Self-Definition and the Bhagat Bani*. New Delhi: Oxford University Press.

Singh, Mohan. 1937. *Gorakhnath and Medieval Hindu Mysticism*. Lahore: Oriental College.

Singh, Vijaypāl. 1992. *Gorakṣa-darśan*. Gorakhpur: Gorakhnāth Mandir.

Śivapurāṇa: Hindī ṭīkā sahita. 1987. Mumbai, India: Khemarāja Śrīkṛṣṇadāsa.

Śivasaṃhitā. 1999. Eds. Svāmī Maheśānanda et al. Lonāvlā: Kaivalyadhāma Śrīmanmādhava yogamandir samiti.

———. 2004. Translated by Rai Bahadur Srisa Chandra Vasu. Edited with an Introduction & Notes by J. L. Gupta. Delhi: Chaukhamba Sanskrit Pratisthan. [The 1914 edition was published in Allahabad by Sudhindra Natha Vasu, at the Panini Office.]

Sivayogisivacarya 1993. *Siddhāntaśikhāmaṇi*. With the commentary *Tattvapradīpikā*. In *Śivadharmagranthamālā* 36. Ed. Candraśekharaśivācārya Mahāsvāmī. Vārāṇasī, India: Śaivabhāratī Bhavan.

Solaṅkī, Komal Singh. 1966. *Nāth panth aur nirguṇ sant-kāvya*. Agra: Vinod Pustak Mandir.

Subhagodaya of Śivānanda. In Madhu Khanna, The Concept and Liturgy of the Śrīcakra based on Śivānanda's Trilogy, 338–47. Ph.D diss., Oxford University.

Sukthankar, Visnu S. et al., eds. 1933–1960. *Mahābhārata*, 21 vols. Poona: Bhandarkar Oriental Research Institute.

Svacchandapaddhati. Madras Government. Library, Madras: 81 B 3 Beta.

Svacchandatantram. 1921–1935. 6 vols. Ed. Madhusudan Kaul Shastri. Kashmir Series of Texts and Studies 56. Albany, NY: SUNY Press.

Svātmārāma. 1975. *Haṭhayoga Pradīpika of Svātmārāma*. With the Commentary *Jyotsnā* of Brahmānanda and English Translation. Madras: The Adyar Library.

———. 1980. *Haṭhapradīpikā: Svātmārāma kṛta*. Eds. Svāmī Digambarjī and Pītāmbar Jhā. Lonāvlā: Kaivalyadhāma Śrīmanmādhava yogamandir samiti.

Taylor, Charles et al. 1994. *Multiculturalism: Examining the Politics of Recognition*. Ed. by Amy Gutmann. Princeton, NJ: Princeton University Press.

Thornton, Edward. 1854. *A gazetteer of the territories under the government of the East-India company, and of the native states on the continent of India compiled by the authority of the Hon. Court of Directors, and chiefly from documents in their possesion by Edward Thornton, Esq*. London: Wm. H. Allen & Co.

Tovstych, I. A. 1988. *Šekch Pchojdžulla: Pobeda Gorokcho: Gorokho bidžoj*. Moskva, Russia: Nauka.

Upadhyay, Nagendranath. 1991. *Gorakṣanātha*. Delhi: Sāhitya Akademi. [First edition published in 1976 by Nāgarī Pracārinī Sabhā in Varanasi, India.]

———. 1997. *Nāth aur sant sāhitya*. (*tulanātmak adhyayan*) Varanasi: Amṛt Prakāsan. [First published in 1965.]

Urban, Hugh B. 2001. *The Economics of Ecstasy: Tantra, Secrecy, and Power in Colonial Bengal*. Oxford and New York: Oxford University Press.

The Vāmakeśvarīmatam. 1945. Ed. Madhusudan Kaul Shastri with the commentary of Rājanaka Jayaratha. Kashmir Series of Texts and Studies 56. Srinigar, India: Mercantile Press.

Van Buitenen, J. A. B. 1981. *The Bhagavadgītā in the Mahābhārata: A Bilingual Edition*. Chicago: University of Chicago Press.

Varenne, Jean. 1976. *Yoga and the Hindu Tradition*. Trans. from the French by Derek Coltman. Chicago: University of Chicago Press.

Vasudeva, Somadeva. 2000. The Yoga of the Mālinīvijayottaratantra. Ph.D diss., Wolfson College, Oxford University.

———. 2004. *The Yoga of the Mālinīvijayottaratantra: Chapters 1–4, 7–11, 11–17*. Pondichérry: Institut Français de Pondichéry: École française d'Extrême-Orient.

Vaudeville, Charlotte. 1974. *Kabir*. vol. 1. Oxford: Clarendon Press.

———. 1991. Chokāmelā: un sant intouchable du Maharashtra. In *Littératures médiévales de l'Inde du nord. Contributions de Charlotte Vaudeville et de ses élèves*, ed. Françoise Mallison, 65–80. Paris: École Française D'Extrême Orient.

Vidyapati. 1984. *Gorakṣa-vijaya*. Ed. Harimohan Miśra. Patna: Bihār Rāṣtrabhāṣā Pariṣad.

Wallace, Vesna A. 2001. *The Inner Kālacakratantra: A Buddhist Tantric View of The Individual*. New York: Oxford University Press.

Wayman, Alex. 1982. The Human Body as Microcosm in India, Greek Cosmology, and Sixteenth-century Europe. *History of Religions* 22, no. 2: 172–90.

White, David Gordon. 1996. *The Alchemical Body: Siddha Traditions in Medieval India*. Chicago: University of Chicago Press. [Republished in 2004, Manoharlal in Delhi.]

———, ed. 2000. *Tantra in Practice*. Princeton, NJ and Oxford: Princeton University Press.

———. 2001. The Exemplary Life of Mastnāth: the Encapsulation of Seven Hundred Years of Nāth Siddha Hagiography. In *Constructions hagiographiques en Inde: entre mythe et histoire*, ed. Francoise Mallison, 139–61. Paris: Éditions de l'EPHE.

———, 2003. *Kiss of the Yoginī: "Tantric Sex" in Its South Asian Contexts*. Chicago: University of Chicago Press.

———. 2009a. Never Have I Seen Such Yogis Brother: Yogis, Warriors, and

Sorcerers in Ancient and Medieval India. In *Ancient to Modern: Religion, Power, and Community in India*, ed. Ishita Banerjee-Dube and Saurabh Dube, 86–113, New Delhi: Oxford University Press.

———. 2009b. *Sinister Yogis.* Chicago: University of Chicago Press.

———. 2011. Yogic and Political Power among the Nāth Siddhas of North India. In *Asceticism and Power in Asia*, ed. Peter Flügel and Gustaaf Hartmann. London: Routledge.

Woodroffe, John. 1997. *The Serpent Power: Being the Ṣaṭ-Cakra-Nirūpaṇa and Pādukā-Pañcaka.* Madras, India: Ganesh and Company. [First published in 1919.]

Yoga-karṇikā [by] Nath Aghorānanda: An Ancient Treatise on Yoga. 1981. Ed. by Narendra Nath Sharma. Delhi: Eastern Book Linkers.

Yogatattvopaniṣad. 1920. In *The Yoga Upaniṣad-s: With the Commentary of Śrī Upaniṣad-Brahmayogin*, ed. A. Mahadeva Sastri, 363–89. Madras: The Adyar Library Research Centre. [Originally published in 1920.]

Yoginīhṛdayatantra. 1988. Ed. Vrajavallabha Dviveda. Delhi, India: Motilal Banarsidass.

Zbavitel, Dušan. 1976. *Bengali Literature.* Vol. 9, *A History of Indian Literature*, fasc. 3. Wiesbaden, Germany: Harrassowitz.

Zvelebil, Kamil V. 1973. *The Poets of the Powers.* London: Rider & Co.

Contributors

Purushottam Agrawal is a member of the Union Public Commission of India. He was formerly a professor at the Jawaharlal Nehru University. His most recent books are *Vichar ka anant* (Rajkamal Prakashan, 2000) and *Nij brahma vichar: dharma, samaj aur dharmeter adhyatma* (Rajkamal Prakashan, 2004).

Ishita Banerjee-Dube is professor of history at the Centre for Asian and African Studies, El Colegio de México. Her most recent books are *Religion, Law and Power: Tales of Time in Eastern India 1860–2000* (Anthem Press, 2007) and *Divine Affairs: Religion, Pilgrimage, and the State in Postcolonial India* (Manohar, 2001).

Ann Grodzins Gold is professor of Anthropology and Religions at Syracuse University. She is the author of *A Carnival of Parting: The Tales of King Bharthari and King Gopi Chand . . .* (University of California Press, 1992) and coauthor, with Bhoju Ram Gujar, of *In the Time of Trees and Sorrows: Nature, Power, and Memory in Rajasthan* (Duke University Press, 2002).

Daniel Gold is professor of South Asian Religions in the Department of Asian Studies, Cornell University. He is the author of *Aesthetics and Analysis in Writing on Religion: Modern Fascinations* (University of California Press, 2003) and *The Lord as Guru: Hindi Sants in the North Indian Tradition* (Oxford University Press, 1987).

Csaba Kiss is a member of the Early Tantra Project at the Ecole Française d'Extrême Orient, where he is preparing a critical edition of the *Brahma-yāmala*. He has published a Hungarian translation of the *Haṭha-yoga-pradīpikā* (Terebess Kiadó, 2000) as well as *Szép indiai mesék*, a translation of a collection of Hindi tales (Mágus Kiadó, 2001).

David N. Lorenzen is professor of History at the Centre for Asian and African Studies, El Colegio de México. His most recent books are *The Scourge of the Mission: Marco della Tomba in Hindustan* (Yoda Press, 2009) and *Who Invented Hinuism?* (Yoda Press, 2006).

Adrián Muñoz is professor of Comparative Literature and Religion in the Faculty of Philosophy and Letters, at the National Autonomous University of Mexico. His first book is *La piel de tigre y la serpiente: La identidad de los Nāth Yoguis a través de sus leyendas* (El Colegio de México, 2010).

Lubomír Ondračka is a researcher and research project manager at the Institute for Philosophy and Religious Studies, Faculty of Arts, in Charles University, Prague. He has edited several books and written numerous articles in Czech.

David Gordon White is professor of Religious Studies at the University of California, Santa Barbara. His most recent books are *Sinister Yogis* (University of Chicago Press, 2009) and *Kiss of the Yoginī: "Tantric Sex" in its South Asian Contexts* (University of Chicago Press, 2006).

Index

29195761R00159

Made in the USA
Middletown, DE
10 February 2016